Tales of the Dandelion Commune
(1977–1983)

Tales of the Dandelion Commune
(1977–1983)

Richie Graham

Burlington, Vermont

Onion River Press
191 Bank Street
Burlington, Vermont 05401

Copyright © 2019 Richard Graham

All Rights Reserved. No part of this publication may be reproduced, distributed, or transmitted in any form or by any means, including photocopying, recording, or other electronic or mechanical methods, without the prior written permission of the publisher, except in the case of brief quotations embodied in critical reviews and certain other noncommercial uses permitted by copyright law.

Cover photo: Johan Neven from Borgloon-Gotem, Belgium [CC BY 2.0 (https://creativecommons.org/licenses/by/2.0)]

Commune photos courtesy of the Robbie Sproule and the author.

Author photo by Juliette Horton

ISBN 978-1-949066-31-9

Printed in the United States of America

Dedication

For the People Who Shaped My Behavior before Community:

Ann Graham (my mother)　　Arthur Graham (my father)
Ed Graham, (my brother)　　Dr. Ira Perelle (psychology professor)
Tony Rizzo, (my best friend)　　Dr. Suzanne Kessler (psychology professor)

For the People Who Shaped My Behavior in Community:

Gordon Sproule　　Alison Feuerwerker
Jane Kilthei　　Larry Linsky
Donald Sproule　　Dakota Morningstar
Deirdre "Maple" Hillary　　Ira Wallace
Douglas Norman　　Raphy Wallace
Robbie Sproule　　Peggy Fitzgerald
Dondi Kimelman　　Sandy Fitzgerald
Mory Macleod　　David "Tango" Rheingold
Douglas Truman　　Sean Purcell
Lisa　　Janet Rix
Bruce "Timothy" Hale　　Sean Hayes
Jeffrey Spears　　Mark Poppam
Jonathan Stokes　　Isabelle Fortin
Bill Svoboda　　Alice "Louis" Adell
Greg Bates　　Randy Friesen
Maura Rudden　　Andrew "Bede" Secord
Jeffrey Alexander　　Cath Poesehn
Faye Walsh　　Miriam "Mert" Jacobs
Matt Walsh　　John Darby
Casey　　Parrish Sproule
Craig　　Devon Sproule
Kat Kincaid　　Chantal
Pat　　Rene
Brian Otto　　Lewis

In memory of B. F. Skinner

"Richard, what the fuck are you doing with your life?"
—Tony Rizzo (best friend)

"Bucks, the prime function!"
—Ed Graham (brother)

"Rich, did you ever stop to think that if you had made $10,000/year for the past five years you would have made $50,000 by now?"
—Ann Graham (mother)

"Rich, remember to always be true to yourself. Good luck."
—Art Graham (father)

"Go! Try out community while you are still young."
—Ira Perelle (psychology professor)

"Richie, you were the soul of Dandelion."
—Julian Svoboda (Dandelion member)

Contents

The Journey Begins, October 1977 | 11
My First Day | 16
My Second Day | 25
Robbie's Visit | 35
My Clearness Meeting | 39
Edible What? | 42
Visitors | 44
Christmas 1977 | 45
January 1978 | 50
Spring 1978 | 58
Arrival of Our First Antioch Student | 60
Noncompetitive Volley Ball | 70
Visit of my Parents | 71
Conference | 75
Tamari | 78
Safety First | 81
The Dandelion Disco Scene | 84
Meeting B. F. Skinner | 85
The Film Project | 90
Orgies? When? Where? | 91
Dinner Conversations | 94
Fall 1978 | 95
Go, Go, Gonads! (Dandelion plays Basketball) | 100
Jonestown Massacre, November 1978 | 101
Winter 1979 | 102
Trip to Los Horcones | 103
ABA Conference, February 1979 | 116
March 1979 | 120
Behavior Code Madness | 123
Spring 1979 | 125
Front Porch Gatherings | 128
Tee Shirt Inequality | 131
Visit of Gerry | 132
New Moneymaking Schemes | 135
Rocky Horror Picture Show Trip | 137
Open Door Policy | 139

Transitions | 143
January 1980 | 148
Behavior Seminar | 151
Bus Ride to New York | 154
Spring 1980 | 156
Cabaret Night | 158
First Baby Born at Dandelion! | 160
I Post My Leaving Paper | 162
The Summer of Alpha Research | 164
Living in Rochester | 167
Summer of 1981 | 169
My 30th Birthday Celebration | 173
The New Children's Building | 176
Moon Madness | 178
Dandelion Builds a Dome | 181
Night of New Games | 183
Behavior Psychology | 185
Late August 1981 | 190
Fall 1981 | 192
Wind Spirit | 194
Staying or Going | 195
December 1981 | 196
January 1982 | 199
Quest for Firewood | 201
Spring 1982 | 202
The Dandy Awards | 208
Cruise Missile Blockade | 210
Tapping the Maple Trees | 211
Devon's Birth | 213
My 31st Birthday | 214
Summer 1982 | 216
Fall 1982 | 217
Craft Show Madness | 218
Spring 1983 | 221
Summer 1983 | 223
Lost in Translation | 224
October 1983 | 231
Where Are They Now… | 233
Acknowledgments | 236
About the Author | 237

Preface

In the late 1960s and early 1970s, six "intentional communities" were established across North America inspired by the Utopian novel *Walden Two*, written by behavioral psychologist B. F. Skinner. These were a series of kibbutz-like collectives where members shared all resources. They built their own buildings, grew their own food, developed their own money-making industries, and raised their children communally. They were collectively called The Federation of Egalitarian Communities.

Although each community was unique, all shared a common philosophy. The founders established these communities to build an alternative society that did not contribute to racism, sexism, poverty, nor the many other inequalities and injustices they had experienced in society. Income sharing, a working democracy, and non-personal shared ownership of the land were some of the basic foundations for all the communities in the Federation.

The stories you are about to read are all based on actual events that occurred at Dandelion Community, which was one of the communities in the Federation. Time and memory may have embellished or slightly distorted the truth, but I have tried to describe as accurately as possible my six-year experience (1977–1983) living an egalitarian lifestyle.

a new culture is emerging FROM THE OLD

The expansion of human consciousness to include more wholistic, global perspectives is creating new social and economic structures that are more compatible with increased awareness. A society based on small, semi-autonomous communities affords a basic unit of manageable size which can serve as a supportive environment for personal growth, a workable base for the appropriate use of resources and technology, and a stepping stone to eventual peaceful existence of humans on planet Earth.

We are a group of communities offering a genuine alternative to a competitive, consumption-oriented lifestyle. We are trying to synthesize the advantages of rural and urban living into a viable social alternative.

We uphold equality and ecology, encourage diversity, and reject competition, violence, and sexism.

The Federation of Egalitarian Communities hopes that you will come live with us and help in the flowering of this new culture.

Please write:

Federation of Egalitarian Communities
Box 6B2
Tecumseh, Missouri
65760
(417) 679-4460

(Please mention where you saw this poster.)

ALOE, NC · DANDELION, ONT · EAST WIND, MO · NORTH MOUNTAIN, VA · TWIN OAKS, VA

PLEASE DISPLAY THIS POSTER

The Journey Begins, October 1977

The mailbox read "Dandelion Community." I turned my car into the long driveway and headed toward the house at the end of it. At the front of the house, I parked behind a dark blue 1962 Pontiac station wagon that had a large dent in the rear-passenger side door.

I got out and looking to my right saw a cow behind a wooden corral staring at me intensely. Not impressed with the stranger, the cow nonchalantly turned, lifted its tail and defecated in my general direction. Welcome to Dandelion Community. Have a nice day.

Shaking my head, I closed the car door and took in the rest of the landscape. The small, two-story wooden farmhouse (at least a hundred years old) had a large screened-in front porch. White paint was peeling off the sides and the front cement doorstep had cracks in it. The house was located on a slight elevation with pleasant views of the surrounding countryside.

Attached to the left side of the house was a new addition and I smelled the freshness of the lumber. I also smelled wood burning and looked up to see smoke billowing from the chimney on top of the green tiled roof.

About one hundred feet to the right of the house stood a small wooden barn. A wooden corral surrounded the barn and enclosed the cow that had so graciously welcomed me. Just beyond the small barn was a larger wooden barn with wide cracks in the walls.

Looking back down the driveway, I saw a large garden with the stubble of the last cornstalks. Just below the garden was a small industrial building made of unpainted wood that also had a green-tiled roof. The fading light of sunset coming from behind the building created an almost mystical setting. There were open fields in all directions and, except for the wind blowing, absolute silence.

Geez, what am I getting myself into this time? I thought. *This was the result of five years of college? Was this the place where I was going to help build Utopia?*

I walked up the cracked doorstep and opened the door.

"Hey, Richie's here!" Donald called out excitedly as I walked into the living room. We hugged each other warmly. Donald was a twenty-one-year-old native-born Canadian, a gentle soul with long brown curly hair, sparkling grey eyes, and in excellent physical shape. He looked like he should always be dancing and projected an aura of quiet self-assurance.

Gordon, Donald's cousin, came in from the kitchen and hugged me as well. "Hey, Richie, how was the trip up?"

"No problem." Earlier that morning, I had left the suburbs of New York City and driven all day to arrive in Enterprise, Ontario, in time for dinner. I had modestly said good-bye to my parents and brother, knowing that I was ending a chapter of my life. I was twenty-six years old, just out of college, and ready for a new adventure.

I had battled all kinds of traffic and weather on my drive up, but crossing into Canada was a breeze. All the Canadians I met were so polite, even the customs agent at the border crossing.

I had worried that I might have some hassles at the border, with all the stuff in my car. I had a mattress, a lamp, a mirror, boxes of clothing, an army cot, a bulletin board, a small desk, a set of weights, and a box of corn flakes.

When asked about the contents of my car, I told the customs agent that I was donating it all to my friends in Kingston. After answering a few more questions, I was waved onto the ferry.

On the ferry ride over the St. Lawrence Seaway, I saw the beginning of a beautiful sunset and told myself that I did not want to lose my connection with the wonder of life.

In my part-time and summer jobs in high school and college, I had met many people who hated their jobs and dreaded going to work in the morning. I was determined not to become one of them.

Now here I was, a 1977 graduate of the State University of New York—College at Purchase, with a degree in psychology, ready to help the six members of Dandelion Community build the *Walden Two* visionary community we hoped it would become.

Gordon was one of the main reasons I had decided to join the community. When I first met Gordon on my trip up last year, I quickly realized that he was committed to behavior psychology as much as I was. We were the same age and same size (5'7"), and were both raised as Unitarians. I admired Gordon for taking an active stand against the Vietnam War in the 1960s. While in high school in New Jersey, he had refused to stand during the morning Pledge of Allegiance. Gordon was married to Jane who were both among the founding members of Dandelion.

Our only difference was that I had short brown hair, brown eyes and no beard, while Gordon had long brown hair, grey eyes, and wore a goatee. By his looks, manner, and passion for behaviorism, I often thought of Gordon as "Frazier," the main proponent of Skinner's ideas in his novel *Walden Two*.

"You're just in time for dinner, Richie," Gordon said.

We all headed towards the kitchen and found Mory standing over the six-burner industrial-size black stove cooking a stir-fried vegetable and tofu dish. She looked up and said, "Hi, Richie, welcome to Dandelion." She walked over and gave me a hug.

Mory was a twenty-year-old from Ottawa who had recently joined Dandelion after dropping out of college. She was a friendly, attractive woman with long brown hair and piercing grey eyes. She was responsible for taking care of the community's accounting.

Chantal, a visitor from France, was also in the kitchen setting the table. She was a French beauty with long brown hair and brown eyes who practiced yoga daily. She smiled at me and with an enchanting accent said, "Hallo, welcome to Dandelion."

Durin, another member, was there as well and said, "Welcome to the nuthouse." He also had long brown frizzy hair and always seemed to look intensely at people over his glasses as if he were inspecting an insect. He was a recent dropout from the United States Army and had grown up in Texas. He and Gordon managed the fledgling hammock-making business on which the community had just embarked.

Gordon grabbed a few beers from the fridge while Mory placed food on the table in the center of the room. The six of us then stood around the table and silently held hands, a small ritual the community had practiced since day one. After fifteen seconds of hand-holding, we sat down to eat.

I answered a bunch of questions about my trip up, and then the conversation shifted to the upcoming craft shows. The community was preparing for its annual onslaught of tinnery orders.

Tinnery was the name the members gave to their recycled tin can business. They took used tin cans and burned designs into them, turning them into candleholders, lampshades, pencil holders, and hanging planters. They were then dipped into a mixture of varnish and paint thinner and hung up to dry. The varnish really made the colors of the can sparkle, and the finished product was dazzling. To its continued astonishment, the community made about $50,000 a year selling these products made from recycled garbage. To sell the cans, the community went to various craft shows all over Canada. They had a mail-order business as well.

After supper, we all retired to the living room and continued our conversations. Gordon took out a guitar and began playing some songs originally recorded by Cat Stevens, such as *Peace Train* and *Moon Shadow*.

Tinnery Craft Show display

The living room was modest but very homey. All the essentials were there to make one feel at home—a soft well-worn green couch, a comfortable sitting chair, and a long table in front of the window looking out over the driveway. In addition, a large shelf held a stereo and a wide collection of records and cassettes. A large painting of a dandelion hung on the wall.

The only thing missing was a television. The community had decided that with so much violence portrayed on so many programs along with sex-role stereotyping (particularly in television commercials) and low representation of minorities that it would go against the values of cooperation, equality, and nonviolence that the community was trying to promote. I thought it would be a worthwhile trade off to give up watching *Star Trek* reruns.

The wallpaper seemed a little tacky (light green with prints of grass and small rivers running on it) but I felt I could live with it.

As Gordon played the guitar, people drifted in and out singing with him. On the couch, Donald was reading *Co-Evolution Quarterly*, later published as the *Whole Earth Review*. A magazine committed to the emerging environmental movement, it was cheap enough for the community to afford a subscription.

The living room atmosphere was symbolic of Dandelion's spirit. Everyone set their own pace in all areas of life, work, and play. If things weren't done one day, they would get done the next.

One of the conversations focused on the anticipated return of Jane and Maple, who had been at Twin Oaks Community (in Virginia) attending the second assembly of the Federation of Egalitarian Communities.

I had met Jane before but not Maple. Jane was a committed behaviorist and shared my enthusiasm for building a real Walden Two community. I had great admiration for her.

The more I heard about Maple, the more curious I became. She sounded even more enthusiastic about building an egalitarian community than I was. In addition, two women hitchhiking down to Virginia and back had to have courage and some good stories to share.

After a while, people began to retire for the evening. Donald helped me unload my car and showed me my room. I would temporarily stay in the visitor room, located just off the living room, which held two bunk beds and a small desk.

It would be another week until I got my own room, which would be in the new addition to the farmhouse. Chantal, the only other current visitor, was staying in Jane's room until she returned.

Donald spoke about Dandelion's future, saying it was the beginning of an exciting time for the community. Several recent visitors were seriously considering becoming members. The new shop building, which they had been working on for over a year, was finally nearing completion and Chrissie (the cow), was expecting a calf in January.

After a few more updates, Donald left, and I turned off the light. Exhausted from my drive up, I fell asleep immediately.

My First Day

I woke up the next day reflecting on my new surroundings. Although the drive yesterday had sapped me physically, and I felt a little bit disoriented, emotionally I was revved up and ready to go. However, where exactly was I now? Oh yes, that *Walden Two*-inspired Dandelion Community.

I smiled and recalled how exhilarated I felt reading that book in my behavior psychology course taught by Ira Perelle, one of the most influential teachers I had ever had.

Walden Two had described a fictional community of one thousand people living a Utopian lifestyle. What had caught my passion was that it was set in modern times and based on behavioral principles. By the end of the course, I had developed a solid understanding (and appreciation) of behavior psychology and the assumptions the novel was based on.

Ira had also passed out a brochure about Twin Oaks Community, which described itself as a Walden Two community and had existed since 1967.

I had always thought I would one day teach a class on behavior psychology, and I wanted to try out living in a Walden Two community first. That was because it seemed to me a Walden Two community was the ultimate outcome of applied behavior analysis, a psychological theory that focused on behavior and its consequences. (At that time I believed I would eventually teach a class at a local college while living at Dandelion.)

When I asked Ira why he didn't live in a Walden Two community himself, he replied that he was older now (he was forty-five) and was reinforced by his car, and family, etc. He said that if he were young and single, he would not hesitate in trying it. He knew I had contacted some of the Walden Two communities and encouraged me to try it.

I jumped out of bed and got dressed. Looking out the window, I was delighted to see it was one of those glorious October days with the sun shining brightly and not a cloud in the sky. Grabbing my towel and toothbrush, I headed for the bathroom.

Built for a standard single-family farm, the bathroom consisted of one toilet, one bathtub/shower and one sink. Above the sink was a small wooden rack that held six toothbrushes.

Next to the toilet was a bucket with grey water in it. (This was leftover bath water.) Above the toilet was a sign saying, "If it's yellow, let it mellow. If it's brown, flush it down." This was the community's attempt to use a septic system designed for four or five people.

I washed up in the bathroom and then returned to the kitchen. As I boiled water on the stove, I grabbed a bowl from the kitchen shelf and went to the pantry to dig up some oatmeal. I scooped out the oatmeal from the large five-gallon white pail and saw some small oval-shaped raisins mixed in with the oats. *What a treat*, I thought.

I grabbed a glass from another shelf when I noticed that many of the glasses, via masking tape, had the names of members on them. Finding a glass with no name on it, I took out a can of frozen orange juice from the fridge, scooped out a teaspoon into my glass, and added water. On my last visit, this is what I had observed members do, another money-saving practice.

When the water boiled, I stirred in the oatmeal. I smiled, as I was getting a great start on my first day at Dandelion. Life was good.

When the oatmeal was ready, I took the bowl out into the living room. I sat at the long table facing the large window and saw multiple trees in their full fall foliage.

My car blocked some of the view and I'd move it as soon as possible. I began eating my first breakfast at Dandelion, feeling like I was sitting on top of the world.

Mory came in the front door carrying a large white plastic pail filled with milk. She had just finished milking Chrissie.

"If that cow knocks over the bucket one more time, I'm going to scream," she muttered and grinned at me as she walked toward the kitchen. Once there, she poured the milk into a gallon glass jar. She placed a filter over each jar before pouring to catch any "extras" such as hay, dirt, or cow feces.

"So, Mory," I yelled from the living room, "These small raisins in the oatmeal, never seen that before. Is that a Canadian specialty?" Mory came back into the living room, not sure she had heard me correctly.

"What are you talking about, Richie?" I pointed to the raisins in my bowl.

She took one look, smiled, and said, "Oh, Richie, those aren't raisins; they're mouse turds. The mice must have gotten into the oatmeal bin again." She tried containing herself but burst out laughing.

I jumped up and ran outside, trying to spit out the oatmeal in my mouth. Mory came to the front door and watched me. I thought about trying to regurgitate the contents of my stomach, but then realized I probably hadn't eaten more than a couple of turds. Did someone say Utopia?

After my unforgettable first breakfast, I decided to go for a short walk and get myself a little more oriented.

The community owned fifty acres, half of which were open fields used for gardens and growing hay. The rest was forest and used mostly for firewood.

"Owned" was a slippery word to use regarding anything Dandelion had. The land belonged to Dandelion as a non-profit corporation, and none of the members actually owned the land. In fact, the by-laws stated that the Federation of Egalitarian Communities would be given the land if Dandelion ever folded.

When a new member joined who had any money or assets, he or she could do one of three things: The first was to loan it to the community, to be returned to the member when or if he or she left. The second was to put it in a trust where no one would have access to it while the member lived at Dandelion. The third option was to donate any assets to the community.

Since very few members or visitors had much in assets, this was usually a moot question. On the rare occasion when someone did have some assets, he or she usually loaned them to the community. Gordon's favorite example was that of an anvil. If a potential member had such a thing, one could easily lend it to the community and then leave with it when he or she left. If a member had a car, it could either be donated to the community or left with a relative, but would not be able to use it while a member.

I walked down the driveway, passing the garden on my left and then the industrial building (the "shop"), which was officially called "Adukie," after the bean, as Dandelion was committed to serving a vegetarian diet.

At the end of the driveway, I crossed over the small wooden bridge (made of huge logs strong enough to support cars) and reached the local county gravel road. I crossed the road and entered a large field, which was about the size of four football fields.

Two weeks earlier the last hay had been cut, leaving only stubble. The far end of the field ended in a small, open hill and I climbed up to get a better view. When I reached the top, I could clearly see the main farmhouse, Aduki, and the barns. With the cloudless blue sky, it looked like an Ontario travel brochure.

I smiled, amused that the community had only the farmhouse, Adukie, and the dilapidated barns. Compared to the novel *Walden Two*, which had 1,000 people living in harmony and at least fifty buildings, Dandelion was nowhere near the book's Utopian ideal.

The fresh autumn air gave me a marvelous sense of well-being. I was so excited to begin building the community of my dreams.

Something moved in the upper branches of the maple tree next to me, and I saw it was a small porcupine. Its black color contrasted beautifully with the red maple leaves. "Amazing," I said out loud. A touch of wonder flashed through my mind. "What other wildlife might be around here?"

After looking for some more animals and not finding any, I sat down on a large rock and began thinking about how I had come to be at this place at this time. What was I looking for? What did I hope to find?

Financial gain was certainly not one of my top goals. Wasn't it more about "practicing what you preach" and "staying true to yourself," something my father had always told me?

For years I had nurtured an egalitarian philosophy. Inspired by *Walden Two*, I felt that such a community could be the kind of place I could really live my values. I still could not believe there wasn't already an up-and-running community like the one portrayed in the book. (Twin Oaks Community, which had inspired Dandelion, was larger, but even they only had about forty people and eight buildings.)

Nevertheless, that was what made my adventure here so tantalizing. Could I help to build a real Walden Two community? One based on positive interactions among members, setting up a society that treated people equally, regardless of sex, color, or creed? That was the challenge. That was the quest.

Coming of age in the late 1960s had deeply affected my personal outlook. When I was twelve, President Kennedy was killed. The following years included the Vietnam War, the civil rights movement, race riots, the emergence of the women's movement, and the assassinations of Martin Luther King, Bobby Kennedy, and Malcolm X. The threat of nuclear war with the Soviet Union always lurked in the background. All of that sparked me to do something positive to change the craziness I saw around me.

I also liked that Dandelion had taken a strong stand against having illegal drugs on the property. This was to make sure we kept on good terms with the local police. I had never done any hard drugs myself, Budweiser beer being my choice of drug.

After contemplating more of my surroundings and my values, I headed back to the farmhouse. I came to the bridge in the driveway and sat down to gaze at the small stream below. The wildlife in that creek was astonishing. There were minnows, snails, water bugs, frogs, turtles, muskrats, and small insect-like creatures I did not recognize. Staring into the calm water, I became entranced.

A shadow came up behind me, which was Mory and Gordon returning from their morning walk. Mory asked, "How's it going, Richie? Have you recovered from your breakfast yet?" She smiled.

"Oh yeah, just getting myself oriented now."

Gordon smiled and said, "It takes time."

Gordon and Mory sat down. Gordon picked up a small stone and tossed it into the creek. The splash made twenty ripples and the minnows scattered in all directions.

"The wildlife in this creek is amazing. I also saw a porcupine across the road," I commented.

"Yes, the wildlife around here *is* quite remarkable, Richie—one of the perks of living in the country," Gordon replied.

Mory chimed in and said, "There's a beaver that we sometimes see in this creek. However, since it's so rare, it is like a mystery. We call it the 'Loch Ness Beaver.' In addition, this past summer we saw two giant snapping turtles mating in here. They were rolling over each other. It was quite a sight. Watching them was our entertainment for one evening."

"Well, time for me to get to work," said Gordon, standing up. "What are your plans for the day, Richie?"

"I'm not sure, Gordon. My next stop was to check my labor sheet."

"Well, remember to go easy your first day here," Mory said standing up. "Take it real slow and don't eat any more of those mouse turds."

I stood up and we all headed back towards the farmhouse. The labor sheets were in a large manila envelope hanging on a wall near the entrance to the kitchen. They were the community's way of keeping track of each person's work schedule. It was based on the honor system and each member had one sheet for each week. For each hour worked, one could claim one labor credit.

There were managers for all the different aspects of work in the community. For example, the kitchen manager was responsible for ordering food supplies as well as estimating how many hours were needed for cooking, dishwashing, and cleaning the floor. The tinnery manager was responsible for ordering all supplies needed for the tinnery and estimating the number of hours needed that week. An auto manager was responsible for maintaining cars, etc. The other managerships included labor, house, visitor, cow, public relations, clothing, building maintenance, and recreation.

On Sunday, managers submitted the amounts of time needed for the upcoming week to the labor manager. The labor manager then developed the work schedule for the following week. The idea was to give people as much of the work they enjoyed doing and to divide up and rotate the jobs that no one really enjoyed, like dishwashing.

Richie's labor sheet

Communitarians usually worked forty-five to fifty hours a week, which seemed high to people outside the community. But those hours included all traditional "women's" work—including cooking, house cleaning, shopping, laundry and dishwashing—so the amount was comparatively smaller than a person would have to work in the outside world. When Dandelion had its first child, childcare would earn labor credits as well.

Some of the labor required for the week (cooking, dishwashing, scheduled trips to Kingston, milking the cow, etc.) had specific times entered on the labor sheet. For the majority of work, specifically working in the community industries, people saw on their labor sheet, "twenty hours of tinnery." Those hours could be done anytime during the week so long as they were finished by Sunday evening at midnight.

This gave everyone a very flexible work schedule. Some people did their industry work early in the morning; others late at night. The labor system was one of the best examples of putting the community's vision of equality into practice.

I reviewed my labor sheet and was grateful to find that I did not have any specific shifts scheduled that day. I noticed that during the upcoming week I had ten hours for the firewood brigade. This involved going into Dandelion's wooded areas and cutting down dead trees, then cutting the logs into smaller pieces and stacking them in the basement. Donald had mentioned something about that the night before and I went outside looking for him.

I spotted him bending under the hood of the station wagon, checking the oil. The Pontiac was closer to the barn and now had an old rusted metal hay wagon attached behind it. The wagon was empty and used for the firewood.

Donald closed the hood of the car and saw me coming towards him.

"Reporting for duty, Donald."

"That's great, Richie. I'm really looking forward to working with you. The car is all set. Are you ready to rock n roll?"

"Yes, Sir!" We hopped in the car and started on our mission.

"You brought some excellent weather with you, Richie," Donald commented as we approached the wire fence surrounding the fields behind the farmhouse. "It's also a fine day to be outside cutting wood, eh?"

An electrical wire fence (to keep the cow out) surrounded the field we were approaching. The fence consisted of thin metal poles that had the wire attached to them and were spaced every ten feet.

The entrance to the field had two sturdy wooden posts and the wire at that point (which usually hung between the two posts) lay on the ground.

Since Chrissie was in the corral, Donald just drove over the wire. Unknown to us, however, the wire somehow hooked onto the wagon as we drove off.

"So how does it feel to be living in Utopia, Richie?" Donald asked, smiling at me.

"Magnificent, Donald. I am so excited to be here." I placed my arm on the open car window.

THUNK!

"What was that, Donald?" I asked, curious.

"Oh, nothing. As you can see, this path has a lot of potholes in it. Probably just a hole or rock we ran over."

If we had bothered to look behind us, we'd have seen that what Donald had mistakenly thought was the sound of driving over a rock was the sound of the post closest to the wagon being pulled out of the ground. We continued driving.

THUNK!
THUNK!
POP!
THUNK!
BOING!

"Boy, there sure are a lot of rocks on this path," I commented innocently, looking out the window and admiring the countryside. We continued to drive across the field while behind us the wire and accompanying fence posts were systematically pulled out, one after the other and began to follow the wagon.

Outside the barn munching away on some hay, Chrissie stopped to watch the drama unfolding before her. Her eyes blinked when each fence post popped out of the ground.

A minute later, Donald felt the car begin to drag, looked in the rear-view mirror and said, "What the—" He immediately stopped the car and we both got out. With wild looks of disbelief, we stared at all the poles scattered behind us. We had efficiently managed to pull out fifty fence posts that had surrounded almost two acres of land.

We looked at each other and then back at the tangled mess. We began laughing. "Geez, I don't remember reading about this in *Walden Two*," I said.

We gathered up the fence posts and began replacing them around the field. It took us the rest of the morning to get the wire and the posts back up in their original positions. "So, is this a typical morning at Dandelion, Donald, or is it just me?"

He smiled and said, "Well, you never really know what each day will bring, eh? That's what makes life at Dandelion interesting."

It was close to lunchtime when we finally got the last posts back up, so we returned to the farmhouse. As we walked in the front door the aroma of fresh-baked bread made me realize how hungry I was.

I walked into the kitchen and saw Mory standing over the stove cooking French fries in a frying pan filled with oil. All of a sudden, WHOOSH! the oil in the frying pan caught fire. The kitchen immediately filled up with thick black smoke, and Mory began choking. I looked around for something to cover the pan while Mory went out the back door choking and coughing. My eyes burning from the smoke, I barely managed to find a pot cover and place it over the pan. Coughing as well, I turned off the burner and ran out the back door.

"Phew, that was exciting," I gasped.

"Oh, geez, Richie, you are having some first day at Dandelion, eh?"

I smiled and said, "Oh, man, you haven't even heard what Donald and I managed to do to the fence posts."

"I don't even know if I want to hear about that." She smiled.

When we returned to the kitchen a few minutes later, we opened up all the windows and let out the remaining smoke. The fries, which had been soaking in the oil for so long, were now just long, soggy pieces of greasy potato no one in their right mind would eat. Nevertheless, Dandelion with its commitment to recycling (and saving money), sat down to lunch and ate every one of them, proving that you could never cook enough French fries in community.

Over lunch, Donald and I told the tale of how we had managed to bring down the electrical fence around the field. Then Mory shared the story of my eating mouse turds for breakfast.

Gordon said, "Let's see—so far you have eaten mouse turds, ripped up the fence posts surrounding the field, and helped put out a kitchen fire. Is there anything else I'm missing?"

"I think that about sums it up," Donald said, smiling.

Gordon continued, "And you are only half-way through the day, Richie. Maybe you should just stay in your room until the planets realign themselves."

There was loud laughter around the table. To me, though, the idea did not sound that far-fetched.

After lunch, Donald and I set out one more time to get the firewood. We returned to the Pontiac and headed out into the field. "Let's see if we can do it without knocking down all the fence posts this time, eh?" Donald said.

I smiled and nodded in agreement. I was also starting to realize that the Canadians really did use the word "eh" a lot. They used it for almost anything—questions, comments, etc.

As we approached the wooded area, I reflected on how the whole idea of heating buildings with wood was quite a shock to me. Heating with wood in the twentieth century? That was outright *primitive*. No one in Westchester County would even think of such a thing, unless it was to entertain friends around the fireplace in the living room (in a house centrally heated by oil, gas, or electricity, of course.)

Nevertheless, it was a fact in rural Canada—a fact that became all too real as we reached the forested part of Dandelion's property and unloaded the chainsaw and gasoline.

We came to an area of dead trees, and both put on our hardhats and safety goggles. Donald pulled on the drawstring and the saw bucked up a few inches and then started up immediately. He cut a V wedge into one side of a tree and then very carefully cut a straight line into the opposite side of the V. The tree began to fall, and Donald yelled, *"Timber!"*

Once the tree was on the ground, he began to trim the branches off the tree, then cut the main trunk into eight-foot lengths. I was amazed at how easy Donald made it all look. He was so graceful, it was almost like watching him dance with the saw.

I had always admired (envied?) men who were comfortable with tools and machines, and Donald was one of those men. I, on the other hand, had never used a chainsaw before.

"Wanna give it a try, Richie?" Donald asked. "There is a first time for everything, right?" I was a bit hesitant, but learned quickly under Donald's gentle guidance: "I like the way you are holding the chainsaw and the way your legs are wide enough to take a sturdy stance. I also like that you are not letting the blade get too close to the ground."

Once I got the knack of it, there was no stopping me. We took turns the rest of the afternoon cutting the wood and then dragging the logs back to the wagon. Four hours later we headed home, the wagon filled to the top.

Richie at the woodpile

My Second Day

The next day I was determined to get things right. While stirring my oatmeal, I inspected it carefully to make sure there were no mouse turds. Finding none, I smiled. "Yup, gonna be a good day."

While eating my oatmeal, I reviewed my labor sheet and found out that I was to spackle my new bedroom with Donald. I didn't know what spackling was, but I looked forward to working with Donald again.

After breakfast, I walked over to inspect my new room, which was located in the new addition to the house. I went through the door that separated the living room from the new addition and found a large room about twenty by twenty feet long. On the left wall were two doors. The one in the far corner led to my future bedroom, the other one to the front porch.

On the right wall, two large windows let in an abundance of light and at the wall facing me, there were two tinnery cutting stations. Gordon sat at the one on the right using a small torch to cut intricate designs into a one-gallon size can. There was also a slight smell of burnt metal in the air.

Cutting stations involved three sheets of metal that made for a "hood" over each station: one for each side with a third sheet going across the top. At the back of each station, a small fan covered a hole in the wall, which took away the fumes created by the oxygen-acetylene torch. There was also a ½-inch-thick metal pipe, one foot long, attached to the edge of each station using a C-clamp. The pole acted as a brace to lean the back of the hand across while it made designs on the can.

The can Gordon worked on sat on top of another can. The can on the bottom was upside down and had a small metal wheel on top of it. The wheel sat horizontally on top of the can and had eight white dots painted around the outer rim of the wheel.

The wheel sat on a set of ball bearings and after each straight line was cut down the can, the wheel (along with the can on it), could be turned so that a new line could be cut. This process was called "ribbing."

For a twenty-eight-ounce can, there were eight lines. The lines started just below the rim of the can and then went down, before stopping about an inch from the bottom. That way before putting designs on the sides and bottom, the bottom edge was bent out and a gentle curve added to the can.

An official from the Canadian Occupation and Safety Board had inspected the whole set-up and had deemed it safe enough to take away any toxic chemicals found in the cans themselves or fumes from the torch.

Gordon was listening to the news on the radio and I couldn't believe what I was hearing: "In the Middle East, the United Nations peace-keeping force is fighting the Christians." Wasn't there some kind of irony in that statement?

Gordon lifted his mask. "Ah, good morning, Richie. Any mouse turds in your oatmeal today?" he asked with a grin.

"Nope, I think I learned from my experience yesterday."

"That's good, Richie. Skinner would be proud of you. But did you check for cow feces in your milk?" I felt a sickening feeling in my stomach, as I realized I had mixed some milk into my oatmeal that morning. I asked, "Is there…"

Gordon cut me off and said, "Just kidding. That rarely happens." Gordon turned, pulled his visor back down, and began working on the can again. Small sparks flew all around the can as Gordon deftly moved the torch.

I walked closer to get a better glimpse of Gordon's newest creation. The can already ribbed and bent, Gordon now cut small swirls on the side of the can and then turned the can over so that just the bottom was showing. There were a number of basic designs used by the communitarians. There were small "swamp" designs, which consisted of three small, curved lines. Then there was the design of just using an "S" pattern. Each communitarian was free to come up with a new pattern as long as it looked "sellable."

As Gordon gracefully moved the torch around the bottom of the can, I could see the outline of a beautiful rose begin to appear. It was almost as if Gordon were choreographing a dance with the torch and can, the whole process making him one with the can. Like Donald, he made it look easy.

"What's on the agenda for you today, Richie? You want to cut some cans with me?"

"Well, I'm assigned to work with Donald this morning doing the spackling on my new room. I haven't seen him yet, though."

"He had to go into town to get a part for the car. He probably won't be back for an hour or so."

"Well, okay, in that case I'd be happy to work with you, Gordon."

"Excellent."

Gordon turned off his torch and set it on the table. Then took off his denim gloves and lifted his mask. Turning off the radio, he said, "Let's put some music on first. What would you like to hear?"

I had grown up on Motown music and religiously watched the TV dance show *Soul Train*. I was also actually once in a band, called "White Soul," which consisted of five white guys playing Motown music. I played bass guitar. (We were missing something, so we didn't stay together very long.)

"Anything by the Temptations?" I asked.

"I have just the album," Gordon said and went into the living room, and put on the *Temptations Greatest Hits* album and returned to the room. As the sound of *Ain't Too Proud to Beg* began to fill the room, I sat down at the other cutting station and put on a pair of gloves and apron. I then reached for the mask hanging up on a peg right next to the cutting station. When I was finished putting on all the paraphernalia, I felt like a Samurai warrior ready for battle. I wondered what my college friends would think if they saw me now.

"Ah, yes, nothing like Motown music to start off the day, eh?" Gordon mused as he placed his gloves and mask back on. He then sat down and grabbed his torch with his left hand. With his right hand, he slowly turned the small knob located near the tip of the torch, releasing the gas mixture. Keeping the torch in his left hand, he then grabbed a "striker" (a flint and steel contraption), and placed it right next to the tip of the torch. He squeezed the striker tightly. This produced a large spark and the torch lit up instantly. "Baby, you can light my fire," Gordon mumbled. He then turned to me and asked, "Remember how this all works, Richie?"

I had worked in the tinnery the first time I visited, and I watched Gordon carefully, just to refresh my memory. "Yeah, no problem, Gordon." I picked up my own torch and repeated the ritual. The only difference was that instead of singing the chorus to the song *Light My Fire* (which Gordon had just used) I had my own way of starting the ritual and shouted "Flame On!" It was the same battle cry used by the comic book character The Human Torch, from the comic book series *Fantastic Four*. I had almost the entire collection when I was a teenager. I also had the first *Spider Man* comic book. (Unfortunately, my parents had thrown away my whole comic book collection when I went off to college.)

I picked up a small empty soup can and began ribbing it. I was pleasantly surprised to find my hands immediately remembered the task before me. "Like riding a bicycle," I commented as sparks flew all around the can and table. I was grateful for mask and apron.

"So, you heard Jane and Maple are hoping to be back by tomorrow evening? I'm so excited to hear how the Federation assembly went and any new ideas they came up with," said Gordon.

"Can you tell me again which communities are actually in the Federation, Gordon?"

"Let's see, there's Twin Oaks down in Virginia, the granddaddy of us all. Then there is East Wind out in Missouri, Aloe in North Carolina, and North Mountain in Virginia."

"There is a new community interested in joining called Sandhill, also located down in Missouri. They apparently are an organic farm cooperative. We also just heard rumors about another community called Los Horcones, down in Mexico. They have expressed an interest to find out more about the Federation as well. They seem to be a bunch of radical behaviorists trying to apply behavior principles in an even more systematic way than we are."

I had visited Twin Oaks Community in the Summer of 1975, after stopping out of college and wanting to see for myself if a Walden Two community could actually exist. I attended the Twin Oaks Communities Conference over Labor Day weekend along with 400 other conferees. What a turning point in my life that had been.

Twin Oaks was located in Louisa, Virginia, and it was the first commune I had ever visited. I was impressed at how well organized it was. The members there seemed to be so responsible, competent, and friendly. I was exhilarated to find out that this kind of lifestyle actually worked for people and that I wasn't alone with my wild ideas about going communal. There I met Doug Norman, one of the founders of Dandelion. I had corresponded with Doug during the year after that conference and visited Dandelion in the spring of 1976.

Gordon finished the can he was decorating and tossed it into a large wooden box with wheels on the bottom of it. "Jane and I were actually thinking of joining Twin Oaks, but we thought the summers in Virginia would be too hot. We also had the dream of building a more behaviorist Walden Two community here in Canada."

A Canadian who had majored in journalism at college, Jane had discovered *Walden Two* in her junior year. After visiting Twin Oaks with Gordon, she was convinced that they could create a similar community in Canada.

"How did you come up with the name Dandelion, Gordon?"

"Well, we were looking for a catchy name and Dandelion came up almost by accident. We were just brainstorming about something attached to the land. I think it was Donald who first came up with it. We thought the Dandelion flower was a rugged plant with many uses and a survivor. It could also be used to produce wine." Gordon smiled and continued, "And Jane thought we could call our newsletter *Pappus* in honor of the seeds the Dandelion produces. Suburbanites think of it as a pest."

I smiled at the story of Dandelion's origin. One of my passions was learning about where names and rituals came from. As part of joining Dandelion, members were free to choose a new name for themselves if they wished. I had always liked "Richie," so I decided to keep it. (However, over time, I took on many nicknames.)

I finished ribbing the soup can and placed it on the counter between Gordon and me. "A great story, Gordon. Now here I am a part of it."

"Yes, and we are so happy to have you with us, Richie."

We continued working on the cans the rest of the morning, listening to songs by James Brown, The Four Tops and the Supremes. By the time we stopped for lunch, we had filled two large boxes with cans. They would later be dipped.

The dipping mixture was made of paint thinner and varnish and held in a large, white five-gallon plastic pail. Members who dipped the cans wore dishwashing gloves and a filtered mask over their nose and mouth to keep out the fumes. Cans were hung by bent paper clips and placed on a series of thick strings that had been strung up horizontally wall-to-wall.

A trough at the bottom of the strings caught the excess drippings. They would later be used for another batch. In the summer, the cans were hung up outside, but in the winter, they were hung up in a separate room.

The room that was soon to be mine had been the one used for dipping. However, two weeks before I had arrived, Donald moved the set up down to the new industrial building.

"Let's go see what Durin cooked up for lunch, shall we?" Gordon said, as we turned off our torches, hung up our gear, and turned off the fans.

"So, what's on for lunch today, Durin?" Gordon inquired as we walked into the kitchen.

"Oh, just the usual—leftovers from last night along with some extra sauce and rice I added." Mory and Chantal entered the kitchen, and we all sat down and began eating. While we were eating, Donald returned from town and joined us.

"Sorry about the delay, Richie, but one thing led to another and the next thing I knew it was 11:30. Hope you found something else to do."

"No problem, Donald. I had a great time cutting cans with Gordon and getting back into the process." I then paused and added, "I was wondering if we could do the spackling this afternoon. I'm eager to get my own space."

"Sure, Richie, I was planning on that. We all want you to have your own room as soon as possible."

"What actually is 'spackling' anyway, Donald?" I asked.

There were a few groans and chuckles from around the table.

Mory piped up and said, "You don't really want to know, Richie."

Donald smiled and said, "Oh, it's really not that bad. Can even be fun if you're in the right head space. It's actually pretty simple. We use a mixture of glue-like paste to fill in the cracks where the sheetrock lines up. After it dries, we sand it down and then paint over it, making a smooth surface all around."

"How long does it take to dry?"

"About twenty-four hours. So if we spackle today, we can probably paint your room tomorrow afternoon. Then you can move in the day after that. Sound workable to you?"

"Sounds like a plan, Donald—but don't forget how our plan yesterday worked out." We both chuckled.

Mory then added, "Don't forget that you'll need about half an hour to clean the spackling off your face."

After lunch, Donald and I gathered the spackling supplies and went to my room. The room was eight feet square and had a small window that faced the driveway. Even though the room was small, I was looking forward to having my own space.

There was a large white plastic pail halfway filled with water. We both put on paper masks over our mouths and noses. Donald lifted a twenty-five-pound bag of powered spackle and poured a bunch of it into the pail. Setting the bag down, he then picked up a paint stirrer and began stirring the powder into the water.

"Double, double, toil and trouble," he chanted, smiling over at me. When the powder and water finally gelled, he picked up a trowel, took some spackle and began putting it along the crack where the two pieces of sheetrock met. After watching him for a minute, I picked up another trowel and began working on the other side of the room.

We finished in half an hour, and I went to the bathroom to clean up. I looked in the mirror and saw that I had all kinds of white paste across my face, eyebrows and hair. Mory was right.

As I cleaned my face, I was happy knowing that I had just acquired another new skill and tomorrow would paint my room as well. I felt like I was a pioneer building my own room from scratch.

I finished washing, then went to my labor sheet and wrote, "three hours tinnery, half hour spackling." Then I met Donald outside and we spent the rest of the afternoon bringing the logs we had cut yesterday into the basement and stacking them.

"Nice job, Richie. That should keep us warm for a couple of months at least." We shook hands and I returned to the visitor room. I felt a little tired from all the physical work I had done that day and decided to lie down for a few minutes.

A little while later, I awoke to the aroma of tomato sauce and went into the kitchen to investigate. Durin was standing over the stove with his long beard, stirring some homemade tomato sauce. There were some meatballs made of texturized vegetable protein (TVP) also cooking in some oil. The combined smells made my mouth water.

Durin had a rice kernel stuck on the lower right side of his beard, left over from lunch. (The joke around Dandelion was that by having a beard, others could always tell what you ate at your last meal.)

"Smells great, Durin. Anything I can do to help?"

"Well, you can cut up some slices of that Italian bread, if you want, and then set the table. That would be a big help. Thanks." I went to the shelves, took out some plates, and began setting the table.

"So, have we heard from Jane or Maple yet?" I inquired.

"Oh, yeah, haven't you heard? Gordon drove into Kingston to pick them up. They should be back anytime now."

I finished setting the table and at that moment, the front door opened, and I could hear the animated voices of Gordon, Jane, and Maple. Durin walked into the living room as Donald came down from the second floor and entered the welcoming home celebration as well. Mory was there, and I went in to join the festivities.

I saw Jane and Gordon standing by the window and Donald was hugging a woman who could only be Maple. Her back was to me as I walked up to them.

When I reached them, Maple stopped hugging Donald and said, "Hi Richie, welcome to Dandelion." She gave me a quick hug.

"Nice meeting you as well, Maple." The first thing I noticed about Maple was her radiant smile with perfect teeth. She was twenty-one and had long, beautiful reddish-brown hair and striking blue eyes—attributes that reflected her Irish heritage. She had high cheekbones and her smile lit up the room.

Jane walked over to me with a big smile on her face, hugged me tightly, and kissed me on the cheek. "Hi, Richie, so glad to have you back. Hope your time here has been going well."

"Great to see you as well, Jane, and yes, it is great being back." Jane had long blond hair and penetrating grey eyes. I was delighted to see her again.

Then Gordon piped up and said, "But wait till you hear how his first day went, Jane. It's a wonder he's still here." Donald, Durin, and Mory laughed at that remark.

"Sounds like a story there," Jane commented, looking at me.

"Supper will be ready in two minutes," Durin said, and returned to the kitchen.

As the crowd wandered into the kitchen, Gordon pulled out several beers and passed them around. After Durin had placed the spaghetti, meatballs, and salad on the table, we all gathered around and held hands.

After the daily ritual, Gordon asked, "So, any good stories from the road?"

Maple began, "Well, as far as road stories, we were lucky to catch some very friendly truckers on the way down and back. They called ahead on their CB radios to transfer us to other truckers."

Jane added, "Yeah, that's true, but the thing that really annoyed both of us was being referred to as 'beavers' in the trucking lingo."

Gordon said, "Well, small price to pay for free transportation, eh?"

Jane said, "Maybe, but it was so humiliating. I think next time the community should come up with enough money so that we can afford a bus. We'd both feel a lot safer."

"That's right. Hitching worked for us this time, but it can be so unpredictable," Maple added.

I hadn't hitch-hiked for years, having had my own car for the last seven years. That would change though. As part of living at Dandelion, I would either have to sell my 1972 Pontiac or donate it to the community. I had discussed that idea already with Gordon, but apparently the community was committed to smaller cars with better gas mileage. So I would sell it when I went back to New York over Christmas.

"Please tell me how my old community, East Wind, is doing," said Durin.

"Well," Jane began, "They are building a very large industrial building to house their blossoming hammock business. They are also planning on building a new child-adult residence building, updating their sewage system, and leasing more land for corn and soybeans. There was also talk of starting a peanut-butter business."

Maple added, "There has also apparently been a cultural revolution with a proliferation of art, music and dance."

Jane continued, "Twin Oaks is expanding their agricultural and child programs and have added a new steel industrial building. They are also requesting articles for *Communities* magazine."

Maple then said, "We emphasized our need for a new residence building for next summer and the Federation issued a statement of support encouraging skilled construction workers from other communities to come up and help us with this project. We talked about setting up a formal labor exchange with other communities. They come up and help us, and then sometime in the future we will help them with a project. The Federation said it would subsidize the transportation, which would really be a big help."

Gordon got all excited and said, "Far out, extra labor would really help with that project."

Maple continued, "A big issue we talked about was our need for outreach. We want to attract more members, including people from groups who have been unrepresented among us: working class people, racial minorities, women, gays, and older people. Posters were sent to a bunch of food co-ops and a brochure is being produced that will highlight each of our communities. In March, Chip from Twin Oaks will give a talk about the Federation at Harvard."

I stopped eating my meatballs and exclaimed, "Wow, Harvard? You have to be smart to go there." Donald and Gordon groaned and shook their heads. Maple, not sure of my sense of humor, stared at me for a moment, and then smiled. "Yes, you're right, Richie."

Jane picked up the conversation, "And we all agreed that continuing to have conferences was one of the best ways to get our message out."

"That's all encouraging news," Donald said. "Sounds like a lot is going on and I hope we can get a bunch of new members with all this publicity and outreach coming up."

I sat there eating my dinner, taking it all in. The conversation had really touched something inside me. When I heard Jane talk about the Federation "statement of purpose," I tuned in. "We support activities that benefit those people who do not receive an equitable share of society's resources."

That last statement clearly matched my own personal values of the communal movement, as I wanted so much to help build a more egalitarian society. To me, community was more than a way of life. It was a political statement. After reading *Walden Two* and studying behavioral psychology, I was ready for a change. For far too long at college and with my family and friends, I had felt like a "cultural mutant."

I tried explaining my new-found enthusiasm to people and most just wished me luck. I realized though, that I would have to find a group of like-minded people who were committed to building an egalitarian community.

Jane and Maple finished telling their stories, and then Donald told them what had been going on at Dandelion. He highlighted how we had managed to knock over the electric fence, and it seemed with each retelling, the story grew. Now it seemed like Donald and I had knocked over every fence post on the property and almost brought the farmhouse down at the same time. Jane and Maple just smiled and shook their heads in amusement.

After supper, we all retired to the living room and continued catching up with Jane and Maple while Gordon played the guitar. There was much laughter and joking over the rest of the evening.

The following day, I painted my room white (since the community had bought several cans of that color on sale and it was the only color available), then I scrounged around the community looking for miscellaneous items to help decorate my room.

I took a mattress from the visitor room and found in the storage barn an old bed frame for it. I also found a small table there and set it up next to my bed. Then I placed on it the lamp I had brought with me.

With some old bricks and wooden boards, I built a couple of shelves, which I used for storing my clothes. I placed my father's painting on the wall facing my bed. To cover the window, I found an old towel and hung it up with pushpins. For the final touch, I found two tin can candleholders (along with candles) and set them on top of the shelves.

The first night in my own room I lit the candles and was mesmerized by the shadows they made on the ceiling. What a great invention the candleholders were. And to think they were originally just garbage! A little while later I blew out the candles and went to sleep.

Robbie's Visit

The following week, Donald's brother Robbie came for a visit. Robbie had spent so much time at Dandelion that he was an honorary member. He had helped build the new addition to the farmhouse as well as the new industrial building. An accomplished photographer, he had documented much of Dandelion's history.

Robbie had a quiet reserved manner but under that, had a dry sense of humor. During his time here, I was to work with him and replace the bottom steps on the staircase leading to the basement.

"No sweat," I thought to myself. "Another new skill I'll learn."

We met on Monday morning and Robbie, who had much more carpentry experience than I did, examined the staircase carefully. He realized that the whole staircase had rotted wood and was ready to fall apart. With his melodious Canadian accent, he said, "Well, looks to me like we might need to replace the whole staircase, Richie." He turned to me and asked, "What do you think?"

I imitated Robbie's inspection technique and then declared, "Yup. I have to agree with you Robbie. Where do we start?"

"Well, the first thing we will have to do is take down the whole staircase itself. I believe there is enough wood left over from building Aduki that we could do it."

I began thinking to myself that on my labor sheet I had only one hour assigned to replace the step. Now here we were getting ready to rebuild the whole staircase in one hour. I didn't think so. "What about our labor sheets, though, Robbie? We've only been assigned one hour for this." Robbie smiled, seeming to have been through this kind of questioning before.

"I think the building maintenance manager miscalculated the severity of the situation. I'd say this is a potential safety hazard and think we should just do it. If you want, you can just help me for an hour and I can finish it off myself. On the other hand, you can check in with Donald (the current building maintenance manager) and see what he says. I'm sure he would justify the extra time."

I thought about the amount of time it would take to track down Donald and decided to just go with my gut and help Robbie. In addition, I liked Robbie's warm friendly approach to life and wanted to work with him. On top of that, I had always prided myself on following safety protocols.

We spent the rest of the morning building the new staircase and by lunchtime, a brand-new staircase was in place. I was very pleased with myself. I was using a hammer for the first time in ages, and I felt very comfortable working with Robbie.

Robbie talked about his work (for an engineering company in Montreal) and reported that he felt like a capitalist drone there, while at Dandelion he felt like a socialist drone. We both chuckled at that.

After lunch, Donald, Robbie, and I were to move the tinnery stations down to Aduki. This would be an historic event for Dandelion. The industry was moving out of the farmhouse, leaving space for two additional bedrooms.

The three of us met in the tinnery workspace in the house. "Well, how should we approach this?" Donald asked.

Robbie said, "I could start cutting holes in the walls down in Aduki while you and Richie dismantle the cutting stations up here."

"Does that work for you, Richie?" Donald asked.

"Sure, sounds like a plan."

Robbie left.

"Okay, how about you take care of that one and I'll take care of this one?" Donald said, pointing to the cutting stations in front of us. I nodded.

The first thing we both did was to remove the C-clamps that attached the metal poles to the table. We placed them and the poles in a large cardboard box.

We then pulled the metal hoods away from the wall. This was very easy because they were not attached to anything. We then took out the fans.

"Wasn't there some quote during the Vietnam War that said, 'We had to destroy the village in order to save it.' or something like that?" I mused out loud.

Donald smiled and said, "Yeah, I vaguely remember that. However, luckily, we are not really destroying anything, just recycling it."

The environmental movement had just started gaining steam the last couple of years, and Dandelion members were committed to recycling as much as they could. In fact, they could not believe that they were taking other people's garbage, recycling it, and then selling it back to them at a profit. They were laughing all the way to the bank, as the saying goes.

"We should probably get some insulation and stuff those holes. That will keep the cold air out," Donald commented. "I'll run down to Aduki and get some. Be right back." He picked up the box with the poles and left.

While Donald was gone, I began to realize how everything around here seemed to take longer than the time planned for it. Patching up the holes in the wall would be another whole task. I placed all the aprons, masks, strikers, and gloves into another cardboard box.

Donald returned a few minutes later with some pink fiberglass insulation, and began stuffing it into both holes and said, "That ought to hold it for a while, at least temporarily. On the other hand, it may be another case of temporarily permanent." He laughed at his own joke.

I smiled, and then asked, "Does that happen a lot around here, Donald? Temporary fixes becoming permanent?"

"Oh, yeah, just you wait. You'll see for yourself how common that is. Unbelievable."

After putting the fans in the boxes, we were ready to bring the table down to the shop. We pried the door to the porch open, then lifted the table and carried it out across the porch. The table was just narrow enough to fit through the porch doorway and then through the screened doorway leading to the driveway. We then slowly crab-walked the table down to the shop and maneuvered it through the front doorway.

My arm muscles ached as we entered the shop and placed the table down on the cement floor. To the right of us, was an open space, about ten by fifteen feet. This was where finished cans would be on display for the occasional customers who stopped by.

To the left of us was a door which led to the new tinnery room where the new cutting stations would go. The room already had large wooden shelves that covered the wall on the right, from top to bottom. We entered to see how far Robbie had gotten.

Robbie had already cut out two holes on the wall opposite the doorway and was just finishing up with drilling out a third hole on the left wall. This would later hold an extra cutting station. We could feel the wind coming through all the openings. "There, that ought to do it," Robbie said, as he stepped back to admire his work.

Donald agreed saying, "Nice job, Robbie. I think we are ready to install the table and christen the new tinnery. How about Richie and I bring the table in and set it up while you go get the tinnery hoods and other stuff?" Robbie nodded in agreement and left the building.

While Robbie was gone, we retrieved the table and moved it against the wall with the two holes in it.

A few minutes later, Robbie returned with the two hoods, placed them on the table, and said, "Here you go."

"Ah, the *piece de resistance! Merci beaucoup*, Robbie," Donald said.

"*De rien, mon frère.* Be right back." He left the building for the box of aprons, masks, and torches.

On his way back down to the shop, he passed Donald and me going up. "We're getting the tanks and will be down shortly," Donald said.

While we were getting the tanks, Robbie maneuvered the hoods to fit against the holes. We rolled the tanks in and set them up in the far corner of the room. Donald hooked up the torches while Robbie and I set up the C-clamps on the table. A half hour later, the new tinnery was completed.

Donald sat down at one station, placed a mask on and said, "Let's see if this thing actually works." He smiled, turned the torch on and squeezed the striker. He began singing *Fire* (by the Ohio Players), his ritual for sparking the torch.

Whoosh went the flame. Donald adjusted the torch until he had a thin steady blue flame and then turned it off. "Gentlemen, as tinnery manager, I now declare the new tinnery open for business."

Before we left, we entered the main room of the shop, to show Robbie the new dipping room. This was the space for the budding hammock and hammock-chair business. In the middle of the room stood two wooden hammock jigs and a smaller jig for the chairs.

On the right side of the room, was a smaller room, where the dipping of cans took place, and Donald gave Robbie a quick tour. "A lot more space, eh?" Robbie commented.

At the back of the main room, opposite the front door, were two large swinging doors, which led out to a small parking lot that overlooked the stream. Four small vertical windows lined each of the walls.

Over in the corner was a small oil furnace, and since the shop was not currently in use, it was off. The building temperature was about forty degrees.

Robbie rototilling the garden

My Clearness Meeting

As part of the ritual for joining Dandelion, new members went through a "clearness" meeting—an hour-long meeting where the new members shared with the community why they wanted to join Dandelion, what skills they brought to the community and what their areas of interest were. It was also a chance for members to share what they liked about the new member as well as to voice any concerns.

By the time a visitor had asked (or been asked) to become a member, it was usually clear that there was a mutual attraction and that the community was willing to give the person a try. In reality, because Dandelion was so small and so new (with plenty of work to be done), the community was eager to have new members. As long as a potential member had at least adequate interpersonal skills and could complete the weekly work quota, he or she was usually accepted.

As part of the preparation for the meeting, the potential member was to read the Dandelion Behavior Code, which was a set of community agreements that the community had developed over the past year. By joining Dandelion, the member was agreeing to live by the following agreements:

- We clean up after ourselves and return articles to their proper place so that others can enjoy them.
- We maintain a positive environment by talking about things we like and by exhibiting other positive behaviors. We do not publicly grumble or gripe about things we don't like in the community, but instead take our complaints to the appropriate person or manager.
- We expect members to do their weekly work quota.
- We arrive and start meetings on time.
- We maintain a non-sexist environment.
- We maintain a safe environment.
- We maintain ecological practices.

My clearness meeting took place in the living room one evening, and Jane was facilitating. We began with the song *Peanut Butter and Jelly*, then Jane reviewed the agenda, which was on a large piece of paper on the wall. The meeting would end with a critique of how the process went.

Jane said, "We are all excited to have you applying for membership, Richie, and think you will make an excellent member. So, without further ado, why don't you share your opening statement?"

I began, "I love that we are pioneers trying to build an alternative society that includes all people and the emphasis on positive interactions among people. My skills include a solid understanding of behavioral principles, my writing skills, my teaching skills, and my sense of humor. I am interested in expanding our positive verbal environment as well as helping to develop the cultural side of Dandelion. I would also like to write some articles for *Pappus*. I am also very interested in learning some practical skills like construction and auto mechanics. My only concern is that I owe $1,500 in college loans and am not sure how to pay that off. I realize that Dandelion requires all loans to be paid off before a member joins, but I understand sometimes a compromise can be worked out."

I sat on a chair in the middle of the living room with an empty chair in front of me. Each member then took turns facing me, holding my hands, telling me what they felt about living with me.

Everyone had only good things to say about me and reported that they loved my positive attitude, crazy sense of humor, my commitment to behaviorism, my sense of wonder, and my egalitarian philosophy. The only concern put out was that they hoped I would be able to cope with the long Canadian Winters.

Mory stated that the community thought investing in me was a good idea and that the community was willing to take on paying off my college loan ($37/month) under the following conditions: For the first six months while I was still a provisional member, the community would pay the monthly fee. If I left at any time during those six months, I would agree to reimburse the community for any money already paid back. After I became a full member, though, the community would continue to pay the loan off and any money the community had paid off would not have to be paid from that time forward. That seemed agreeable to all around and was music to my ears.

At the end of the meeting, I left the room while a discussion took place. This was in case there were any concerns about me that a member did not feel comfortable discussing directly with me. A vote was also taken at that time.

After five minutes I returned and was given a summary of the closed discussion. There were no added concerns.

"You are now officially a member of Dandelion Community, Richie." Jane stated. "Welcome aboard!" There were smiles all around and people came up and hugged me.

"Way to go, Richie. Now you can officially go out and destroy more of Dandelion's property," Donald said with a big smile on his face. Gordon walked in from the kitchen with bottles of beer in his hands, which he happily passed around.

I was now officially a provisional member. The only difference between a provisional member and a full member was that provisional members could not vote on issues. (Voting was rare. Most decisions were reached by consensus.) At the end of six months, another clearness meeting would be held and, if the provisional member had proved him or herself, he or she was voted in as a full member.

I left the meeting feeling exhilarated that I was now an official member of Dandelion and went to bed thinking about the community of my dreams.

In the morning while eating breakfast (sans mouse turds), I again reflected on my journey and how much change I had gone through the last couple of weeks. I had graduated from college (leaving behind all the friends I had made there), left my family, my best friend Tony, a lifestyle I was familiar with, a familiar diet, my hometown and my country of origin. Big changes indeed.

At the same time, however, a new sense of purpose and freedom was growing inside me. Every day I woke up with a sense of excitement and looked forward to what the day might bring, knowing my values and behavior were finally matching up. I felt like I was a true behaviorist, changing my environment to change my behavior, a pioneer in building an egalitarian society. Just being at Dandelion felt more meaningful and important than anything else I had done with my life.

I was learning to trust my fellow communitarians as they developed their trust in me. Like the others, I was learning to live within an income-sharing group with little personal spending money. I felt as if we were all out to change the world and nothing could stop us.

Pictures taken of me that fall showed a gleam in my eye and a smile so wide that my face could barely contain it. I felt so connected to what I was doing and felt so alive. It was almost as if I were a child again and that everything would be okay, no matter what.

Edible What?

I had only been on the commune a couple of weeks when the dinner conversation turned to "edible underpants." I had never heard of such an animal and thought it was absurd. (This may have been due to my limited sexual experience.)

I was trying to figure out why anyone would want to eat their own underwear, and without thinking, blurted out, "I don't get it, why would you want to eat your own underwear?"

Forks of tofu on the way to the mouth froze in mid-air. The slicing of bread halted half-way through the loaf. Conversations came to an abrupt halt and a silence befell the table as eight heads turned in unison and stared towards the end of the table where I was sitting.

"What?" I asked innocently.

Donald, sitting directly across from me, realizing that I was serious in my quest for knowledge, explained as gently as he could. "Well, you see, Richie, the idea is to get someone *else* to eat your underwear."

I felt my face turn red-hot and I stammered, "Ohhh…"

The whole table burst out laughing. Inside my head, I had picked up a new Mantra, "You get someone else to eat your underwear, you get someone else to eat your underwear." I then said, "Well, thank you for clearing up that mystery, Donald."

I joined in with the laughter still echoing around the table. Then with a grin I asked, "Does Dandelion actually have any of that underwear?"

More laughter.

"Not yet, but it is on my list for birthday presents," Gordon replied.

The next morning, I found myself in the hallway up on the second floor of the farmhouse, in community clothes (which the community had affectionately come to call "Comedy Clothes"), picking out my clothes for the week. (This was still in the time of sharing everything, not only shirts and pants, but socks, undershirts, and underpants as well.)

I returned to my room and picked out a clean pair of underpants for that day and put it on. A little later while walking down to the shop, I noticed an uncomfortable sensation in my groin area.

When I got down to the tinnery, I dropped my pants and saw that there was a hole in the middle of the underwear about an inch wide, and my penis had slipped through it and stayed there. This situation caused the tip of my penis to rub up against my corduroy pants, causing an unpleasant burning sensation.

I immediately pushed things back into place and returned to Comedy Clothes for a replacement.

I took off the underpants and threw them into the small wastebasket by the dresser. I was into recycling as much as the next communitarian, but this was going way beyond the expectations of what the recycling movement stood for. (Recycling yes, but getting your penis burned in the process was not what I had signed up for.)

A week passed, and I found myself once again getting my weekly allotment of clean underwear and while searching through the underwear drawer, stopped and looked in amazement. There, back in the drawer, were the "holey" underpants. I couldn't believe it. Someone must have thought the underwear had ended up in the garbage by "accident" and believed there was still some life left in it.

In hopes of having no one else suffer the way I had, I got a pair of scissors, cut the underwear to pieces, and tossed the remains into the garbage pail. (I always thought it might have been Gordon on laundry detail that week, but never confirmed my suspicions.)

Visitors

Dandelion had some interesting visitors that fall who contributed to my first impressions of community life. Chantal, the French visitor, had the habit of doing her early-morning yoga routine in the middle of the living room, which I stumbled onto my first morning at Dandelion. With her leg twisted around her head, I had almost asked her if she needed any help.

Then there was Ekima, a woman who was a professional astrologer and did my astrological chart. I had long ago given up reading my daily astrological horoscope, once I got into science, but nevertheless thought it would be fun to see what my chart might show. My most vivid memory of Ekima was early one morning when I was watching her do her Tai Chi routine out in the fog-shrouded field. With the changing colors of the trees in the background, surrounded by the fog, the scene looked magical and I stood there for minutes spellbound by what I was witnessing.

In November, Bruce visited, and after a week he was interested in membership. He had visited other communities within the Federation, but he said Dandelion felt like home to him. I took an instant liking to Bruce, as we both had similar senses of humor and would often do comedy routines from Monty Python.

Then there was Doug Grass. Doug was one of those visitors the members would talk about for weeks after he left. Friendly and outgoing, Doug worked as a costume designer for a theatre troupe in Toronto. He had the endearing habit of singing while he worked. Members would joke about him, saying that he would probably not make a good bank teller, singing, "Here's your money."

He also happened to be gay, and I learned from him a lot about the oppression of gay people. He told me how hard it was for him to find places where he could just be himself, that he often had to hide who he really was, and how he could not openly express his affection for men in public.

I remembered reading somewhere that to conceal his race, Charlie Pride (the black country-western singer), had his first three albums released without a photograph of him on the cover. What kind of message does that send to a person? How do you cope with that kind of daily discrimination?

Now here was Doug talking about a similar situation. Was it any wonder that Doug was attracted to a community that was part of the Federation of Egalitarian Communities?

Christmas 1977

In trying to be as egalitarian as possible, Dandelion did not endorse any religious practices. Spirituality was a private matter. Members were free to practice or celebrate any religion they chose so long as it did not conflict with Dandelion's basic agreements. For many members, the Dandelion vision was a spiritual as well as a political and practical set of beliefs.

The community did celebrate some holidays. (Again, we had all grown up in modern Western society with most of us coming from a Christian or Jewish background.) Community celebrations took place on the spring and autumn equinoxes and on the summer and winter solstices. On the evening of December 21 (the winter solstice that year), the community gathered around the solstice tree (a small hemlock tree from our property) in the living room that had been decorated with various ornaments and popcorn strings.

Maple and Donald cooked a large feast and there were cocktails of dandelion wine. In addition, several presents were under the tree. After supper, we opened our presents and Gordon played some traditional Christmas songs on the guitar. We all sang along and enjoyed a true sense of community.

The next day, I drove down to Mamaroneck, New York, to visit my parents and brother for Christmas. I was excited to see my family and Tony and share with them how much I had learned in my three months at Dandelion.

I got to Mamaroneck, and by coincidence, driving down Fenimore Road, Tony spotted me driving in the opposite direction and tooted his horn. We stopped, got out of our cars, and hugged each other affectionately.

"Tony! So great to see you! How did you recognize me?"

It had snowed the night before and Tony, laughing, pointed to the top of my car with four inches of snow still on it and simply said, "It didn't take a genius to see that you were coming from a more Northern climate." We both laughed.

Then I said, "I'll call you later and we can get together later in the week, okay? Right now I'm past due at my parents'."

"Sure. I'm looking forward to hearing about your adventures. Ciao."

As a joke, I had brought with me a black, bearskin-like coat that looked like something a French-Canadian trapper might wear. I also had a straw farmer's hat that had a wide green visor. I thought it would be fun to walk into my parent's apartment wearing the coat and hat.

"Hey, look, it's the Canuck!" My brother Ed cried out when I walked in the door.

"Oh, my wandering son has returned!" My mom exclaimed.

"Good to see you again, son," my father commented. We were all excited to see each other and shared hugs.

Then my brother jokingly said, "I think it's time for some deprogramming." He walked me to the kitchen, sat me down, and then took out his credit cards and held them in front of me saying, "Bucks, the prime function! Master Card, Visa, American Express! There are no countries, just Exxon, IBM and AT&T!" We were all laughing as he flashed the cards three inches from my face.

Over dinner, I told them about my adventures at Dandelion, emphasizing all the new skills I had learned. They all seemed interested and happy for me, but I picked up a perception that they were waiting for me to say that I had tried out communal living and was now ready to get on with my "real" life. Nevertheless, it was great being back with my family and spending time with them.

I spent the rest of the week catching up with Tony and other friends. Like my parents, they were happy for me but wondered when I was going to get a real job.

Since the community did not need my car, I sold it with no regrets. I realized I was solidifying my commitment to Dandelion by saying goodbye to my car. From now on, I would rely on the bus or hitchhiking to visit my folks.

I saw the movie "Saturday Night Fever" with my brother and Art Bruno. Art (a friend of Ed's) often referred to me as "the innovator" because I could always get people up and dancing. When he heard that I was now making things out of tin cans, he jokingly referred to me as the "Tin Man."

During that time, Lisa, a friend from my college days, called to say hi and see how I was doing. Lisa was twenty years old, had short, cropped, brown hair and happened to have a phenomenal body, with all the right curves in generous proportions. Her major was art and she was a talented poet as well.

The down side of her creativity, though, was that she was an extremely sensitive woman, which seemed to have led to her more easily developing emotional problems.

I had struck up a casual sexual relationship with Lisa the summer before I joined Dandelion. We had been intimate only twice, and since I was headed off to Canada, I didn't think anything long-term would come out of the relationship. I had not pursued it further and didn't correspond with her once I arrived at Dandelion.

Now here she was calling me to say hi, and see how I was doing. I found myself excited to talk with her and fill her in on my past three months. (That she was the last woman I had made love with may also have had something to do with it.)

I shared with her my more notable stories of Dandelion and then asked how she was doing.

"Well, to be honest with you, Richie, this past semester was very hard on me, a lot of stuff going on in my personal life. In fact, I've decided to drop out this coming semester and take a break from school."

"Oh, sorry to hear that, Lisa. Well, what are your plans now?"

"I'm not sure, taking things one day at a time. But, you know, after listening to you describe Dandelion, I was thinking that maybe I could visit there for a while."

I felt my heart leap and said, "Sure, that'd be great, Lisa. I think you might like Dandelion and we could sure use the extra help. Let me make some phone calls to set things up and I'll get back to you, okay?"

"That would be much appreciated, Richie. Thanks so much."

Two days later, we drove back up to Dandelion in Lisa's 1972 Volkswagen bug. We had some very interesting conversations along the way, about community, college, art and the purpose of life.

We arrived at Dandelion by early evening and as a joke, I once again wore the bearskin coat and straw hat along with my sunglasses. We walked in the front door and headed straight to the kitchen where dinner was in progress. We got to the kitchen. I put my arm around Lisa and shouted, *"Bonjour, mon amis!"*

Gordon, Mory, Donald, Durin, Jane, and Timothy all cheered and laughed. At the table was a new visitor named Alabama who had just arrived from that state. He looked up from his plate of tofu and beans and declared in a heavy Southern accent, "Wellll, what do we have here?"

After catching up over dinner how everyone's Christmas vacation went, Lisa and I went to her car and unloaded it. Gordon, the current visitor manager, had assigned Lisa to the visitor room, so we moved her suitcase and sleeping bag there. I thought that was a wise move. It would be good for Lisa to have her own space, since she said she was planning to stay for a month.

After helping Lisa put her stuff away, I went to my room and unpacked. I felt good being back at Dandelion. I had just finished unpacking when there was a knock at my door. It was Gordon, with Lisa standing behind him. "Uh, Richie, I have a request. (He began scratching his chin.) As visitor manager, you know I originally thought of putting Lisa in the visitor room, but, Alabama is in there currently, and Lisa said she felt uncomfortable sharing a room with a strange man. I was thinking that if it's okay with you, maybe she could spend the night here until we can make other arrangements?"

I thought of the various sexual positions I had not yet tried with Lisa, but I was hesitant, concerned about Lisa's emotional balance. I didn't want to set up any expectations that this would be her space for the unknown length of time she would be at Dandelion.

However, I was horny as hell, especially after that long eight-hour drive.

"Sure, Gordon, that would be fine. Come on in, Lisa. We can debrief more about Dandelion." She smiled and said, "Thanks so much, Richie."

Lisa entered with her suitcase and set it down on the bed. "Sorry to intrude on your space, Richie, but it just felt too weird to even think of sharing a bedroom with a man I don't know."

"That's fine, Lisa. I was actually going to invite you to stay here for the night anyway." I smiled and walked over to her and gave her a warm embrace. "It's the least I can do to thank you for driving me back here." She smiled again.

I continued, "As you can see, I only have a twin bed mattress. So you can have it and I'll just sleep on the cot." Feeling proud in my forethought of bringing up my army cot, I immediately reached under the bed and pulled it out. I began setting it up and felt as if I were in some kind of Woody Allen movie.

"Oh, you don't have to give up your bed, Richie. I'm happy to sleep on the cot."

"Well, maybe we can both try sleeping on my bed and see what happens." I smiled.

Lisa smiled back and said, "That would be fine."

"First things first. Let me light some candles." I lit two candles, placed them in the tin can holders, and turned off the light. Then I placed her suitcase next to the wall. "That's better, yes?"

She looked up at the flickering shadows on the ceiling and said, "Those are so beautiful." She smiled at me and then stepped to the corner of the room, turned her back and slowly removed her sweater, shirt and jeans. I realized I was about to have my first sexual experience in community. In the candlelight, she looked like a dream fantasy.

She was wearing black panties and a black bra. She turned around to face me, and her large breasts came spilling out over the edges of her bra. I felt like they were taunting me to reach out and touch them, hold them, and squeeze them. I felt a sudden intake of breath.

"Lisa, you are even more beautiful than I remember." I walked over to her and began kissing her at the same time squeezing her breasts. She began unbuttoning my shirt as I searched for the clasp on the back of her bra. I was so excited my hands actually fumbled and I kept missing the clasp.

"Here, let me do it," she said smiling. I watched in wonder and with gratitude as the bra parachuted to the floor and two of the most perfect breasts I had ever seen rose up to greet me. Her nipples were pointing straight up, and I immediately began sucking them. Things then began happening very fast.

Soon we were both naked on my bed, feeling and squeezing each other. "Lisa, just to make sure, you're still on your birth control pills, right?" She smiled at me warmly and said, "Yes, you don't have to worry about my becoming pregnant. That is the last thing I need to happen in my life right now."

With that discussion out of the way, and a mounting urgency, the next thing I knew, Lisa had turned over onto her hands and knees and spread her legs apart. Her perfectly shaped ass was slightly raised and I lined up behind her and quickly inserted myself. She was very wet and I easily slid all the way up inside her. I began thrusting and grunting. Within seconds, I ejaculated and let out a loud "Ohhh," collapsing on top of her. I pulled out and we just lay there watching the shadows on the ceiling until we fell asleep.

The next morning, we didn't get up until after nine and I was still in shock with what had happened to my body the night before.

We finally stumbled out of bed and headed for the bathroom to take a shower together. This was another historic moment, the first time I would take a shower with a woman. Since we had gotten such a late start, the living room, bathroom and kitchen were deserted.

In the shower with Lisa, I watched in amazement as my hands washed her breasts and in between her legs. She in turn gently washed my chest and lower body. We both smiled at each other, and I felt so peaceful.

After getting dressed, I cooked up some oatmeal for both of us and we ate breakfast in the living room, gazing out the large window. It was one of those glorious, sunny days in January and the sky was cobalt blue. "How about I give you a tour after we finish breakfast, Lisa?"

"Sure, I'd like that. I'd also like to see the cow, which I hear is expecting to deliver any day now."

We finished breakfast and put our dishes in the appropriate basins. We then put on our coats and went outside. The brisk cold air immediately struck and astounded both of us. I grabbed Lisa's hand and said, "Welcome to Utopia."

We walked down to the shop and found Bruce and Gordon working away at the cutting stations in the tinnery. Gordon turned, lifted his mask, and with a slight grin on his face asked, "Did you guys sleep okay last night?"

I winked at Gordon and said, "Oh, yeah, it was a very reinforcing evening."

Lisa smiled and said, "The accommodations were most pleasant." I smiled at Lisa and we all laughed.

"Did Richie remember to set up the candle holders?" Bruce asked.

"Oh yeah, the shadows on the ceiling were almost hypnotic," replied Lisa. "I think I am really going to enjoy my time here."

January 1978

For the rest of January, Lisa did spend all her nights with me. We took many long walks together and it was an unforgettable month for me. It was the first time in my life that I was getting laid on a regular basis. What a phenomenal feeling. How fulfilled I felt.

I taught Lisa how to do tinnery, weave hammocks, and milk the cow. She was an excellent cook and made some very tasty meals for the community, especially the veggie burgers, which tasted like real meat.

The community hosted a "Coffee House" one evening and Lisa shared some of the poetry she had written about Dandelion. She seemed to be making a fine impression on everyone.

But something was missing in Lisa's commitment to the community. Although Lisa and I had gotten to know each other much better, I was still hesitant about any long-term involvement with her. She had talked about becoming a member, but I felt it was because she wanted to be closer to me, rather than understanding what Dandelion really stood for. I shared how that made me feel uncomfortable and she decided to go back to New York and think about things.

When January ended, and she drove down the driveway, I thought that might be the last time I would see her. I soon found out, however, that it was only the beginning of the story.

For the community, January turned out to have many surprises. Chrissie gave birth to a calf, and because the birth was so easy, the community named her "Easy." Bruce (who had now changed his name to Timothy) and Alabama decided to become members, had their clearness meetings and were accepted.

Alabama had the amazing ability to sweat down one half of his face whenever he ate cheese. I, with my commitment to science, wanted a demonstration when I heard about this. So one evening I asked Alabama to demonstrate this ability. While Alabama ate the cheese, I stared at him, eyeball to eyeball. Then, lo and behold, I observed one side of his forehead grow bright red, and then, right before my very eyes, I witnessed Alabama begin to sweat only on the left side of his face.

"That is absolutely amazing, Alabama. How do you do that?"

With a goofy "I-told-you-so" expression, Alabama smiled and said, "I have no idea."

Durin, Alabama, Mory, Jane, Martin, Donald, Maple, Richie, Hans, Gordon (sitting)

The other Dandelions witnessing this event began applauding and laughing. "How can we turn that into a money-making scheme?" blurted Gordon.

That month also saw the arrival of the first wave of people from Katimavek, a program sponsored by the Department of National Defense. *Katimavek* was an Innuit word meaning together.

The program offered Canadian youth (seventeen-to-twenty-one-year-olds) a ten-month group learning and working experience. During the ten months, they spent time in several locations across the country, working at various labor projects, learning to live together as a group, and developing various personal and professional skills.

Dandelion took on four Katimaveks at a time, for two-week periods. This turned out to be a beneficial experience for all of us. The Katimaveks were all polite, generally easy-going young people. They contributed much-needed energy to the community and built two new bedrooms in the space where the original tinnery used to be.

Anita and Robert, two behaviorists who were interested in starting a Walden Two community in upper New York State, also visited during that time. They stayed the whole month of January and I had some thought-provoking discussions with them about behaviorism and the vision of Dandelion. By the time they left, they too were seriously thinking of becoming members.

With that many people around, there were always lively discussions going on, and the farmhouse felt like it was bursting with people as well as energy. Members talked seriously about the need for a new residence building. In addition, work was more easily distributed and the work quota dropped to forty hours a week. Members got a glimpse of the benefits a larger community could offer.

After Lisa left, I returned to my normal routines. Not having a lover/significant other in my life left something to be desired. I thought about her often and realized how much having a lover in community added to the richness of life here. I missed talking with her and making love with her.

February was an interesting month for me. I worked hard and got caught up with all my reading and correspondence. Then one evening, late in February, while I was down in Aduki, Maple walked in.

The lighting was very soft when she entered the shop and had an almost dream-like quality. It was about nine p.m. and I was in the large hammock area, putting records away. No one else was in the shop. The song *Rhiannon* by Fleetwood Mac was playing softly in the background. I heard the door close and turned to see who it was.

She came directly toward me smiling and upon reaching me, wrapped her arms tightly around my neck and stared at me intensely. I wondered what was going on behind her beautiful blue eyes as I smiled and returned her gaze.

"You are the most gentle, kindest, non-sexist man I have ever met," she said. I was surprised by that statement and was sure she had mistaken me for someone else. I also felt a little uncomfortable as well, as I was just beginning to grasp the many issues around the women's movement. Nevertheless, her words certainly sounded nice.

"Well, um, thank you," was all I managed to say. Maple smiled at me one more time, released her arms from my neck, then turned and left the shop. I was in a daze as I watched her leave.

After she left, I found myself thinking, "What was that all about?" Then, "What would happen if I got involved with Maple?" Nothing much, except she was in love with my best friend. I immediately put the thought out of my mind, finished putting the records away, and left the shop.

After that night, things were different between Maple and me. I caught myself thinking more and more about her and what a beautiful woman she was. I wasn't sure, but it seemed when I hugged her now, the hugs seemed to last longer. Was I imagining that or what?

Adding to my confusion was my relationship with Lisa. Although I missed having her around, I felt no long-term potential there. Maple, on the other hand, was committed to Dandelion as much as I was. On top of that, I was now much more open to the idea of getting involved with a Dandelion woman even if she were involved with my best friend. However, a three-way relationship sounded too difficult—or maybe crazy was the more appropriate word. How could I consider getting involved with her when she and Donald had their own relationship?

But I also knew that Donald had a sexual relationship with Jane. Donald had two lovers, and I had none. I felt no jealousy, just confusion. How did that actually work?

To make matters worse, I had never had a girlfriend in either high school or college, so I had no experience with long-term relationships. Lisa had been the first woman I was involved with for any length of time.

Three days later, Donald went away to do a week-long craft show in Peterborough. That evening, I was lying on my bed reading when there was a knock on my door.

"Come on in." It was Maple.

"Hey, Dicky, was wondering if it would be okay if I read with you tonight?" She flashed her glorious smile.

Communitarians would often read together, either reading the same book aloud or reading their own books separately, lying next to each other. Lisa and I had done that, but I had not done it with any of the women at Dandelion.

I had my head against my pillow, which was leaning against the wall, and said, "Sure, that would be fine." She took off her shoes and lay down on the left side of me. She placed my other pillow next to mine and began reading *Ms. Magazine*.

"How did your day go today, Dicky?"

"Fine, mostly doing tinnery and answering some correspondence."

"That sounds like an easy day."

"Yup, it was." We both went back to reading.

A few minutes later she asked, "How's your book going, Richie?"

"Very interesting." I was reading *Be Here Now* by Ram Dass. Ram Dass (who was originally Richard Alpert), was a Harvard professor who got involved with LSD and then became a Buddhist. He dropped out of Harvard, became a proponent of using LSD to enhance one's spirituality, and had a big following.

"I'm starting to believe that Skinner and Ram Dass are saying the same thing, but with different words. It seems like 'karma' means 'action' and 'vipako' means 'results.' To me, that is almost the same as 'stimulus-response,' right?" I turned to face her and smiled.

"That sounds interesting, Dicky. Maybe you are on to something there," she said with a slight grin on her face.

"I think the Buddhists also believe, as I do, that there is a very fluid boundary between a person and his or her environment."

"Maybe if we're lucky, we will eventually get some Buddhists to join us," Maple said and again beamed that radiant smile of hers.

I then became aware that she was staring at me with a different kind of look. Was it a look of invitation, expectation? I also realized she was staring at my lips and that now there was a certain tension between us. I smiled back at her and returned to my book. I realized my heart was beating a little bit faster and that it was hard to concentrate on what I was reading. What was going on here?

A few minutes later, without a word said, Maple casually reached out and took my left hand. She held if for a few seconds, and then ever so slowly, moved my index finger up to her face, and slowly inserted it into her mouth. Seemingly, as if it was the most innocent/natural thing to do, she then sensuously began sucking on it. She continued to read her magazine.

"Holy smokes!" I thought to myself. I felt like I was living a male fantasy. I put my book down and stared at Maple. Keeping my finger in her mouth, she just kept reading her magazine.

Before I could comprehend my actions, I pulled my finger out of her mouth and leaned towards her. I put my right hand on her shirt and began feeling her stomach. She put her magazine down and offered no resistance.

I leaned over to kiss her—and at that moment, the telephone rang. (Saved by the bell.) "Let me get that," Maple said. She bounced out of the bed and ran to the phone. I got up and followed. Mory and Timothy came out of Mory's room to see who was calling at nine p.m.

Maple picked up the phone and said, "Hello, Dandelion."

Hi, this is Ron Gainseke calling," he said in a friendly manner. "Just so you know your cow is right outside our house. You might want to come and get her."

"Oh, geez! We'll be right over, Ron. Sorry about that."

"No problem." Ron hung up.

She turned to me, Mory, and Timothy, and said, "Chrissie's escaped again. We need to get over to the Gainsekes' and bring her home."

The four of us bundled up and headed out in the sub-zero weather. The moon was bright and there were a billion stars. The air was invigorating.

We found Chrissie and managed to return her to the barn within fifteen minutes. Maple and I then found our way back to my room. She lay down on the bed as I lit some candles and placed them in candleholders. The wondrous shadows appeared on the ceiling.

I turned off the light and lay down next to Maple. As before, I had doubts about my behavior. What would Donald think? How would things change between me and Maple?

I looked at her in the flickering candlelight and saw the young beautiful woman lying in my bed, with her long red hair and appealing blue eyes. She looked up and smiled at me and then leaned her head up and kissed me. It was a long, slow kiss and felt like pure magic.

Even though we spent the night together (fondling and touching each other), we did not have intercourse that night. My introduction into the mechanics of multiple sexual relationships in community was about to begin.

For months when I first arrived at Dandelion, I would see members go to bed at night all in happy moods. The next morning I would find a bunch of arguments going on, crying, and overall not-happy campers. That made me very wary of getting involved with any of the women there. I had a hard enough time relating to one person, let alone being involved with two. I even wrote my behavior psychology professor asking him his opinion on three-way relationships. I was in new territory here, with no map or sense of direction. I would tread carefully.

The next day, Maple and I went about our normal routines as if nothing had happened, but something had definitely changed between us. We now stood closer to one another when we spoke. We sat next to each other at lunch and at supper. We both were animated talking with each other about our lives before Dandelion, feeling very comfortable with each other. There was a sense of anticipation in the air and I wondered who had actually known about our rendezvous last night. Nevertheless, out of respect or non-nosiness, community life went on as usual.

A couple of days later, Maple burst into the shop and shouted, "Alabama's gone; he's left." She was crying. She ran over to me, threw herself into my arms, and grabbed tight. Alabama had really begun to fit in at Dandelion and I was saddened to hear the news.

I don't remember what happened the rest of the day. There were plans for a party that night (to celebrate Timothy's birthday), and even though I felt in the pits, I was going to celebrate. Moreover, even though I didn't have anything to drink, it turned out to be a fun evening. Maple and I danced a lot and hung out in the corner and talked.

I left the party early and was feeling sad as I lay down on my bed. I was thinking about Alabama as well as Maple.

I had really liked Alabama, and for him to leave with no note or anything, did not make any sense to me. It was true that the community had started to have some problems with Alabama, as he seemed to be drinking excessive amounts of alcohol lately. (Members had started to suspect that he might have been a closet alcoholic.) However, I was optimistic about his overcoming that problem.

There was a scratch at my door and it opened slightly. "Richie?" Maple asked quietly. "Do you want to be by yourself tonight?"

"No, not tonight, it would be nice to have some company."

I got out of bed, hugged Maple and then lit some candles so I could see her more clearly. I absolutely loved the way she looked. Moreover, this time, I could no longer control myself. I wanted her, and I wanted her now.

We lay down next to each other and began kissing each other. I took off her shirt, kissed her breasts, and explored the rest of her body with my hands. I was again plagued with guilt. She believed in the same things I did, was such a beautiful person, and was so in tune with life. But she was my best friend's lover. How could I face Donald when he returned? How would he react? What would he say? How would he feel? I had never been in such a situation and felt so confused.

However, I could not stop kissing Maple, and in an instant, we were both naked, under my blankets with the candlelight casting shadows on the ceiling. One thing led to another, and soon I was inside Maple and it was the most intense sexual feeling I had ever had. Within a minute, she moaned out loud and said "Richie…Richie… Ohhhhhhhhhh…"

A woman who could so easily have an orgasm astonished me. (That was my first time with a woman who had one.) Moreover, after thrusting for a minute, I moaned, "Maple!" and then collapsed on top of her in pure ecstasy. What an incredible, easy lover. At that moment, I was falling madly in love with this amazing woman who was committed to Dandelion as much as I was.

Donald returned at the end of the week and I was feeling guilt and regret—not that I had made love with Maple, but that I had now jeopardized my friendship with Donald.

Therefore, for the first couple of hours after Donald's return, I just kept busy with tinnery, hammocks, and other routine stuff.

I knew that once Donald returned, Maple would spend more time with him, since they were primary partners. Nevertheless, I hoped that my turn would once again come with Maple.

I finally met up with Donald later that afternoon, outside by the Chevy and started out by saying, "Donald, I guess you heard about me and Maple spending the night together. I am so sorry if I hurt your feelings and hope it doesn't change the friendship between us."

Donald, in his soft, gentle voice just said, "It's okay, Dicky. This is community life and these things happen. I only wish you could have talked to me beforehand."

To which I responded, "Well, if I had thought something like this was possible in my lifetime, yes, I would have spoken with you beforehand, Donald." We both smiled. "It was just such an intense experience for me, Donald, caught me totally by surprise. Moreover, just so you know, I realize she is your primary partner and I don't plan on pursuing anything long term with Maple." (Was I lying to myself as well as to Donald?)

"Yeah, we'll see, Dicky. Relationships in community are such unpredictable animals. You never know where they end up. But, just so you know, I have no hard feelings towards you." We hugged and I felt a sense of clearing the air and was relieved that Donald handled the news so well.

When I later spoke with Maple, I told her I had no expectations and would just take it one day at a time. Maple hugged me and said, "I think for now, that is a good idea, Richie. And, just so you know, I loved spending the night with you. You are such a gentle lover." She smiled and walked off to milk the cow.

Spring 1978

Maple, Donald, and I continued our three-way relationship over the next couple of weeks, but there was tension in the air. This became most noticeable whenever we were all doing something together.

It turned out to be torture for me, as I waited every night, hoping that Maple would return to my room and want to "read" with me. Then I became disappointed when she didn't. It seemed to be her choice whom she would sleep with. Even though I continued to sleep with her about once a week, the unpredictability was very frustrating.

In addition, just to be clear with Lisa, (who had been writing me saying she would like to see me again and make a commitment to Dandelion), I wrote her a letter explaining that I had developed a sexual relationship with Maple. Lisa wrote back, saying that she wanted to give Dandelion another chance and we could talk more when she got there.

Lisa arrived two weeks later in late March, and I was happy to see her again. We went for a walk and had a long conversation and I told her how much I missed her and the status of my relationship with Maple.

A part of me was hoping that something long-term would develop with Maple, but my more practical side knew that was a very remote possibility. Maple had clearly asserted that Donald was her primary partner. But here was Lisa, saying she was willing to give Dandelion and me a chance, saying *she* wanted to be my primary partner.

After walking and talking for an hour, we made it back to Dandelion and went straight to my bedroom. We undressed each other and to my delight, found myself making love with Lisa.

Lisa and I went back to being a couple, which came as a relief to Maple as well as to me. Even though I still had strong feelings for Maple, I realized it was just too complicated being in a three-way relationship with her. I now had to be considerate of Lisa's feelings as well. Therefore, Maple and I reluctantly agreed to go back to being just friends.

For the rest of the spring, Lisa and I re-established our commitment to each other. Part of me, however, was still holding back in regard to anything long-term with her.

She applied for membership and at her clearness meeting, when it came to my turn to share my feelings with her face to face, I once again expressed my hope that she would join Dandelion as a member, not because of her feelings towards me, but because of what Dandelion stood for. Lisa acknowledged that and said she hoped for the same thing.

Maple building the chicken shed

Arrival of Our First Antioch Student

Dondi Kimelman arrived April 1, the first of several student interns from Antioch College in Ohio. As part of her school year, she had chosen to spend three months at Dandelion, earning college credit for her time there. Along with her student advisor, she had been communicating with Dandelion the last couple of months and it seemed that it would be a beneficial experience for all involved. Dondi had written a letter explaining what she hoped to learn at Dandelion and the skills she had to offer the community in return.

She was a sophomore at Antioch, about five feet tall with long frizzy black hair that hung down to her lower back. She had bewitching hazel eyes, a welcoming smile and a gentle personality. Her major was psychology and she wanted to see what a Walden Two community might be like.

She arrived at the Kingston bus station at eight p.m. and was picked up by Gordon. By the time they made it back to Dandelion, it was after nine p.m. Gordon escorted her into the kitchen for some refreshments.

Jane and I were in the kitchen when they walked in. "Hi. Welcome to Dandelion," I said.

"It's nice to be here," said Dondi. "I'm really looking forward to learning about Dandelion."

Dondi debriefed about her trip and then was shown the essentials—bathroom, food supplies, etc. After that, Jane showed her the visitor room. There were no other visitors, so she had the room to herself.

I was immediately taken by Dondi's friendly manner and felt she was destined to fit in well at Dandelion.

Dondi turned out to be a dependable and well-liked temporary member for Dandelion. She easily adapted to the Dandelion routine. Very quickly she learned milking, tinnery, and hammock weaving. I developed a special relationship with Dondi.

She was from Long Island and we both had an interest in theater and acting. We even hosted an evening of Theatre Games. (Theatre Games are warm-up exercises that actors use, improvising scenes, doing theatre exercises, etc. as a way to tap into their creativity.) They went over so well that I thought it would be a great icebreaker for the community conference coming up in August.

Dondi also loved dancing and had taken ballet lessons for years. Since dancing was one of my passions, I asked her if she would teach me some ballet

Richie and Dondi with kittens

moves some time. She happily agreed and for a few evenings down in the shop, you could find us doing ballet together. We would often go for walks around Dandelion, talking about behaviorism and *Walden Two*.

April became May and brought some exhilarating warm weather. After the long Canadian winter, it was so liberating to be able to walk outside without wearing a bulky coat, boots, hat, gloves, and so on. I realized that the absence of a dislike turned out to be a big like.

In the spring, the community seemed to blossom along with the flowers everywhere, around the farmhouse, in the garden, along the road, and out in the fields. Living in the country certainly had its benefits. It was also a real treat for me to be part of the garden crew and help plant the tomatoes, carrots, lettuce, cucumbers, corn, green peppers, potatoes, and watermelons.

There also were projects springing up all over the place. The community had decided to buy twenty-five chickens so we could have fresh eggs in the morning. Timothy went to pick them up, and because the community lacked proper carrying cases, he improvised and used some old mail sacks to transport them. He and Maple, the new chicken managers, built a small chicken shed behind the dairy barn.

The chickens turned out to be a real hit. In the morning, you could walk out to the shed and pick up some fresh eggs for breakfast. Often they were still warm—another benefit of living at Dandelion.

Timothy's parents graciously donated a washer and dryer to the community and the weekly trips to the Laundromat became history. Donald installed some long lengths of black plastic pipe along the south side of the farmhouse roof and with a large water tank (painted black) successfully created Dandelion's first use of passive solar power to heat water.

Next to that, he built a simple outdoor shower (connected to the black tank), that communitarians could use in the summer. The shower consisted of a large three-sided box (made out of plywood), with the showerhead attached to the top of the back wall. Everyone was very pleased at making this first step toward becoming more energy self-sufficient.

We had started advertising for our Communities Conference to be held in August, and already a trickle of registrations was coming in. Many workshops about communal living would be offered.

I proposed that we contact the band The Village People to see if they might give us a free concert. I ended up writing them and received an eight by ten glossy photograph of the band with the written words, "To Richie: Be Cool. Glen Hughes—The Leather Man." That became one of my treasured possessions.

There were also plans for something we were calling a Walden Two Week. This was to be a chance for fifteen people to gather at Dandelion the week before the conference and form their own temporary community. They would live in a large army tent (across the field) and help Dandelion build numerous picnic tables for the conference. It would give the group a chance to experience what building a community might be like.

During this time, I began to have some issues with Lisa. She had her own room now, but I realized there was no long-term commitment between us. I explained to her, in my most gentle voice, that I felt things were not working out the way I hoped they would.

Lisa became very upset and yelled at me, cried, and threw things. I had never been in such a situation, and in trying to accommodate her, said I would work on things. This seemed to calm her down, but I was really starting to worry about her emotional side.

May 9 was my birthday and the community decided to give me a birthday party. It was a perfect spring evening. The frogs were peeping in the creek and the sky was cloudless. We all got into some maniacal dancing in Aduki that evening and by now I had grown very fond of Canadian beer, La Blatt Blue being my favorite.

I was sweating and went outside the shop to cool off. I saw Dondi up by the farmhouse leaning against the picnic table, watching the stars and walked up to join her. "Tis another fine evening at Dandelion, eh, Dondi?" (I seemed to be using that word "eh" a lot lately.)

"Yes, it sure is, Richie. Love looking at the stars here," she responded and smiled at me.

"I'm sure gonna miss you when you go back to Antioch, Dondi."

"Well, you know, Richie, I've been thinking about that."

"Oh?"

"Yeah, I'm having such a great time here, that I'm thinking of seeing if I can get a three-month extension to stay over the summer. Do you think the community would go for something like that?"

A huge smile appeared on my face. "Dondi, that is music to my ears, and, yes, I think the community would love to have you stay on for the summer." I grabbed her shoulders and hugged her tightly.

After a few more minutes of watching the stars, we headed back down to the shop. Walking down the driveway, I grabbed her hand and she reciprocated. I realized I was developing a crush on Dondi.

Back at the shop, Dondi, Donald, and I continued perfecting our disco moves with each other. When the song *We Are Family* came on, everyone joined in a circle and changed the lyrics to "We are community." By the end of the night, Donald and I were voted best disco dancing couple of the evening, and we were the last ones to leave the party.

One week later was the Tulip Festival in Ottawa. Dondi and I were scheduled to do the second week of the fair.

On the way to Ottawa (a two-hour drive), we were listening to the *Deja Vous* album by Crosby, Stills, Nash, and Young. We kept replaying *Our House* because it was a favorite for both of us. There were all these winding roads, going through farmland and meadows and the temperature was just perfect, about seventy-two degrees with no humidity.

Dondi wore a white dress with a bright flower pattern on it and looked gorgeous. Even though we had done some harmless flirting over the past two months, we were still just friends. Nevertheless, we both could tell that an attraction was growing between us.

We arrived late in the afternoon at the downtown park where the festival was located, found the Dandelion booth, and took over for Maple and Donald. The craft show was located on a hillside overlooking the river and you could see the Parliament building on the other side. Maple said it had been a good show so far and the tin cans had been selling briskly. Tulips were blooming everywhere.

We settled into the booth space, which had great views all around. Maple was right, and we did sell many cans over the next two hours.

At six o'clock, the fair closed for the night, so we cleared off the shelves and packed all the tinnery in the large tent behind us. We then headed for the house where we would be staying.

When we got there, an easy-going young man named John, who was a college friend of Donald, greeted us, "You must be the new folks from Dandelion. Come on in."

The house was a co-operative housing situation, which six people shared. John showed us around the first floor, which included the kitchen and living room. We then went upstairs, and John showed us where we would be sleeping.

This turned out to be a large closet space with just enough room for a queen-sized mattress. A flower-patterned curtain hung on a bar over the doorway to give a semblance of privacy. There was another, normal-sized closet outside in the hall where we could store our clothes.

"This is all we have available right now—sorry for the cramped headquarters. Tomorrow, Jennifer is going away for the week and you can crash out in her bedroom after she's gone. Everyone else is out for the evening, so just make yourselves at home. I'm off to work so I probably won't see you until tomorrow evening. Enjoy!" John left us and we unpacked our clothes.

We cooked up some supper and ate in the kitchen. "Seems like a nice place, eh, Dondi?"

"Yeah, and it's so nice having the whole house to ourselves. How rare is that?"

After supper we took showers and then hung out in the living room listening to some French music (Barde). We then went up to our "bedroom."

Being the gentleman that I was, I let Dondi into the closet space first, so she could get undressed in private. Out in the hall I just stripped down to my black undershirt and underpants. That morning one of the underpants I chose had "Home of the Big Whopper" written on it, which I was currently wearing.

Dondi called out from the closet, "I'm ready when you are, Richie."

I smiled, pulled back the curtain, and stepped into the closet, pulling the curtain closed behind me.

Dondi was lying there on top of the sheet wearing a thin, white T-shirt. The fabric was so thin I could see the shape of her large breasts and pink nipples. Dondi saw the underpants, and jokingly said, "So that's what you call it?"

"Well, it was the one of the few clean underpants left in the drawer." I smiled and lay down beside her, staring up at the ceiling. Then I turned towards her and said, "I'm not sure what might happen tonight, Dondi."

To which she replied, "I'm not sure either, Richie, but I'm curious to find out." With that said, I moved closer to her and we kissed. We did end up making love that night and it was another magical time for me. It was as if we just fit together perfectly and her body scent was intoxicating to me.

While making love, Dondi did something that no woman had ever done before. As she was lying on her back and I was inside her, thrusting back and forth, she lightly wrapped her legs around my back and crossed them. What an incredible sensation and the behavior caused me to push up even further inside her. In addition, the sexual sensation was immediate.

After being inside of her for what seemed like the blink of an eye, the effect of her legs wrapped around me caused me to come within seconds. Immediately after that I felt her legs tighten slightly around my back, gently relax and then slowly, ever so slowly, slide off my back. What a gentle, erotic, loving behavior and it took me a couple of minutes to catch my breath. Dondi turned out to be an incredible lover. In our post-coitus conversation, Dondi had shared with me that she had been making love since she was fifteen. In contrast to that, I shared that I had been a virgin until I was twenty-five.

We snuggled in each other's arms, spoke for a little while longer, and then Dondi drifted off to sleep. I on the other hand, was wide-awake trying to absorb what I had just experienced with Dondi and what had happened to me sexually over the last couple of months.

I reflected that I had made love only a couple of times before joining Dandelion, once at college, and once at the Dandelion Communities conference last summer. Then there was Lisa, with whom I had made love with three times before joining Dandelion. Then Maple, this past winter, and now here I was with Dondi. Was it true what they said about people living on communes—that everyone slept with everyone else?

Was I just trying to make up for lost time or perhaps on a steep learning curve? I smiled at that last thought, for as far as learning a new skill was involved (and learning that the fastest way possible), I certainly was not complaining. I was enjoying the journey immensely.

The next morning, we got up at nine and had a leisurely breakfast of eggs and bagels. (We didn't have to be at the fair until eleven.) Again, we felt lucky, to have the whole house to ourselves.

We had a romantic time the rest of the week, making love every morning and every night. We took showers together. The days at the fair blended into each other. In the evening, we would go to various restaurants and have dinner. One night it was pizza, the other night it was Lebanese. Everyone we met was so friendly.

We walked along the canal (known throughout Canada as a famous landmark) and found a bar where we listened to a rock and roll band. We saw two movies that week, *Harold & Maude* (a favorite of mine) and *Coming Home* (the anti-war film starring Jane Fonda and Jon Voight). Other nights we enjoyed listening to the records of the co-op house as I fell deeply in love with the Antioch intern.

At the end of the week, the fair ended, and we packed up all the unsold tinnery and loaded up the van. Since we were having such a good time, we decided to use one of our vacation days and stay an extra day and just explore the city. We called Dandelion to let them know our plans.

The following day turned out to be another beautiful day with bright sunshine and temperature in the mid-70s. We had a leisurely start to the day, walked along the canal again, visited the Parliament building, stopped in some secondhand stores, and listened to a band play in the park. For dinner, we picked a nice Chinese restaurant. Over dinner, we debriefed about the fair and our week together.

I raised my wine glass and said, "This is going down as one of the most beautiful weeks in my life, Dondi. Everything was just perfect."

She smiled back and raised her glass. "Yes, I agree, Richie, and here's to you and me!" We clicked our glasses and then leaned over our food and kissed.

Dondi continued, "And to see all the tulips and other flowers in bloom along with their fragrance everywhere was just magnificent."

"And I'll never forget that night those folks stopped by our booth with the helium balloons and firecrackers. In addition, how we helped them set it afloat and the firecracker went off fifty feet in the air. I felt like we were little kids." We both laughed.

We made love one more time that evening and headed out early the next morning.

On the drive back, Dondi matter-of-factly said, "Lisa is going to hate me."

I grabbed her hand and assured her that wasn't the case. "I'm not sure how things are going to unfold, Dondi, but I only know that I would really like to spend some more time with you." Dondi agreed that she would like to spend some more time with me, as well, but didn't want to cause any undue conflict once we got back to Dandelion.

Dondi's caution hit home with me as I had been processing my feelings regarding Lisa. Now, after this week, what would happen with my feelings for Dondi?

We returned to Dandelion, parked the van near the shop, and began unloading it. We saw Lisa, Maple, and Jane working in the garden. "Hey, Dicky and Dondi," Jane said in a friendly manner. Maple said, "Welcome back." Lisa smiled and started walking towards the van.

"Hi, Richie, I hope you had a good time in Ottawa." She gave me a hug, ignoring Dondi completely.

"We did and sold about $5,000 worth of tinnery."

"Good for you. You can tell me all about it later." She returned to the garden.

About a minute later, Lisa, Maple, and Jane left the garden and walked towards the field on the side of the house. Each had their elbows wrapped between the others' elbows. I watched them for a few seconds wondering what the topic of conversation might be.

"That was pretty rude of Lisa to ignore you like that, Dondi," I said.

"I told you she was going to hate me."

"Well, I'll take care of things with Lisa. Don't worry about it."

We began to unload the van when Gordon came out from the shop. He was very curious about the fair and asked, "So, how did it go, Richie? Anything interesting happen, any good stories? Did we sell many cans?" Gordon smiled at us.

"Oh, we had a great time, Gordon. The weather was perfect, and yes, we made about $5,000."

"Way to go! My thanks to both of you."

I added, "Dondi was a great saleswoman, too, Gordon, very friendly with the customers." Gordon's eyes got even bigger. "Well, all right then. We'll put that woman to work again sometime soon." We all smiled.

"Did we miss anything here while we were away?" Dondi inquired.

"No, not really, although it seems that spring is definitely in the air. Just feels like there are big changes happening." After some more debriefing about the fair, Gordon said he would be happy to unload the rest of the van, and Dondi and I headed up to the farmhouse.

Gordon's words about "big changes" turned out to be prophetic, but not in the way I had hoped. The week after we returned from the fair in Ottawa, some big changes did happen. First of all, much to my great surprise (and disappointment), Dondi started up a relationship with Durin. I didn't see that coming, as I was so sure that what we had shared at Ottawa would blossom into something far deeper once back at Dandelion, even though we had not been intimate since our return.

To be fair, Durin had not been involved with anyone since I had joined Dandelion. Nevertheless, I could not understand the attraction. Dondi was so outgoing and enthusiastic, while Durin was just the opposite—methodical, serious, etc. However, for whatever reason, that was the reality, and I had to accept it.

Dondi came to my room one night and said, "Richie, I am so sorry about what has unfolded between me and Durin. It just happened. I can't explain it. For now, it just feels right being with him. On top of that, I don't want to alienate Lisa any more than I have."

I listened to what she was saying, and for the most part understood and wished her all the best. I once again felt that I was being given the short end of the stick—and it was because I was involved with Lisa. I thought Dondi was a much better match for me, and I felt frustrated. When would I find the right partner for myself? I wondered how the rest of the summer would turn out.

To take my mind off the emotional turmoil I was experiencing, I often wandered the grounds surrounding Dandelion, thinking of what I could make out of all the junk lying around. I found various wooden planks, a large, vintage Coca Cola sign (four feet by five feet long), various bottles (in all sizes and shapes), bits and pieces of antique furniture, farming tools left over from the last century, an old covering for a street lamp, and a dozen bald tires along the side of the barn.

The old street lamp first captured my imagination. I thought about painting the top part yellow (as in the color of a Dandelion) and the bottom part green. I could then attach it to the post the mailbox sat on. That way, we could tell visitors to look for the large 'Dandelion' on the mailbox. I smiled thinking how clever I was.

The second thing I thought of was that maybe there could be a creative "sculpture" made out of all this junk. This could be added to or taken away from, depending on who was interested or maybe who was visiting.

The third thing I thought of was as a Trekkie, I had always wanted to build a replica of the bridge from the Star Ship Enterprise. I began to see the old tires set up as "transporters," a table (made out of the old boards and saw horses), could be built for the navigation consoles for Sulu and Chekov, and a separate console could be set up for Mr. Spock's station. Some of those old, blue bottles were perfect as dilithium crystals to power the ship. I could even get dressed up in my Captain Kirk look-a-like pajamas and then go explore the Universe. I got all excited.

I was sure the Star Trek idea would be a big hit with the children who visited that summer. Since Dandelion did not have a playground, this could be an alternative. In addition, my parents were planning on visiting later in June and I knew they would love to see what I had created.

I started pulling out the tires and began setting up my Star Trek replica out behind the farmhouse, so no one could see it from the road. (I was aware that Dandelion's reputation was on the line, and I didn't want the locals thinking we were any weirder than they already imagined.)

After I finished building my Star Trek replica, I then went and found the half-empty paint cans with green and yellow paint in them. I went to work painting the old street lamp. When I finished painting it, I looked at it with pride. Surely, this will become an icon for Dandelion. That night there was a community meeting and I put on the agenda my idea for the lamp going onto the mailbox.

I brought the street lamp to the meeting expecting "ooos" and "ahhhs," but what I got instead were dazed and questioning looks. "What's that, Dicky?" Mory enquired.

"Well, it's my conception of what a giant Dandelion might look like. I thought it would be cool to put it on our mailbox and help visitors locate us more easily."

"Oh," was all she said.

I eagerly waited for the responses from other members. Gordon was the only one who could see the genius of my idea and said, "I like it, Richie." Others were more cautious.

Jane said, "I always admired your creativity, Dicky, but this one seems a little, umm—how can I say this gently—maybe a little too tacky to me."

Timothy said, "I like that it's made from recycled items, but I think the metal really doesn't look like a flower at all."

Donald perked up and said, "Well, what if we tried it out for a week to see if it looks any better over time? If more than three people think it's still tacky, we can take it down. Would that be a workable compromise?"

Maple said, "That sounds fine with me. As Richie likes to say, let's experiment."

There were general, although reluctant murmurs of agreement around the room and the next morning, using old fence wire, I tied the lamp to the mailbox post.

After the first day of the lamp being up, even I began having second thoughts. It did look tacky and it did look like a street lamp painted yellow and green. What was I thinking? Waiting a whole week was too long to admit what I already knew the others were thinking, so I removed the lamp and brought it back to the barn.

Noncompetitive Volley Ball

The summer also brought out the volley ball net, and volley ball games became a favorite activity after supper. With the extra visitors the community had during that time, there were always enough to have at least five people on each side of the net.

No one kept score. People rotated around the whole playing field, switching sides every few minutes. The only score we kept was the number of times the ball went over the net without hitting the ground. This turned out to be the greatest challenge of all. No matter how hard we tried, the best we could do was five or six times over the net.

This became very discouraging—so discouraging in fact, that I thought of a way out of the mess. "Hey, I have an idea, how about each time the ball goes over the net, we count it as *five* times over? That way we could easily jack up our score." By this method, if the ball went over the net ten times, it sounded like we had made it to fifty.

"Way cool idea, Richie. Let's try it," Donald said. The other members and visitors agreed, and we were very pleased with ourselves when we made it to twenty-five.

Visit of my Parents

It was a gorgeous, sunny day, late in the afternoon, when the yellow Gremlin (a Ford car) pulled up in front of the farmhouse and my parents stepped out. I was working in the garden and yelled, "Hello, Mom and Dad! Welcome to Dandelion!"

"Hello there, son," my dad replied.

"Hi, dear," my mother said and waved.

I left the garden, went up and hugged them. "How was the trip up?"

"Oh, no problem, son, you gave good directions. So this is the place, huh?" said Dad, looking around.

"Such a large garden. What are you growing, dear?" My mother asked.

"We have tomatoes, corn, watermelon, carrots, lettuce, peppers, and strawberries. You name it, we got it. Come on into the house. You can freshen up and have some lemonade and banana bread. Then I can give you a tour."

We walked into the kitchen and ran into Timothy and Jane. "Jane and Timothy, these are my parents."

"Hi, and welcome to Dandelion," Jane said warmly and extended her hand.

Timothy said, "Nice to meet you."

"Timothy is a lot like Ed, Mom. We do comedy routines together." I smiled at Timothy.

He groaned and said, "Well, we're not going to do any right now, are we Richie? At least give your parents a chance to get settled in." We all laughed.

We grabbed some lemonade and banana bread and went out to the porch. "So how's Ed doing these days?" I asked.

"He's doing fine. Just got a job working for a computer company down in the city. Starts in two weeks," my father said.

"Is he still thinking of applying to law school?"

"He'll have to see. He wants to save up some money first."

Mom piped in and said, "This banana bread is delicious. I'd like to get the recipe before we leave."

After we finished our refreshments, I took them down to the shop. Along the way, I introduced them to Maple, who had just started working in the garden. Maple walked over to the fence, stuck out her hand and said, "Welcome to Dandelion. Richie has spoken highly about both of you. I'm so happy to meet you."

"Maple is one of the main people in charge of the garden this year. She's also the new chicken manager."

Maple smiled and said, "Yup, that's me. Call me Chicken Woman."

"Maple. Is that your real name?" My father asked.

"No, Mr. Graham, it's a name I took because it sounded Canadian. My real name is Deirdre." She smiled and said, "Well, I hope you have an excellent visit." We said our good-byes and continued down to the shop.

Gordon and Donald were working in the tinnery room.

"Hey, guys, my parents are here." They stopped cutting cans and lifted their goggles.

"Hello, very nice to meet you," Donald said.

"Welcome to Dandelion," Gordon added. "Richie has shared some great stories about both of you. It's nice to meet you in person."

"This is where we churn out all our recycled cans," I said, pointing to the cutting stations.

After some more small talk, I took them out to the main area of the shop. "Here is where we make out chairs and hammocks. That's Mory and Dondi at the hammock jig."

Dondi said, "Hi, Mr. and Mrs. Graham. It's nice to have some other New Yorkers here."

"Oh? Where in New York, Dondi?" My dad asked.

"Hempstead, Long Island."

"Dondi is the woman I told you about who's been teaching me ballet," I said and smiled widely at Dondi.

My mom added, "My son has always had a passion for dancing. Did he ever tell you about the movie he made about square dancing in Westchester that was shown in American Embassies around the world during the bicentennial?"

"No, he never said anything about that, Mrs. Graham." Dondi and Mory looked over at me with a look of surprise.

I said, "It never came up in a conversation, that's all."

"What else didn't you tell us about, Richie?" Mory inquired in a teasing tone.

"We all have our secrets, right?" I winked and smiled.

"Well, got to give my parents the rest of the tour. See you later." I took them out the back doors, and walked over to the bridge.

"We've been talking about building a new residence building. Before doing that, we would have to replace this wooden bridge with a cement one."

"That looks pretty sturdy to me," my father commented.

"Well, it will have to be strong enough to hold up the cement-mixing truck, along with a bulldozer and other trucks bringing in lumber and ceiling joists.

The last thing we need is one of those trucks caving in our bridge."

"Will you actually help build the new building?"

"That's right, dad, I'm hoping to learn some carpentry and construction skills. The women will be helping with it also."

My mom smiled and said, "I'm happy for you, dear. Keep learning all those new skills. It sounds like this is going to be a very interesting summer for you."

Arthur and Ann Graham, my parents

"That's what I've been saying to myself as well, mom." Secretly I was saying, "If she only knew..."

"Hey, speaking of the new residence building, let me show you what I already built on the site where we're hoping to build it." We walked back up the driveway and went behind the farmhouse. I pointed and said, "Look, mom, there."

We were looking at a set of five tires laid out on the ground, in the same order as the five circles on the Olympic flag. Ten feet in front of that was an eight- by three-foot wooden plank set across two wooden sawhorses. The planks sagged dangerously in the middle and there were some empty paint cans on top of it. A rusted metal folding chair was behind the planks. "What is it, son?" My father asked.

"Don't you see it, dad? It's the bridge from the Star Ship *Enterprise*."

We walked over and pointing to the tires, I explained it was the transporters. Then pointing to the chair, I said, "Here, you sit over here mom, at Sulu's station, and dad, you stand on one of the tires. Get ready to be beamed up."

I had my camera and said, "Let me take a picture of you." They shook their heads humorously and took their assigned places. "Smile and make like you're having a good time." I said, and then took some pictures and imagined what they were thinking.

"Dear, you have such a vivid imagination. Where do your ideas come from?" My mom said lovingly.

"I think I inherited it from you and Dad, mom." I smiled.

My parents left early the next morning and even though they didn't really understand what I was doing, I was grateful they had the chance to visit, *Star Trek* and all.

The warmer weather always brought an increase in visitors—some staying for the entire summer and some returning later to become members. It became increasingly clear that Dandelion needed that new residence building.

This need had been talked about for years, but it now was about to become a reality. It would be a juicy time for the community, as members could see an actual physical expression of their dreams coming true.

Ah, but first things first. Dandelion already knew it needed a new bridge and had consulted with an architect to determine what kind of bridge would be required to support heavier trucks. With blueprints in one hand and picks in the other hand, members began digging large holes (three feet wide, ten feet long, six feet deep), on each side of the bridge.

While I took my turn swinging the pickax into soil and rock, I said out loud to Donald (who was on the other side of the bridge doing the same thing), "My mom always said if I didn't get a college education, I'd end up digging ditches somewhere."

Donald building the bridge

Conference

As we dug holes for the new bridge, Dandelion continued to receive more and more registrations for our conference. By the week before the conference began, we had received over one hundred registrations (mostly from Canada and the U.S., but some from France and Germany).

A few days before the conference, there was excitement in the air as members from other Federation communities began arriving to help set up the conference and to lead some workshops. They included Piper from Aloe Community, another female behaviorist, heavily influenced by *Walden Two*; Larry from Twin Oaks, who was committed to "process" and basing community decision-making on consensus; and Ira, an African-American woman, also from Aloe Community, who was committed to raising children in an egalitarian world and had a passion for gardening. (She also had a reputation for being one of the best cooks in the Federation.)

Ira held a special place in my communal journey. When I thought back on my first communal conference at Twin Oaks in 1975, Ira was the one who clearly stood out in her passion for community and all that it stood for. Hearing her speak at that conference convinced me to pursue my dream to live in a Walden Two community.

Chantal and Ira

So much still needed to be done before the weekend. The field across the road had to be mowed for parking spaces, food had to be ordered for all the people we expected, and a childcare program would have to be in place. Ten children were registered and Ira and Maple would be in charge of that detail.

We purchased a large used army tent and set it up in the middle of the field. That would act as the main area for food serving. (Food would be cooked in the farmhouse and transported over.)

For dishwashing, a new large oil drum was purchased and cut in half with the community torch. This was set up over the fireplace in the middle of the field and both were filled with hot water, one with dishwashing soap. Conferees would camp out in the wooded area beyond the field. Temporary outhouses were set up as well.

Tours of Dandelion were scheduled. We also needed a labor system set up, with conferees helping to run the conference. They would help in the food preparation, garbage disposal, wood gathering, clean up, and childcare.

Dondi and I volunteered to set up entertainment for Friday and Saturday evenings. Moreover, we narrowed down which workshops we would offer.

Conferees began arriving late Friday afternoon. After supper, Dondi and I led an informal gathering of Theatre Games as an icebreaker. (Some of the games we did were Robots, The Village, Machines, and Space Rebound.) Conferees really enjoyed the exercises and it sparked many new friendships.

The conference started at 9:30 Saturday morning with a large circle of over a hundred people gathered in the field outside the army tent. Jane was the main facilitator and said, "Welcome, everyone! We are so glad to have you here with us today and that you chose to spend your weekend learning about community."

After the morning announcements, conferees went to the main shop building to watch the twenty-minute Federation slide show. The slide show portrayed all the communities in the Federation with a soundtrack of music and commentary—a polished show, professionally done. (A little propaganda never hurt anyone.)

After that presentation, conferees had their choice of workshops for the rest of the day. Some of the workshops offered were, "Alternatives to Punishment" (hosted by Gordon and me), "Community and Social Change" (Jane and Ira), "Community Economics" (Larry and Mory), "Rituals in Community" (Julian and Maple), "A Community Behavior Code-Why Have One?" (Gordon and me), "Children in Community" (Ira and Jane), "Community Values and Agreements" (Maple and Mory), "Construction of the Physical Environment" (Donald and Gordon), "Interpersonal Relationships" (Jane and Larry), "Industries and Economic Self-Sufficiency" (Larry and Ira), "So You Want to Start a Community?" (Jane and Donald), and "*Walden Two*—What Does it Mean?" (Gordon and Piper). The workshops were held at Aduki, the farmhouse, the army tent, out in the field, and other various locations.

I started my "Alternatives to Punishment" workshop with, "When someone does something that you don't like, how do you inform that person without making the other person feel bad? Here at Dandelion we have what we refer to as a positive verbal environment. In our day-to-day living, what that actually means is that people say out loud what they like about the people they live with and the work they do. We find that emphasizing the positive makes it a lot easier to hear a negative, which eventually happens in any work or home situation."

Gordon added, "We found that a lot of times people will think something nice about you, but they don't usually say it out loud. When they voice a dislike

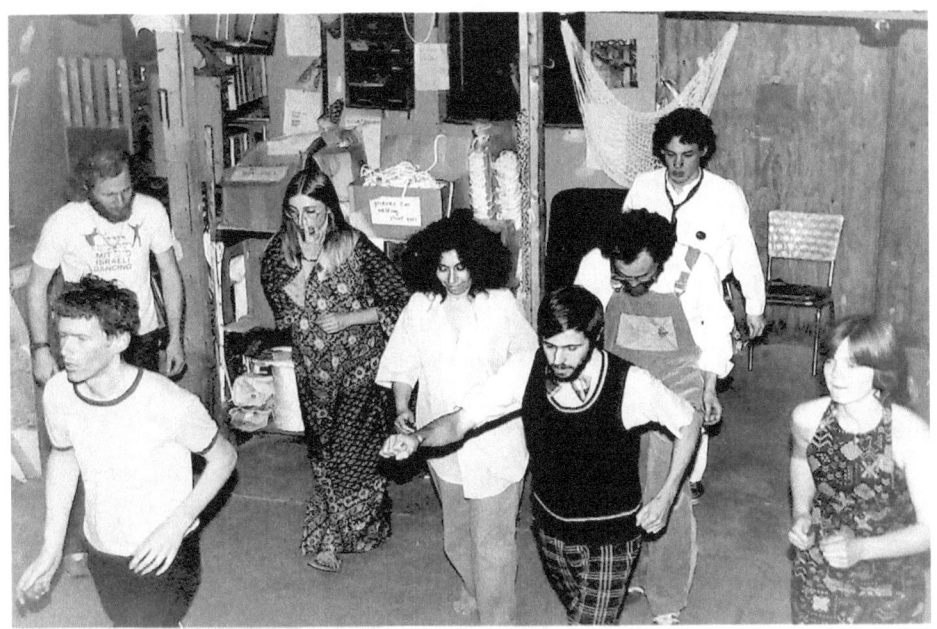

Disco night, Gabriel, Paul, Jane, M'lissa, Richie, Jonathan, Donald, Dakota

about your behavior, it is not heard in the right balance. That is why having our Behavior Code is such a critical piece of our lifestyle—stating clearly what our expectations are, and being particularly aware of language and how that affects us."

Many meaningful conversations were sparked by each of the workshops, reflecting the variety of people who attended.

For the community members (from Dandelion as well as from Twin Oaks and other communities) it was such a juicy time to talk about what was so important in our daily lives. It was also exciting to see so many visitors unfold and warm up to the idea of community. I observed "the light" begin to shine in some of the conferees' eyes as they grasped what Dandelion stood for.

That night a dance was held at Aduki, and more than fifty people showed up. The room was packed, and disco songs dominated the evening.

The next day was filled with more workshops. In the evening, people gathered around the campfire for folk songs accompanied by Gordon on guitar.

The conference was officially over after breakfast on Monday morning, and most cars were gone by noon. There was a general sense of relief around the community (many members felt exhausted), but at the same time we felt exhilarated for having had our egalitarian lifestyle validated.

Tamari

Gordon spent a lot of his time that summer planning the new residence building. There were so many topics to research and details to take care of. Where would we get lumber and nails at the best price? Who would manage the project? What new tools would we need? Which electrician would we hire? Finding a bulldozer, a cement company, getting any village building permits needed, etc.

After hours and hours of planning, Gordon finally presented a general design of the new residence building at a community meeting in early August. "Well, as you can see, it is a basic rectangular shape and there would be a set of covered stairs at this end. It would be cheaper if we didn't have to cover the stairs, but in the winter, we would have to devote hours to shoveling snow off them. It would also be much safer that way."

"That sounds like a good idea, Gordon. Thank you for thinking safety first," I commented.

Gordon continued, "It will hold five bedrooms on the first and second floors and four bedrooms on the top floor. Each floor will have a small open area for the wood-burning stove and living area, which can hold couches, chairs, desks, etc. Each bedroom will be ten by ten feet, with a window in each room. I've designed it so that one of the longer sides will face south. That way we have the option of adding a greenhouse to that side of the building. I also added a steep incline to the roof to make it easier for snow to fall off. The only drawback is that there is no bathroom planned for the building. Perhaps in the future, we will have enough money to add one."

There were murmurs of approval, as members were quite impressed with Gordon's vision.

"Who would be responsible for the actual day-to-day supervision of the project, Gordon?" Mory asked.

"Well, that remains to be seen. I've sent out letters to other communities in the Federation asking for help in that department as well as help with anyone who has experience in carpentry or construction. Shiva from East Wind has shown a strong interest and has helped build some of the buildings there. I think he would make an excellent candidate for that position. I know he also has a Master's Degree in music and I'm sure he could add to our cultural scene as well."

"This is all so exciting," Jane said. "When can we start?"

"Well, for starters we would have to clear the land behind the farmhouse, going down six feet. I've contacted Bill Eisner regarding renting him and his bulldozer. He says he has an open day two weeks from Thursday. So, I set him up for that time."

"It all sounds great, Gordon. Thanks so much for all the planning you did," Donald commented.

The rest of the meeting dealt with the most critical part of the project, which was naming the new building. This went on for over thirty minutes. I proposed "Star Ship," which was met with groans. Jane proposed calling it "Tamari" in keeping with the tradition of naming buildings after beans. A few other names were proposed.

After much haggling and joking, the community finally approved the name "Tamari." The meeting closed with a group hug and a general sense of excitement for this new project.

The next two weeks everyone was excitedly talking about the new residence. An area directly behind the farmhouse was staked out. It was in the same area I had built the replica of the bridge from *Star Trek*, which I disassembled and stored in the barn.

The bulldozer arrived two weeks later, plowed under the top layers of soil, and went down about six feet. Because of all the dirt accumulated, a small hill began to form to the right of the farmhouse. Then a surprise—the top of a large boulder, six feet long, stuck out of the ground about a foot. The bulldozer could not plow that away. The community would have to rent a jackhammer to break it down.

Dealing with that rock became a symbol of the community's spirit. The jackhammer we rented was about four feet tall, and the community took turns wielding it onto the rock. People would jackhammer away for a few minutes, with their long hair bobbing, wearing eye and ear protectors. It was particularly inspiring to see Dondi go at it, as she was almost the same size as the hammer.

When my turn came, I briefly flashed on the scene in the movie *Shane* where in the beginning of the film Shane helped Joe Jared cut down the remaining tree stump in front of the ranch. While I used the jackhammer, I imagined I was Shane whacking away at that tree stump, except now I was battling a rock.

To help speed up the process, after a few cracks appeared in the rock, a small fire was lit on top of it and then doused with water to further break down the rock. After many hours, the rock was finally level enough for the pouring of cement.

Dandelion was lucky to get a labor exchange commitment from East Wind and Shiva agreed to become head honcho for the project. Tomo from Twin Oaks Community showed up on labor exchange as well.

Two German men (long-term visitors) showed up that summer and said their dream was to help build a house in Canada. Along with that hard-core group, Dandelion could provide two members working eight hours each day. Any visitors who had experience in carpentry were assigned to that work crew as well.

In its quest for equality, Dandelion made sure that any woman member who was interested in developing carpentry skills was able to do so, and all of them took turns working on Tamari.

The men on the site were very accommodating to these women and took time explaining construction tips in detail (correct tools to use, how to build a load-bearing wall, proper way to put shingles on the roof, wiring, etc.). I often reflected that compared to a woman finding a job in construction in the outside world, how different that entire experience might have been.

Then a funny thing happened once actual construction on Tamari began. Our usual positive verbal environment, for some unknown reason, was replaced with the vocabulary found on any construction site. Swearing began appearing randomly at first and then became much more frequent. Was this due to workers' accidentally hitting themselves with various tools and hammers? (As Stephen Gaskin, the philosopher, liked to say, "You can tell how enlightened a person is by what they say when they hit their thumb with a hammer.") Was it just part of doing traditional men's work? Or maybe it was just a way to deal with the frustration when lumber and other materials were not delivered on time.

Whatever the reason, phrases like, "Please pass the fuckin' hammer," or "Has any one seen the fuckin' power drill?" dominated conversations at the site. Even the women seemed to pick up this vocabulary.

Safety First

Summertime always brought a host of visitors—college students, people on vacation, and folks from other countries, some of whom would eventually become members. Jeffrey was one of them. He was a young man from California who had long blond hair, blue eyes, and looked like he could easily be a surfer. Because he was a talented drummer, he quickly developed the nickname of "Sticks."

Sticks and I hit it off instantly, probably because we both had such a zany sense of humor. This led to one of the most talked about stories that summer.

To help members feel more comfortable with our bodies, Dandelion had a "clothes-optional" policy for dress. That is, it was okay if you wanted to walk around naked, walk around in underpants, just wear a top, or whatever. It was open to personal interpretation.

Now like most of the other communards, I had grown up in middle-class society, with its collection of norms and values regarding appropriate dress. Walking around nude in public was not one of them.

However, Dandelion in its Utopian vision, had agreed (in its bylaws no less), that nudity, if one chose that style of "dress," would be okay. However, few, if any, practiced that option.

Therefore, as the tale is told, there was one day in late August when Sticks and I were assigned to collect firewood for the upcoming winter. As always, this involved using the chainsaw to cut down dead trees.

We were out in the back woods of Dandelion far away from any public roads and had been cutting wood for about an hour. The summer heat and humidity had become oppressive and both of us had steadily taken our clothes off. We were down to our shorts and steel-toed boots, along with the required safety goggles and helmet.

Beads of sweat were running down our foreheads, chests, and backs, as we took

Jeffrey aka Sticks

turns using the chainsaw. We then dragged the fallen trees out to the open field where they would be picked up later.

We stopped for a water break, and wiping the sweat off his forehead, Sticks said, "Man, it's hot out today."

"You can say that again," I replied smiling.

To which Sticks responded, "Man, it's hot out today."

We both started laughing.

"You know, it's *so* hot that I almost feel like taking the rest of my clothes off," I said half joking.

Sticks looked at me, grinning, "Well, if you do it, I will too."

We both started laughing again and I said, "Well, it's in our by-laws, right?" We stared at each other with big smiles on our faces, then began slipping our shorts and underpants over our boots, and just stood there in all our glory, laughing and feeling empowered that we had broken a cultural norm. We felt like little kids who unexpectedly found themselves naked, but didn't care.

I picked up the chainsaw and yanked on the pull string. The chainsaw sprang into life at once and bounced up a couple of inches. I then stepped up to a tree and began cutting a V-shaped wedge into it. Something about "safety protocols" briefly flashed through my mind, and I double-checked to make sure I was wearing my goggles and helmet. (In my state of grace, any other thoughts of safety were temporarily repressed.)

As Safety Manager, I took great pride in being a good role model when it came to safety issues and practices. (For example, I had removed all flammable material from the basement and relocated it to the tool shed. I had initiated fire drills and had members try out using fire extinguishers. In winter, I always made sure there was adequate salt and sand for icy paths.)

As we watched the tree fall safely down, I swung the chainsaw over to the next tree. Certain body parts were swinging gloriously free in the air. Being out in nature, and not having one's male genitals confined by a pair of "tighty whiteys" gave one such a sense of freedom.

Some friendly locker room banter started up and Sticks casually mentioned, "Looks like you got a third leg there, Richie."

I smiled and remembered when a fellow male gives you that kind of compliment, you must, in turn, offer one back as well and affectionately said, "Yeah, and you be careful not to accidentally step on your penis."

To which Sticks replied, "I did that the other day when I was taking a shower, and man did that hurt. Don't you hate when that happens?" We both laughed out loud.

Then I added, "My brother once told me he found a way to make his penis twelve inches long—he folds it in half." We roared at that one.

We both realized we would treasure this moment for a long time. For the first time in our lives (except for maybe when we were young children and allowed to play at the beach naked), we felt totally free in the wild, and at one with nature. We just laughed the whole way through the next hour, taking turns cutting down more trees.

When we finished (and still feeling like little kids), we decided to see how close we could get back to the farmhouse without someone noticing we were naked.

We walked through the fields and ran up behind the barn, laughing as if we were doing something naughty. Then we ran behind the small tool shed, closer to the house, seeing no one so far. Then we ran in the back door of the farmhouse and still found no one around. "Where is everybody?" I said out loud, disappointed.

Feeling let down, we made some orange juice and just stood in the kitchen drinking it slowly. "Ah, that hits the spot," I said.

Even though we were still naked, we both had now lost our sense of freedom. We took showers, and after cooling off, went back to our rooms, put on fresh clothing, and returned to our normal lives.

Before nodding off to sleep that night, though, I reflected on my activities of the day. As gruesome images of slashed penises and castrated testicles lying on the ground flashed through my mind, one thought seemed to break through loud and clear: *What were we thinking?*

The Dandelion Disco Scene

It was 1978, the peak of disco mania. The radio blasted out hits such as *I Will Survive* by Gloria Gaynor, *YMCA* by The Village People, *Do You Think I'm Sexy* by Rod Stewart, and *Hot Stuff* by Donna Summer, and the members loved to dance.

With the summer weather making travel easier, where else would you find the commune members on a Saturday night? That's right, downtown Kingston at one of the many dance clubs (such as the Commodore Hotel), shaking their booties and doing their thing.

Except there was one small difference—the members of Dandelion did not fit your typical description of disco kings and queens. Oh, no, in fact, they were quite the opposite of the Kingston dancing scene and the disco crowd never fully comprehended what had hit them whenever the members of Dandelion invaded their clubs. And invaded was the right word, as in an alien culture coming to town.

The Dandelion members would show up in torn jeans, mismatched clothes, old shorts, and men with long hair and ponytails. The exceptions were that Maple had her pair of four-inch platform shoes and I had managed to import my blue and white paisley 100% polyester disco shirt. I also happened to own a pair of 100% polyester plaid pants.

Once on the dance floor, there was no stopping us. In solidarity with the few gay men dancing on the floor, Donald and I danced as a couple, confirming our reputation as the best dancing couple of Dandelion.

Gordon would do some wild flinging thing with his arms. Maple, Jane, Mory, Dondi and Timothy, would be shaking their luxurious long hair. Lisa was spinning around on the dance floor.

Dancing, for most of us, was a great way of expressing our joy in being alive. Sure, we were out to create an alternative culture, but we wanted to make sure we had fun on the journey as well.

So there we were, nine Dandelion members dancing away. It was the summer of 1978 and I felt so alive, so connected to what I was doing, and so enjoying my journey.

For the rest of the summer, I enjoyed my time with Lisa, but still carried a torch for Maple and Dondi.

Meeting B. F. Skinner

The really big news for me that summer was that my thesis sponsor from S.U.N.Y. (Dr. Suzanne Kessler), informed me that she had submitted my thesis to the American Psychological Association's annual conference, to be held in Toronto that year, and it had been accepted. That blew me away. I was so excited, not only for myself, but for the community as well. This would be an excellent opportunity to advertise about Dandelion. Suzanne also had mentioned that B. F. Skinner would be attending, and I was thrilled to hear that as well. I would finally meet "the man."

My thesis had been on sexist language and the effects of using the "generic masculine" (i.e., using the word "mankind" or using the pronoun "he" when it could refer to either a man or a woman) on imaging and recall. I had tested students attending my college as well as people living in community.

I had asked both populations to read a story about people living in the future. There were three different versions of the story; one using masculine adjectives, one using feminine adjectives, and one using neutral adjectives. Each person received one version of the story and was then asked to draw a picture accompanying that version and answer some questions.

The results showed that when people read the neutral version, they tended to draw a neutral image, regardless if you lived in community or in the "outside" world.

In the community population, whichever version people read, they tended to draw neutral pictures. The people from the outside tended to draw masculine images when they read the masculine version and then feminine images when they read the feminine version. The results were "statistically significant," which meant that there was a low probability the results were due to chance.

This was one of the things I loved about science—you didn't argue about what is right or wrong; you demonstrated your point, with experiments and data. I also loved that science was egalitarian—that is, other people could follow the same steps you took, and see if similar outcomes resulted. If not, maybe a new theory could be proposed to explain the difference in results. With this method, science gradually stumbled towards a theory that fit the facts.

The conference was to occur during the same time as the Canadian National Exhibition. The CNE was a three-week-long extravaganza of craft shows, farming exhibitions, Canadian culture, Native American cultures, dance contests, amusement rides, airplane shows, etc. It was in Toronto, next to the lake, and each year millions of people attended.

I was to do one week of the show with Durin, and we stayed with some friends of the community in Toronto.

The CNE was a big event for the community. That exhibition and the Christmas season were where we made most of our money for the year.

Dandelion had a small fifteen-by-fifteen-foot booth in the arts and crafts pavilion. A cutting station was included to demonstrate the making of the tin cans. The sparks flying all over the place was always a crowd attractor and pleaser. There was also a stand for the hanging chair, where people could test out the chair themselves. Durin or I would often take turns in the swinging chair, to attract customers.

On Friday, I left the booth to attend the APA conference, which was at the Royal York Hotel in Toronto.

People attending the conference were mostly professionals, the men dressed up in suits and ties, and the women wearing professional outfits as well. Even though I was wearing a blue short-sleeve dress shirt and clean white pants, I felt a little out of place with my long hair and headband.

I met Suzanne at the hotel an hour before the scheduled time of our presentation. "So nice to see you again, Richie," Suzanne exclaimed.

"Same here, Suzanne." We hugged each other warmly. "How goes your grand experiment?" she asked, smiling.

"Oh, pretty good, and what a summer this has been so far, Suzanne! We just started building a new residence building, our membership is climbing, and we had a successful community conference. We're almost certain to get some new members out of that. In addition, some friends of mine from Purchase are coming in two weeks to make a documentary about us. Moreover, I get to present my thesis here at the APA and later on hopefully meet Skinner."

"I'm so happy for you, Richie. Sounds like you made the right choice joining Dandelion. Speaking of Skinner, what happened with your being summoned for jury duty?"

In December, I had received a letter from the court system in White Plains, New York, requesting me for jury duty. I had never served on a jury before. I wrote back saying that I was a behaviorist and believed that the environment a person lived in had a tremendous influence on their behavior, and that I would have a hard time trying to determine if someone was guilty or not of a crime. (I had included contact information regarding Suzanne, Ira Perelle, and B. F. Skinner as references.)

Four weeks later I received a post card from the justice department that said,

"This person has been taken off of jury duty for the following reasons:" The box that had been checked simply said, "Permanently taken off jury rolls." That was all there was to it, I thought. I imagined that a number of people felt the same way I did, and that I had somehow taken a stand for social justice.

"Jury duty—oh yeah, that was months ago. How did you know about that?"

"I found out about it when the director from the Department of Justice called me and read your letter over the phone."

"What?"

"Yeah, he wanted to know if you were some kind of a nut."

"What? Did he actually say that?"

"Those were his exact words. Then he said, 'What if everyone felt that way?' He also wanted to know what kind of person you were. I told him you were very idealistic and intelligent. Then he asked if he should give this other person, B. F. Skinner, a call as well. I convinced him that he was a college professor at Harvard, way too busy."

"I can't believe it, Suzanne!" I said, laughing. "I didn't mean to put you through that. I thought many people felt the same way I did. Geez just shows you how much I don't know. Wait till I tell the folks back at Dandelion. Here I was thinking I got off jury duty because of a philosophical argument, but in reality, they thought I was crazy!" We both started laughing.

"Anyway, getting back to reality," said Suzanne, "I was thinking that we could make this a joint presentation, Richie. I could present the basic findings and you could talk more about the method of collecting and analyzing the data. Does that work for you?"

"That sounds fine, Suzanne. I can't tell you how excited I am to be doing this with you. I mean, how many new college graduates actually get to present their thesis at a national conference. I feel very honored. Thank you."

"Well, you worked hard for this, Richie. Moreover, I feel honored to be presenting the thesis with you."

We proceeded into a large, open conference room. About fifty people showed up to hear the presentation and Suzanne asked everyone to move their chairs into a large circle. There was a certain energy there and I knew this would be a special day for me. I felt lucky indeed and indebted to Suzanne for arranging this to happen.

Suzanne presented the general outline of the study and there were several questions and comments, many of which supported my thesis. I handled most of the questions on the methodology, and we both answered regarding the results. People seemed particularly interested in the use of non-sexist language at Dandelion.

The whole event was so uplifting for me, a perfect example of "doing"

Richie meeting B. F. Skinner

science. I felt excited that many of my peers and leaders in the non-sexist language movement were treating me as an equal.

After the session, we continued to debrief about the whole event. Suzanne told me that I had done an excellent job presenting the evidence and was very articulate in the way I answered questions. We then went off to the luncheon.

Over lunch, Suzanne shared what she was working on and how things were going at Purchase. The whole time, I felt that I was now being treated as an equal by my college professor, and I would never forget Suzanne and that conference.

After lunch, I spotted Skinner sitting at a table with his daughter Julie Vargas, an emerging leader in the field of education. I said good-bye to Suzanne and went over to Skinner's table. I had corresponded with Skinner over the years, but this would be the first time I would actually meet him.

"Hello, Doctor Skinner. I'm Richie from Dandelion Community."

"Ah, Richie, so nice to meet you in person. Please have a seat," Skinner said warmly. I felt an instant connection with the man.

"It is an honor to meet you, Dr. Skinner. Your books have had such an impact on my life."

"Thank you, Richie, and, please—call me Fred." I became even more relaxed.

"I'm curious to know how your presentation went today." I was humbled by the fact that Skinner even knew I was presenting a paper and gave him the condensed version of my thesis and workshop.

"So, how does using non-sexist language work, in practice, at Dandelion?"

"Well, we don't use words like "mankind" or "man-made" when referring to the whole human population. We use the word "co" instead of "him" anytime the person you are talking about could be either a man or a woman, for instance, like a teacher."

Skinner smiled and said, "You know, I visited Twin Oaks Community this past spring, and heard that word being used there as well. It sounded awkward to my ears, but it seemed well established at Twin Oaks. I will be curious to see how the children adapt to it."

We talked more about Twin Oaks, Dandelion and Walden Two. I was impressed with his humanity and concern for the state of the world. He seemed

Richie talks about Dandelion at his "Poster Session" at the conference with other interested psychologists.

most interested in the children of community and their upbringing.

Skinner also talked about the film crew from *NOVA* (the science TV show on PBS) that had filmed his visit at Twin Oaks and was preparing to show it in January. I had heard about the film project and learned more of the details from Skinner.

Lunch ended and I found myself walking with Fred outside the hotel. I gave him the tin can I had made for him. On the bottom, I had burned in "SR+" which stood for Stimulus Response-positive, which in behavior lingo was the shortened symbol for positive reinforcement and informally was the behaviorist's expression for love. Skinner put it on his head and asked for a picture to be taken. I obliged.

"I wish you all the best with your experiment at Dandelion, Richie. Good luck, and keep me posted on your progress."

"I sure will, Fred."

That conference turned out to be one of the most exciting times of my life. I felt that I was a true behaviorist, living at a Walden Two community, and sharing experiments and data with my psychological peers. I felt like I was on track, enjoying my journey, and that the Universe was in balance.

At the end of the CNE, Durin and I dismantled the booth and returned to Dandelion. The community ended up making $17,000 in three weeks.

The Film Project

Before I got involved in studying psychology, I was a film major. One of my filmmaking friends, Jeffrey Clapp, also had an interest in alternative lifestyles and was interested in making a documentary about Dandelion.

He had contacted me to see if it was possible for him to come up and make the film, which would be his senior project.

I was all excited about the idea, as was the rest of Dandelion. We saw it as a great PR tool, which could be shown at conferences and schools. We coordinated details with Jeffrey, and all agreed that a four-day visit in late August worked best.

The film crew happened to show up while Gordon and Jane were on vacation. That was the only drawback. However, Jeffrey and his crew did manage to capture the essence of Dandelion, and the amazing energy of that summer.

For instance, at that particular moment, I was envisioning myself making a lifetime commitment to Dandelion, which came across on the film. I also mentioned that it was an "Exciting time for the community. The community was growing. We had ten members." (That was expressed in a genuine, optimistic way, as I believed that we would soon be on our way to a population of one hundred.)

The film also captured the zaniness of our infamous basketball games, portrayed the tinnery production, the solar shower and the general positive atmosphere of Dandelion that summer.

Mory and Dondi, the best of friends

Orgies? When? Where?

As a male, I felt particularly lucky in the fact that Dandelion seemed to attract an unusual number of beautiful women. Skinner had written about this in *Walden Two*: "Why our way of life has attracted an unusual number of physically attractive women came as a pleasant surprise to Frazier."

I had come to believe that every woman I met was beautiful in some way. I also came to the realization that, eventually, all the women I lived with became attractive to me on some level. Was this because of being limited to potential partners on the commune, or just learning to appreciate the women? Or maybe I was just turned on because they shared the same dream I did.

I also saw them when they first woke up in the morning and worked with them doing tinnery, hammocks, milking cows, cutting wood, cooking or working on Tamari. I learned to appreciate the uniqueness each one brought to the community.

Generally, the women at Dandelion did not shave their underarms or legs and did not wear makeup. Since this was the "norm" (and because I had not been with that many women before joining Dandelion), unshaved underarms and legs became the norm for me as well. I had no problem with that and even found it somewhat erotic.

The women I was most attracted to were the ones who were artists, writers, or thought outside the box. Moreover, here at Dandelion, they were living with me, in abundance, helping me with my wild and crazy ideas. What better attraction could there be? All of these musings probably contributed to my next great idea.

I had been reading an article in the *Whole Earth Review* about communes in California. In terms of orgies, it seemed like a *lot* was happening out on the West Coast—at least a lot more than was happening at Dandelion.

I had been at Dandelion almost ten months, but as far as I could tell, there were no orgies going on. (If there had been any, I certainly hadn't been invited.)

I now knew a bit about three-way relationships, but in terms of the actual lovemaking, that part usually happened only two at a time, as far as I could tell. I began thinking (or maybe fantasizing is more accurate) about what it would take to have an orgy occur at Dandelion. I knew that all the members had come from mostly middle-class backgrounds with families that never divorced.

We had grown up in the 50s & 60s, watching TV shows such as *Leave it to Beaver, Father Knows Best, The Adventures of Ozzie & Harriet,* and that classic cultural icon "*Queen for a Day.*

Queen for a Day was a show where the host would choose three women from the all-women audience. They would then come up on the stage and each one would take turns describing (in detail) how horrible their lives were. (Their husband died, their child needed an operation, etc.)

After hearing the stories, the host would then hold a white handkerchief over the head of each one, and the audience would clap loudest for the one they thought had the most pathetic tale. They actually had an "applause meter" that would register how loud the clapping was. This was on stage and observed by the audience.

The winner would then get a dozen roses, a tiara and a red cape. She would also receive several household appliances like refrigerators, washing machines or hair dryers. There was also a cash prize included. The winner usually had tears running down her face.

What was the effect on young boys and young girls watching this kind of show?

I began thinking of this kind of conditioning and then it hit me. I was living on a commune that was committed to using applied behavior analysis to shape more communitarian behavior. The bylaws stated this. I started getting excited. What if we used those same behavior principles to break down our previous cultural conditioning and then used those same principles to shape orgies? I was stunned with my realization. Could we do something like that? Such an experiment had never appeared in any of the psychological journals I regularly read.

Had I missed something somewhere, maybe from some psychological journal published in California? I would have to check up on that later.

I began to think of how an orgy could actually be "shaped." I would first have to find members who would be open to this kind of thing. Were there any? As far as I was aware, there were only committed couples at the current time, along with maybe one three-way relationship. I began to fantasize about the paper I might put up with my ideas for *the plan.* Something like this:

> "Dear Dandelions, here is my plan for creating an orgy to be held sometime over the upcoming week. On Monday, I would like all interested couples to make love at nine p.m. in their own beds. The next evening, same time, same place, all couples will make love again, but instead of on the bed, you will now be on the floor. On the third evening, all couples will still be on the floor, but closer to the door. On the fourth evening, still on

the floor, but with the door open one inch wide. On the fifth evening, still on the floor, but now with the door open six inches wide. On the seventh evening, doors open, with your feet sticking out into the shared space in the hallway. On the seventh evening, your whole bodies are in the doorway. On the eight evening, all couples will now be moving towards the center of the shared common space. On the ninth evening, all couples, as they make love with their intimate partner, will be touching some other person. Then on the tenth evening, well, *umm*, we will just have to see what happens next."

Then I realized we would probably have to reach consensus at some meeting, which quickly squashed my fantasy.

Dinner Conversations

"Let's see, what will it be tonight?" Gordon asked out loud, thumbing through the *Merck Medical Manual*, a physicians' reference book. The book listed all the diseases ever discovered by humankind and filled with plenty of details describing the gory symptoms, prognosis and possible treatments.

People would often gather in the living room before dinner and it was Gordon's habit to pick out a "disease of the night" and read it aloud to anyone who would listen, leaving nothing to the imagination. People usually humored him with this quirky habit, but occasionally someone would say, "Okay, that's enough, Gordon. I've heard all I ever want to know about DVT Syndrome."

That would usually hold Gordon for a couple of days, but then he would start up again. Visitors and members were impressed, horrified or humored. I was humored, at least most of the time. In fact, I was so humored that I eventually began reading the book out loud as well.

The horrifying diseases would sometimes spill over into our dinner conversations. Stories about sickness and death would often lead to other morbid conversations about torture and disasters. (We often wondered if this was our attempt to make up for the TV shows we missed watching.)

Fall 1978

By September, all the gardens flourished and it was such a treat for me to eat food that I had helped plant and grow. When my turn came to cook supper, I was overjoyed to pick the carrots, tomatoes, lettuce, green peppers and cucumbers from the garden. The corn on the cob was outstanding, as were the cantaloupe, watermelon and strawberries. I was eating like a king.

Bill Svoboda (another Antioch student) arrived the first week in September. He was six feet tall, had long blond hair, blue eyes, and a wide Slovakian face. He was very laid back and had a "live-and-let-live" attitude. (Some would have referred to him as a "hippie.") Bill was majoring in psychology and although he and Dondi had both chosen Dandelion for their internships, they had not met before.

As the cooler weather approached, Bill (who had decided to change his name to "Julian") expressed a keen interest in gardening and became part of the garden team.

Julian proved his worth almost immediately, as there was an early frost one evening and he took on the job of protecting the plants in the garden by covering them with blankets, tarps, shower curtains, and anything else he could find.

And, after a summer of conflicting emotions regarding Lisa, I gently explained to her that my feelings for her had permanently changed and I did not see any long-term relationship between us. She returned to New York shortly after that.

September turned into October and I reflected on my yearlong journey at Dandelion. So much had changed in my life. I had so met so many new people, visited so many new places, been involved with some beautiful women, and had learned so many new skills.

Donald went off to Aloe Community in North Carolina on labor exchange. (He would be gone for a month, needing some time away from Dandelion.)

We also had several interesting visitors that Fall. A visitor named Greg Bates, an eighteen-year-old who had a strong commitment to social change, and was figuring out what his next adventure would be. He fit in so well that after his first three days many members were asking him when he would join, which he did. He then switched his name to "Max."

Max and I would often have long conversations about freewill versus determinism, the ideal society, and of course, women. These were often thought-provoking discussions, and we both enjoyed them immensely.

Randy Friesen, another visitor, was a tall blond construction worker from Alberta. He said he was tired of living in isolation and getting away from that lifestyle was one of the main reasons he was attracted to Dandelion. He ended up doing many shifts on Tamari.

Then there was the Tamari work crew that had assembled over the summer. Shiva became an excellent team leader and organized the workers into efficient teams. Tomo turned out to be such a valued worker that he became assistant manager for the project. In addition, Robbie once again came up on many weekends to work on Tamari.

Progress on Tamari was beginning to take a tangible shape. The frame of the whole building was completed. By the end of the Fall, the first floor was completed. It was exciting to watch the building take form and see our dreams for expansion become reality.

Recreation sponsored a movie trip into Kingston one night, and many of the members and visitors went. Maple, Max, and I went to see *Who'll Stop the Rain*, which turned out to be one of the worst films I had ever seen. It was just too violent for me, and I left before it ended.

On the ride back to Dandelion I was in the back of the van and deeply engrossed thinking about Maple. With Donald gone, I knew Maple would again be free at night. I somehow sensed that if I got involved with her again, it would become something much deeper than what I had felt before. I also knew that Maple would go back to her primary relationship with Donald once he returned. That fact haunted me the whole trip back. I also wondered what Maple was thinking.

When we got back home, I went straight to my room, preparing for bed. Then there was a scratch at my door. I opened it and Maple was standing there. She came in and said, "Richie, you seemed so serious tonight. What's going on?"

I stared into her eyes and simply said, "You must have some idea, Maple."

She smiled and said, "Far Out!" and put her arms around my neck and kissed me. After a minute of kissing, I began lighting the candles. So began another beautiful month together.

The rest of October was a blur for me. We spent many nights together and often worked on Tamari and many other projects. We often read together at night, which usually ended in making love. For me, it was another dramatic time, both sexually and emotionally.

To balance things out, though, I knew that once Donald returned, this chapter of my life would close permanently. However, in the meantime, I would enjoy it to the fullest.

Speaking of Donald (who was the current tinnery manager), someone had to step up to the plate to cover the day-to-day business of running the tinnery. I felt it only fair that I be the one, since I held relatively minor managerships at the time: Behavior, Safety, and Visitor.

After doing tinnery for over a year, I felt comfortable in knowing the ins and outs of the operation required for the tinnery to run smoothly.

Then a big business surprise hit the community. A company that manufactured tin cans (The Continental Can Company), located in Toronto, contacted Dandelion in early October in hopes of purchasing some cans for its annual meeting.

Gordon took the order over the phone and asked, "How many would you need?"

"Well, we have eighteen hundred employees and we're hoping we can get that amount." Gordon's mouth dropped open and he took a deep breath to calm himself. Never had such a large order been placed in the history of our business.

Max in the tinnery

"When would you need it by?" asked Gordon, calculating the production needed and hoping we would have at least two months to get it done.

"Our annual dinner is on November 1, so we would need it at least a couple of days before then."

Gordon gulped, but said, "Sure, we can do that." He then reviewed the types of cans for sale and they ended up ordering eighteen hundred of the hanging 28-ounce cans (the ones peaches usually came in).

This order gave Dandelion about a month's notice. However, where would we find all those extra 28-ounce cans? Our usual supply of recycled cans from recycling bins and friends would be inadequate for such a large order. The cans would also have to be placed in small boxes, which were gratefully provided by the Continental Can Company.

To meet the challenge, we immediately started serving more meals that included food from 28-ounce cans. We

Richie in the tinnery

contacted local friends and asked for any extra cans they could provide.

Alas, there were still not enough to cover the order. Therefore, Gordon ordered five hundred new cans from a manufacturer in Kingston. He then contacted a local town resident and asked to rent a canner that could attach a lid to a can. That resident graciously let us borrow it with no charge.

With Dandelion now having to "make" its own recycled tin can, a new production step became part of the tinnery process. One member would attach the lid to a can and then hand it off to another member sitting next to him or her. That step provided the "edge" at the lip of the can which would prevent the can from bending. With an electric can opener, the member would then remove the lid just put on it. Then, lo and behold, Dandelion had enough cans for the order.

This project turned out to be the greatest professional challenge I had experienced since coming to Dandelion. The production process was enormous. Along with that order, we had to produce all the other cans needed for other craft shows as well.

To add to the equation, the construction crew was committed to getting the whole of Tamari enclosed by December 1, before the cold weather really set in.

Extra hours were required to make the tinnery deadline. More varnish and acetylene would always have to be on hand along with the labor needed for the extra cans and assembling the small cardboard boxes.

With everyone working extra hours in the tinnery, how would I keep up the morale? I would have to be a role model, never complaining and trying to keep the tinnery a fun place to work. Bottlenecks had to be prevented to keep production on schedule.

We already had a work incentive in effect—for every extra hour a member worked over quota, everyone's allowance went up by ten cents. (Our allowance at that time was $2.50 a week.) This incentive was to reinforce co-operation. Therefore, if two people worked over quota, everyone's allowance would go up by twenty cents, and so on.

I also drew up a chart so people could see how many cans we had made. In addition, when we reached our goal, the tinnery budget would sponsor beer for the Halloween party.

For the most part, things went as smoothly as possible. The day before Halloween the truck arrived to pick up the entire order. Members were still putting cans in boxes as the truck was being loaded.

When the truck drove off, there was a collective sigh of relief felt round the community. We had done it. At three dollars per can, the community had earned $5,400. Subtracting the cost of supplies, the community had made about $4,000 in one month—a true accomplishment.

Donald arrived the night of the Halloween party, which turned out to be another amazing party with incredible costumes. Maple went as Dorothy and I went as (who else?) the Tin Man. I had made my costume out of a cardboard box and covered it with aluminum foil. There was a small door cut in the front of my "chest" and inside was a cardboard heart, painted red. It hung down with some black chain.

I watched the interactions with Donald and Maple and realized my time with Maple was truly at an end. After finishing my fifth beer, I went over to Donald and told him about what a great month I had with Maple. Donald simply said, "It's okay, Richie, everything will work out. I'm glad you got to spend some time with Maple while I was gone."

Maple spent the night with Donald. I went back to my celibate life.

Maple as Dorothy

Richie as the Tin Man

Go, Go, Gonads!
(Dandelion plays Basketball)

I loved playing basketball. In hopes of playing some ball on a regular basis, I had contacted the local grammar school principal and reached an agreement that it would be fine for us to play once a week in their gym late on Thursday afternoons. Dandelion paid local school taxes, but did not have any children at the current time, so this seemed to be a fair exchange to the principal.

The games we played were something to behold. The communitarians, all usually very mild-mannered, gentle people, were transformed into wild, maniacal players when it came to playing basketball. Some of the basketball nicknames reflected this transformation: Gordon "Hawkeye" Sproule, Donald the "Rubber Band Man" and not to forget the most frightening of them all, "Sugar Buns" Graham (me). There was also "Tomo Chi Chi." We would show up in all types of wild outfits, including mismatched socks, full-length dresses, and occasionally some disco shirts.

Visitor, Alison, John, Janet, Richie

As an avid follower of the National Basketball Association, I always tried to model and play according to the rules of the NBA, but alas, it often seemed that rules did not exist once we took the court. Moreover, as in volleyball, we did not keep score. Therefore, it was really all about trying to improve our skills and strategies.

Speaking of basketball, one of the boldest moves I ever made in my life was when I walked into the local tavern at Tamarack, which was home to most of the local farmers. The finals for the hockey league were being broadcast on the television set above the bar. It was also the night of the final NBA game between the New York Knicks and Los Angeles Lakers. No one seemed to be watching the hockey game, so I gently asked the bartender if he would be kind enough to turn the channel to the basketball game. He stared at me for a moment (as if I was some kind of alien), looked around the bar, and then said seriously, "Okay, just this one time." I braced myself for an uproar, but nobody complained.

Jonestown Massacre, November 1978

The Jonestown Massacre put all the communities in the Federation on alert. Jonestown was a religious community located in Guyana, South America and led by gospel preacher Jim Jones.

His congregation of twelve hundred people was originally from San Francisco, but they moved to Guyana to start a new life, living a co-operative lifestyle. Like the communities in the Federation, they shared all income and resources.

Jonestown came to a horrifying end on November 18, when Reverend Jones persuaded/ordered all his congregants to drink Kool Aid injected with cyanide. The drinking of that juice ended in the deaths of nine hundred people, including three hundred children.

The Sunday morning after it happened, Shiva and I were listening to the updated news over the radio. We listened in horror of what had gone down in Jonestown. A senator from California had gone down to investigate rumors of abuse, which triggered a gunfight at the airstrip near the community that killed the senator and members of his team.

The Federation was on alert, fearful that our own communal experiments might be associated with Jonestown. In fact, shortly afterwards, a law was passed in Dandelion's county stating that no more than three "non-married" couples could live together in a single household. (Dandelion was somehow graciously grandfathered in.)

For the most part though, the town folk in Enterprise took it all in stride and did not change their relationship with us. We received no threatening phone calls or hateful letters and believed that spoke to the reputation we had worked so hard to achieve.

Winter 1979

In January, the PBS science show, *NOVA*, broadcast its show about Skinner and Twin Oaks Community. Since we did not have a TV, we decided to rent a motel room in Kingston to watch. There we were, ten communitarians crammed into a small motel room watching the show. There were "ohhssss" and "aaaahhhhhhs" throughout the viewing. Overall, we agreed that *NOVA* had presented an accurate picture of Skinner's philosophy and of Twin Oaks Community in particular.

But the hundreds of inquires we expected after the showing never materialized. Twin Oaks did receive about thirty inquiries, but only a few visitors resulted from that, and we had only two. There was general disappointment in that experience, but we released a collective sigh and got on with the work of building community. It was during this time that Durin left for East Wind Community to pay back our labor exchange hours.

Dandelion in Winter

Trip to Los Horcones

Over the winter, I was reading and hearing more about Los Horcones Community, located in Mexico near the city of Hermosillo. The more I heard about them, the more curious I became.

They apparently were an intentional community dedicated to applying behavior principles on a more systematic basis. Before starting their own community, the members of Los Horcones (all Mexicans) had visited Twin Oaks in hopes of finding a community based on behavior principles. Even though Twin Oaks was founded on Walden Two, the Los Horcones members found it did not live up to their expectations. Los Horcones members believed that the book *Walden Two* was a work of fiction, whereas the science of human behavior, on which the book was based, was real. Therefore, they felt that a "real" Walden Two community should be based on that science, and they would have gladly joined Twin Oaks had they found it to be that kind of community.

After visiting Twin Oaks, the members of Los Horcones decided to build their own community in Mexico. They had the same goals and practices of communities in the Federation (i.e., income sharing, committed to non-violence, raising children communally, etc.), and had joined the Federation. The big difference was that they were much more radical in their application of behavior principles.

I was most intrigued and wanted to find out more.

In January, we had a visitor from Toronto named Jim Kennedy. A recent college graduate with a degree in biology, he had a strong interest in building a community based not on the science of behavior alone, but a community based on all the other sciences as well (solar, nutrition, electronic, etc.). Jim and I had many passionate discussions regarding what that kind of community would be like.

When Jim found out about Los Horcones, he, too, became very interested in visiting them. After much discussion with other members, I proposed going to Los Horcones on labor exchange for a month to see what they were doing. The community felt it would be a worthwhile adventure.

Jim was generous enough to offer his car for the trip (a 1973 Volkswagen bug), if we shared the gas/oil expenses, and together we planned the trip.

Since Jim had never visited any of the other communities in the Federation (and I had visited only Twin Oaks), we decided to visit Twin Oaks and

East Wind on our way down to Los Horcones. They were along the route we planned and we would save money on food and motels. We would drive South to Twin Oaks, then West to East Wind, and then South to Mexico.

Maple was interested in getting away from the community for a while and had arranged to do some labor exchange at Twin Oaks. She would join us on our ride there.

We left early in the morning and arrived at Twin Oaks two days later. We arrived in the evening and when we got out of the car, we heard a lot of cheering and singing coming from the Chai residence building. We curiously approached and went in.

The community was celebrating Gareth's thirtieth birthday and people had gathered in the Chai living room. There were about fifty members in the living room, which included a sunken fifteen-foot round floor in front of the fireplace. No lights were on and numerous candles lit up the room. We could smell incense.

Beer and wine bottles were everywhere. All kinds of food (from chicken wings to hummus) were on the tables. A true sense of celebration and community was in the air.

In the corner, dressed in a toga outfit, was Green Tree, a long-term friend of the community and an actual medical doctor who did not charge the community for his services. He was loudly banging on a snare drum with his long hair swinging wildly.

There was commotion at the side entrance and suddenly the large doors (which led to the hammock shop) opened and four women, dressed in Greek togas, carrying rose petals, along with grapes on plates, entered the room. Four men followed them, dressed in similar togas and carrying a stretcher on their shoulders.

On the stretcher was Gareth. He was leaning on his side, completely naked, smiling, waving, and obviously drunk.

The women threw the rose petals in the air as the four men brought him to the center of the sunken room and gently laid the stretcher on the floor. Gareth flipped over onto his stomach, and the four women began rubbing oil over his back and legs. When that mission was accomplished, they then gently turned him over and began rubbing oil all over his front side as well (discreetly skipping his genital area.) Hoots and hollers erupted around the room.

With the fire roaring and the fifty members sweating and breathing, the room began to get very hot. As this was going on, more and more members (both men and women) began stripping down to their birthday suits.

I started getting excited. Was this the beginning of an actual orgy? Spellbound, Jim and I smiled at each other.

The four women peeled the grapes and slowly inserted them into Gareth's mouth. What an erotic movement. Gareth eagerly ate them up and was really getting into the moment.

Then Tomo (who had earlier that month returned to Twin Oaks), walked into the middle of the sunken floor area next to Gareth, took off his remaining undershirt and underpants and proudly announced, "Who will wrestle me?"

There were more hoots and hollers all around and then Taylor (a woman) stood up and said, "I'll wrestle you, Tomo!" Cheers and applause exploded as now Taylor took off the rest of *her* clothes and stepped into the sunken pit, buck-naked.

What happened next became Twin Oaks lore and anyone who witnessed that event was destined to remember it forever—at least I did. Gareth was removed from the pit (still on his stretcher and still having a giant smile on his face) as Tomo and Taylor began to gently wrestle each other. The competition quickly heated up and became more and more aggressive. At one point, Tomo picked Taylor up by the waist, and she somehow turned upside down and was now facing Tomo's crotch area. A loud cheer went up. She then pinched Tomo's ass and he screamed, letting her go.

They were now rolling around the carpet trying to get a pin, but they were too drunk or maybe just not very good wrestlers. Taylor then had Tomo on the floor, face down and began slapping his behind, which elicited more cheers and clapping from the crowd.

They were both exhausted by now and Tomo called a truce, saying Taylor was a fine wrestler and bowed to her. Taylor returned the courtesy and bowed as well.

The night unfolded with more merriment and craziness, but as far as I could tell, no real orgy developed out of it. However, we would never know, as we were exhausted from our drive down. Jim and I were led to the visitor room while Maple was given a separate room.

We planned to stay at Twin Oaks for only two nights and while there, we met a German visitor named Pitt. He was a twenty-one-year-old outgoing fellow, who had seen the *NOVA* program and was one of many Germans who had come to visit the States to see firsthand what the communal movement had to offer. When he found out about our plan to visit Los Horcones and East Wind, he asked if he could join us. He said he would be happy to help pay for expenses. With that offer, how could we refuse?

Before leaving the next morning, I went to say good-bye to Maple. I once again thanked her for all the time we spent together and kissed her on the forehead when I left. The last thing she said as I was going out the door was, "Don't drink the water."

The trip to East Wind began. It was a cloudy day and snowstorms were predicted for the Mid-West. We made good time crossing Virginia and West Virginia and would never forget the majestic mountains of those states. That was some of the wildest, untamed countryside I had ever seen.

We made it to Tennessee by nightfall and since we had very little money, we decided to skip finding a motel and continue through the night.

Halfway through Tennessee, the snowstorms began. We were on the interstate, our little bug doing fine on the roads, but around one a.m. the heating system went out. The car suddenly became very cold.

The cold air made our breath fog up the window, and whoever was in the passenger seat would press their hands on the window so that the driver could continue to see the road ahead. By this method, we managed to keep open a space about four inches square. The outside of the car began to develop a thin sheet of ice around it.

We finally arrived at East Wind Community at six a.m. after driving for twenty-four hours, and we were exhausted. We parked the car in front of a large building, and when we got out, we saw the entire car was covered in a one-inch sheet of ice. We met a fellow East Winder going into the building and after introductions he invited us into Rock Bottom, which was the community's dining complex.

After breakfast, we were shown the visitor building (a converted chicken coop that was heated and didn't smell of chickens). We all crashed out in the bunk beds and were quickly asleep.

Six hours later, we were all up and eager to explore East Wind Community. We went to Rock Bottom for lunch and met Durin, who was thinking of becoming a member there. He filled us in on the latest news regarding East Wind and then gave us a tour.

We were impressed with all the buildings we saw. There was a huge hammock shop, children's building, auto shop, and four large residence buildings. They had also begun construction on an enormous industrial building, which would later hold their million dollar per year peanut butter business.

The one thing missing was that, except for the children's building, none of the buildings had indoor bathrooms. Instead, they had several two-seater outhouses scattered over the property. One morning, I found myself sitting next to a complete stranger. I was just happy it wasn't a woman.

The other thing about East Wind was that it had only one large public shower room, like a locker room. I found myself in the awkward situation of going into the shower room (with six showerheads) and finding a woman showering.

She was rinsing her hair under the nozzle and I diplomatically coughed just to let her know I was entering the shower room, and then said, "Hi, I'm Richie Dandelion, visiting East Wind for the first time."

"Oh, hi, welcome to East Wind. Shiva has said only good things about Dandelion. I'm Mary," she said in a friendly manner with her back to me.

I stepped up to the shower farthest away and turned it on. Facing the wall, I quickly got under the water and began washing myself. Since she was the first woman I had seen naked in a while, my nether parts were becoming aroused and I did not want to embarrass the woman or myself. I quickly finished up and left the shower.

By the time I had returned to the visitor building, it was getting dark. Pitt and Jim were there and we headed out to Rock Bottom for dinner. We would eat a hearty meal as we were planning to leave early the next morning, hoping to make it to Texas by evening and the Mexican border the following day.

We were on the road by seven and after six hours of driving south, we noticed two things—first, the bitter cold we had been struggling with since leaving Virginia had become much warmer, and second, the scenery had begun to change dramatically. We were leaving behind mature forests of oak and maple trees, and were heading into much more open country featuring cactus trees and small sage bushes. There were even open stretches of sand.

By the time we reached the border of Mexico, it was early evening and we decided to cross the border and find a cheap place to crash. We crossed the border at Nogales and came to a small customs building. The Mexican agent, who spoke fluent English, inspected our car and asked for our passports along with our insurance papers.

Jim assured the agent that his insurance covered him wherever he drove and showed him his insurance card. However, the agent insisted that he needed a special permit to come into Mexico.

We were stumped by this and didn't know what the agent was talking about. However, he made it clear that without the papers, we could not come into Mexico.

Then Jim caught onto what was happening. He politely asked the agent if he could help us. The agent replied, with a straight face, "For a small fee, I could type you up the proper certificate that you need." Jim then diplomatically asked how much that would cost. The agent went to his desk, took out an official looking book, and with hardly a glance at it, replied, 'That would be one hundred pesos. If you have only American dollars, that will be fifteen dollars."

We realized it came to five dollars each, but we had no choice. We paid the agent in cash, which the agent accepted graciously and then he went to his typewriter and typed out a piece of paper stating that we had the proper papers to travel in Mexico. He then bid us a safe journey.

In the car, Jim said, "I've heard of bribery at border crossings, but this is the first time I have seen it up close."

"That was something else," I replied, shaking my head.

Pitt added, "I wonder how much he makes in extra cash each day? That has never happened to me crossing into any countries in Europe." We all shook our heads and then smiled.

After leaving the Mexican customs station, we now found ourselves on the southern side of the border, smack in the Mexican town of Nogales. Things were different here. It was if we had stepped into a movie set for some outlaw town, featuring dim lights, trash on the streets, old cars, rundown buildings, and very few street signs. Very quickly, we found ourselves lost and went into the only lighted building on the street. This turned out to be the local police station.

We walked in and the police officer we found was sitting at his desk wearing two rolls of bullets crisscrossing his chest. *Just like in the movies*, I thought. The officer had black hair, a large gut, and a dark black mustache. When we walked in, he said in a friendly manner, "Ahhhh, *Americanos*, how can I help you?"

After explaining that we were looking for the best route to Hermosillo, the officer described the safest way to get there and bid us a safe journey.

Our journey in Mexico was having quite the beginning. As we left Nogales, our car soon developed engine problems and we had to pull over on the side of the road. We were out in the desert with no streetlights and very few cars driving by. Luckily, after some keen tinkering by Jim, it soon was running again. A little while later, we found a cheap motel and crashed for the night.

The next day, after a cheap breakfast of beans & rice, the real adventure began. We had been driving for about an hour when we came around the curve of a small hill and saw a road worker flagging cars to stop. Apparently heavy rains the night before had shaken loose many small boulders overlooking the highway.

The flagman, using his best judgment, would wait a moment, watch as a small boulder came rolling down the hill, look up to make sure it was okay, and then flag a car through. There was a line of five cars waiting.

We were fascinated as the drama unfolded before us. Would we take a chance and trust the judgment of this flagman? We watched as cars zoomed off as soon as they got permission to proceed.

When our turn came, we were eager to return to our travels, and so we too raced off as soon as the flagman gave the thumbs up sign.

We traveled a couple of more hours and found ourselves behind ten cars stopped before a small bridge that had washed out the night before. At the side of the bridge, a dirt road lead down to the small river, where ten cars had lined up waiting their turn to drive through the riverbed.

Every couple of minutes a car would enter the water, and fighting the current, sometimes dangerously drift downstream with the rapids, bump and weave its way to the far shore. A loud cheer would go up when the driver made it to the other side. Next, cars coming from the other direction would take their chance in crossing the stream.

When our turn came, we took a deep breath and drove our car into the stream. We were immediately tugged, pulled and turned sideways, but Jim somehow managed to keep the car heading for the shore.

Then an amazing thing happened. For a couple of seconds, our car actually floated, with no traction at all with the riverbed below us. I had heard rumors that Volkswagen bugs could float, but this was my first time experiencing it.

With Jim pushing the pedal to the medal, the car touched the stream bed, finally gained traction again, and we hobbled onto the shore. The crowd of onlookers cheered, applauded and yelled, "*Buenos, Buenos.*" We three gringos smiled triumphantly, waved to the crowd and continued our journey.

Along the way, we now saw many poor dwellings, including people living in abandoned freight cars that had been dropped off near old abandoned train tracks. The land was sparse with very few trees, but many sage bushes. We could see for hundreds of miles in all directions and the ultra-blue sky and warm weather gave us all a sense of well-being.

Four hours later, we passed through Hermosillo, which had orange trees growing everywhere. Some trees even grew between traffic lanes and we could see people picking oranges there.

We arrived at Los Horcones in the late afternoon. As we got out of the car, we could see many white buildings spread out over the land. They also had large fields of crops growing all around the outside of the community.

The community was located about ten miles from Hermosillo and they supported themselves by teaching children with cognitive disabilities. We began walking towards the nearest building, looking for Fernando, with whom I had been communicating with since December.

"*Hola, amigos,*" a voice called out to us. We all turned and saw a tall man, with a brown beard, brown eyes, light tan complexion, and wide smile approaching us.

"Are you the folks from Dandelion Community?" he asked in mildly accented English.

"Yes, we are. I'm Richie Dandelion and this is Jim and Pitt."

"Ah, welcome to Los Horcones." We all exchanged handshakes and smiles. After some small talk about the trip, Fernando said, "Grab your stuff and I will show you your rooms." We gathered our bags and followed Fernando to the visitor building on the far side of the community.

On the way over, Fernando showed us the bathroom complex and the outside shower. He explained that we would have to first heat the water in the outside shower tank (which was the size of a small torpedo) before using it. One did this by starting a small fire below the water tank. (A pile of small twigs and logs was conveniently stacked next to the tank.)

We then came to the kitchen–dining building, and Fernando said, "We have communal meals between seven and eight for breakfast, noon to one for lunch, and six to seven for supper. If you miss those times, you can always help yourselves to whatever is in the pantry and fridge."

We entered the building and could see it had two main rooms. The first room was a kitchen which had a six-burner stove, industrial size refrigerator, two kitchen sinks, a wooden cutting table, and various cabinets and shelves. A large black pot on the stove contained frijoles (beans).

The second half of the building was the main dining room. Here were two rows of long wooden tables with about thirty wooden chairs. Large windows on all sides of the room gave picturesque views of the whole community.

We left the kitchen-dining complex and ran into Juan, Maria, Linda, and Ramon, who greeted us enthusiastically. Juan was eager to talk with me and find out more about what Dandelion was doing in terms of applying behavior analysis to community practices. I said, "Well, that is the same reason I came to visit you, Juan." We both smiled widely.

"*Buenos*. We will talk more over dinner," said Juan in more heavily accented English.

We left them and continued our tour, with Fernando pointing out the school and recreation buildings. Looking at the buildings, I realized that one big difference between buildings at Los Horcones vs. buildings in North America was that they did not have to worry about heating them in the winter. Their bigger challenge was keeping buildings cool in the summer. They accomplished this by various building designs and having air conditioners in some of the buildings. The money they saved on heating and insulation contributed greatly to money they used for other projects.

We made it to the visitor building, which had twelve private rooms. Fernando pointed to three doors along the side of the building and said, "We currently have plenty of space, so you can each have your own room."

There was no bathroom attached to this building. When asked about that, Fernando smiled and said, "For peeing, you have your choice." He pointed to the vast open space surrounding the building. "For other, please use the main bathroom complex." He then added, "You've had a long trip. Why don't you rest up and take it easy for a little while. The cooks will ring the bell at six and you can easily hear it. *Adios.*"

"Wow! Can you believe we actually made it here?" Jim exclaimed.

"Yeah, and we are so lucky they all seem to speak fluent English. I was afraid we might have to communicate in Spanish," I replied.

"I wonder if any of them speak German," Pitt said, smiling.

"Maybe you can teach them some German drinking songs," I added, with a grin.

We went to our individual rooms and unpacked. My room was ten feet square with a comfortable bed, small dresser, a chair, and a small table with a lamp on it. It had one large window, next to the door, which looked out on the wide-open land.

I felt too excited to lie down, so I walked across the open land away from the community. As there were no fences, I wondered how far their land actually went. I was walking on red-colored soil, scattered with sage bushes and small trees. The sky was bright blue and the temperature was in the mid-70s. There was to be the same kind of weather for the next couple of weeks, and I felt like I had stumbled into some kind of tropical paradise.

I heard the bell ring at six p.m. and headed back to the visitor building. I teamed up with Jim and Pitt and we headed out to the kitchen-dining complex. We were all hungry and eager to meet and talk with the members of Los Horcones. This would also be our first home-cooked meal in days.

When we walked into the kitchen-dining complex, there were about twenty people there and five young children. There was a cacophony of melodious Spanish heard around the tables.

Juan came up and said, "Ahhh, *amigos*. Welcome to your first dinner with us." He walked us over to a large serving table that was stacked with all kinds of delicious-looking food and my mouth began to water.

There was the large pot of beans, burrito flaps, a large bowl filled with salad (which included lettuce, tomatoes, carrots, spinach, cucumbers and bean sprouts), corn on the cob, grated Mozzarella, Havarti, and Gouda cheese (all labeled in Spanish & English), grilled chicken breasts, and sliced avocados. All kinds of dressings were available. Next to the burritos were sliced onions, mushrooms, cubed tomatoes, and lettuce.

To the right of that table was another table that contained all kinds of fruit, including pineapples, pears, plums, oranges, and apples. Next to that were slices of apple pie. I looked at Jim and Pitt and we all smiled. This was going to be a feast.

After filling our plates, we turned around and saw Juan beckoning us to the three chairs opposite him. "*Amigos*, come, *por favor.*" Fernando came over and sat down opposite us as well.

Juan began, "So, you made it here safely. Any good stories from the road?" Jim shared our experiences of driving through the stream, avoiding boulders and driving to East Wind in the snowstorm and how we had arrived with our car covered in one inch of ice.

"Ah that is one thing you won't have to worry about here," Juan said. We all chuckled.

Fernando then asked, "Are your rooms satisfactory, comfortable enough for you?"

Pitt said, "Ah, so, yes, very strong bed, *muchas gracias.*"

As the conversation continued, I was eagerly devouring my meal, taking large bites of my burrito and savoring every bite of the corn on the cob, which I had generously dipped in butter.

"So, Richie, I am eager to hear more about how Dandelion is applying behavior principles," Juan said with a smile.

"Well, first of all, I know you are well versed in the O.U.R. World Series books that talk a lot about language as a focus of social change."

Juan smiled and said, "*Si.*"

"In fact, I believe Los Horcones is mentioned in the dedication of one of their books, *si*?"

Juan smiled and nodded his head.

"So, to answer your question, our main focus is on maintaining a positive verbal environment, talking about the things we like, trying to shape behavior in a positive way."

Fernando asked, "*Por favor,* can you give us any examples of that, Ricardo?" I liked my new name. I felt like I was already accepted at Los Horcones.

I went on to explain my interaction with my fellow member. "There was a new member who swore out loud a lot of the time. Personally, I do not like swearing and try to avoid it. Certainly it took away from our positive verbal environment. So, I thought of different ways to approach this behavior. One thing I could have done was to say something like, 'You know, I don't like it when you swear around me. If you could keep an eye on that, I would really like that.' In that instance, the person is doing a behavior and the negative feedback would technically be a form of punishment. I thought of a different approach where I could reinforce him in a positive way when he wasn't swearing. So I said, 'I really like that you haven't sworn around me for the last half hour.' The member was smart enough to pick up on what I was saying and his swearing gradually decreased."

Juan said, "Wow! That is a great example, Ricardo."

Being called Ricardo once again made me wonder if I was slowly being shaped to become more used to the Spanish language.

Juan continued, "So, besides positive verbal behavior, what else are you doing?" I thought for a moment and then said, "Well, we have our Behavior Code, which lists all the agreements we live by. Our labor system is set up so that we divide the aversive work as much as possible, usually by rotation. Everyone takes a turn at doing dishes, for example. We also use a non-sexist language whenever possible. In addition, we try to make aversive work situations more fun. For example, sometimes someone will read a book out loud to a member who is doing dishes."

Juan and Fernando nodded to each other, and Juan said, "We do the same thing here."

"Jim, you visited Dandelion last month. Can you think of anything to add to this conversation?"

Jim thought a moment then replied, "Well, there was just a sense of community there that I had not experienced anywhere else. The trust and cooperation everyone shared was just amazing. I also liked the non-competitiveness in all the areas of work and play."

I was eager to hear more about behaviorism at Los Horcones, but dinner was ending, and I sensed that I would have to wait for another time. Just as I was contemplating that very thought, Maria (Juan's wife) came over and grabbed Juan's arm, apologized for interrupting, and said she needed to talk with him. Juan nodded and said, "My wife calls, I must obey." He stood up, kissed his wife, and then said, "We will continue this conversation tomorrow. I especially want to hear more about your behavior code. Rest well, my *amigos*, and tomorrow Ramon will give you a tour of the gardens and fields. We'll meet here for breakfast at eight a.m., okay? *Buenos noches*."

We did get the tour the next day and had some thought-provoking talks with Ramon, mostly about behaviorism and community. I realized that Los Horcones really was much more radical than Dandelion about living a behaviorist lifestyle. For instance, they had behavior meetings twice a week where members could report both the positive and negative behaviors they had witnessed during the week. Since I was a visitor, I would not be invited to those meetings, but I heard they were generally positive.

Their children's program was most impressive. The children had their own building, and the older children each had their own room. Each child was responsible for taking care of some area of the community. For example, Juanito, the six-year-old son of Juan and Maria, was in charge of feeding the rabbits the community raised for food. He also kept track of the amount of food served to each rabbit.

In attempts to teach children non-possessiveness, the adults would refer to items of clothing and toys as "The toy I use," rather than "my toy." Alternative-

Los Horcones: Jim, Pitt and Richie

ly, they would say, "The shirt I wear," rather than "my shirt." Jim and I joked about how far you could take the analogy. Could one say, "The wife I use," instead of "my wife"?

English was taught to the children in the community school, and members always encouraged English-speaking visitors to converse in English with their children whenever possible.

One day after I had finished doing the lunch dishes, Juan approached me and told me they were planning to attend the tenth annual Southern California Association of Behavior Analysis conference, happening in two weeks in Los Angeles. Skinner and some other well-known behaviorists would be there. Would I, Jim, and Pitt be interested in attending with them?

"That would be fantastic, Juan. I'm sure Jim would like to go as well. I believe Pitt is making plans to visit South America, but you can check with him. It would be great to meet up with some other behaviorists and maybe get some converts." We both smiled.

I added that I had a cousin in Los Angeles and Jim and I could probably stay with her.

During the day, Jim, Pitt, and I worked mostly doing simple chores like cleaning or working in the fields, weeding. We were also allowed to observe (behind one-way mirrors), the daily interactions in the school for children with cognitive disabilities. I was again impressed with the community's emphasis of using positive reinforcement to shape the behavior of the students there.

In the evenings, most members retired to their rooms or helped put the children to bed. Jim and Pitt and I would meet in the recreation building to compare notes on how our day had gone.

One evening there was a communal campfire that everyone attended. The sky was full of stars. Members shared stories about their lives before community. Jim and Maria took turns playing guitar. The children roasted marshmallows over the fire. If it weren't for the fluent Spanish being spoken all around me, I could have sworn I was back in suburban New Jersey visiting my cousins and Uncle Eddie and Aunt Marion.

The night before we left, the community had a going-away party for us in the recreation house. The community members took turns singing songs, playing guitar, shaking maracas, and generally having a good time. Corona beers were offered. Much appreciation was expressed at their having had the chance to meet and interact with us "Yankee Gringos."

ABA Conference, February 1979

The next day, Fernando, Juan and his son took off for Los Angeles followed by Jim and me. We had agreed beforehand that we would all meet up at the conference.

Two days later, Jim and I arrived at Los Angeles in the late afternoon the day before the conference. My cousin Jean (whom I had not seen in ten years) graciously agreed to put us up for three days.

Jean was a first cousin of my father, so I had rarely seen her when I was growing up, mostly at weddings. The thing that I always remembered about her was besides having a very gentle and friendly disposition, she had the most gorgeous red hair I had ever seen on a woman.

She was currently living with a lawyer friend and they shared a very nice four-bedroom house. Jim and I would share a small bedroom that had its own bathroom.

"Richie, so nice to see you again! Come on in. Dinner is just about ready," exclaimed Jean as she welcomed us into her house.

"Great seeing you too, Jean. It's been too long." She showed us our bedroom and said, "Dinner will be ready in half an hour. You can get settled in and come on down when you're ready." We both showered and went downstairs.

Jean had cooked a roasted chicken along with baked potatoes and green beans. There was also a bottle of red wine on the table. Larry (her significant other) came into the dining room and introduced himself, "Pleased to meet you, Richie. Jean has talked a lot about you. Make yourselves at home."

Over dinner Jean asked, "So what is this conference all about, Richie?"

"Well, over the past couple of years, I have gotten very interested in behavior psychology and its applications in a variety of fields, like education, child rearing, and prison reform. For the past year, I have been living in an intentional community trying to apply basic behavioral principles to a small group setting. This conference tomorrow is about different aspects of behavior analysis. I believe the mayor of Los Angeles will be making a guest appearance."

Larry piped up and said, "I've read some stuff about your basic philosophy. It appears that you don't believe in free will. Is that correct?"

Jim replied, "Well, we say that the environment a person lives in tends to have a major influence on how that person behaves. Behaviorists are just saying that a person can modify those influences, so in that sense, we are exhibiting free will."

Larry replied, "Well, criminals have to be held accountable for their own behavior, right?"

"Why, yes, of course. But if you look at most criminals now in jail, eighty percent of them never finished high school. That certainly has to be a factor in not getting a well-paying job, which might lead them down a different path."

"I don't buy it. You're minimizing the responsibility of the individual and saying it's society's fault that they turned out the way they did. Isn't that true?"

I then added, "Well, that is one of the main reasons I joined Dandelion. If you say, for example, that humans will always be at war because we have some kind of gene for violence, that is a pessimistic statement about the human condition. But, if you take the alternative view, and say that yes, humans can be aggressive given the right environment, the question becomes: Can we set up an environment where the possibility of violence/aggression is minimized or not able to express itself in the first place."

After some more philosophical exchanges, Jean got up to clear some dishes and brought them into the kitchen. I picked up my own dish and followed her. "I don't know, Richie," said Jean. "That sounds like some pretty radical stuff you are talking about in there."

"I agree Jean, it is radical, and I'm still trying to process it myself. It is a different way of talking about the causes of human behavior. But as far as I'm concerned, what have we got to lose?" I smiled.

We returned to the dining room where Jim and Larry had changed to topics that were more neutral.

The next morning, Jim and I arrived at the Westin Bonaventure Hotel, located in the heart of downtown Los Angeles. We parked our car in the large parking lot at the hotel and walked toward the entrance, where we saw a line of about one hundred people waiting to get inside. We then saw Juan and his son going along the line handing out flyers about Los Horcones.

"*Hola*, Juan," I said approaching him.

"*Buenos dias, amigos.*"

"Busy passing out the revolution manifesto?" I said smiling.

"*Si*. And by the way, at 12:45, we will be showing the Federation slide show in our room to any interested persons, room 445. *Por favor*, pass the word around."

"That's awesome, Juan. Maybe we can get some new converts here. We'll be there."

"See you then. *Adios.*"

We entered the main entrance of the hotel and got on the elevator. At the next floor, the elevator door opened and in walked Skinner. I couldn't believe the timing. "Fred, so nice to see you again!"

Skinner recognized me at once and said, "Ah, Richie, nice seeing you again as well." We smiled and shook hands.

I introduced Jim, who said, "An honor to meet you, Dr. Skinner."

I realized we only had a minute on the elevator and invited Skinner to the Federation slide show. 'Why, yes, I'd love to see that. What room will it be in?" As Skinner jotted it in a small notebook.

"The people from Los Horcones will be the ones presenting it."

"Ah, yes, I've heard a lot of good things about that community and will look forward to meeting them as well."

The elevator doors opened and Skinner left. Jim then said, "Wow, you actually called him 'Fred' Richie. Pretty cool."

I smiled. "Yeah, and I'm dying to see his reaction to the slide show." We got off at the next floor and walked to the main auditorium.

Tom Bradley, the first African-American mayor of Los Angeles was there, and he made some nice introductory comments about the value of behavior psychology in schools. After the keynote speaker was finished, I attended a workshop on prison reform. It was interesting, but I thought the focus should be on how to prevent people from going to prison in the first place.

After lunch, Jim and I met Fernando and Juan at their room at 12:30. There were five other people in the room whom we had not met before and Fernando introduced us.

A few minutes, later Skinner entered the room. There were smiles all around, but perhaps the biggest was mine. I was so excited to share the Federation slide show with Skinner and see what his reaction would be.

After the slide show, Skinner said he was very impressed with what he saw. "It seems like Los Horcones and Dandelion are the ones using applied behavior analysis in the most systematic way. That gives me great pleasure." After some more debriefing about the communities and answering questions, we all left for the afternoon workshops.

Later that day, I ran into Joe Morrow, another radical behaviorist who taught psychology at the California State University in Sacramento. I had communicated with Joe last year, as he was the editor of the psychological journal Behaviorists for Social Action. I'd had my thesis published in that magazine as well.

"A pleasure to meet you in person, Richie. How are you doing?"

"Great, Joe. It's been a thrill being around all these behaviorists." I then introduced Jim and gave Joe an update on our travels and Los Horcones.

Joe then asked, "That is all exciting news, Richie. Listen, would it be possible for you and Jim to take a side trip and come speak to my graduate seminar class up in Sacramento? I know my students would love to hear about what Dandelion and Los Horcones are doing. I have plenty of room in my house where you and Jim could stay."

I looked at Jim to get his reaction. Jim was a little hesitant, as we had already made plans for our trip back. "Well, I'm not sure about that, Joe," he said. "We're on a pretty tight schedule."

To which Joe replied, "I'm begging both of you. Please! It is only a four-hour ride from here. You can follow me back tomorrow and you can present on Monday afternoon and then be on your way on Tuesday. Please?" Joe clasped his hands together and looked desperate.

Jim gradually smiled, and we both agreed it would be a fine detour. Anything to help the cause. Who knew? Maybe we could meet some possible recruits.

After speaking at Joe's class (which had about one hundred students), Jim and I planned our route back to Canada. We would go straight through the Western United States, driving twelve-hour days, arriving in Detroit three days later.

We accomplished that and then arrived in Toronto the following day. I stayed at Jim's apartment overnight and then took the bus back to Dandelion the following day. I had enjoyed my time on the road with Jim, particularly visiting Los Horcones, but now was eager to get back to Dandelion and share what I had learned.

March 1979

When I returned to Dandelion in early March, it was a different place. Maple had decided to try out living in the real world and wound up working for the National Survival Institute in Toronto. Dondi and Donald had left as well—she to Twin Oaks, feeling she needed a larger community to live in, and Donald to visit his parents and figure out if he wanted to apply to medical school. In addition, Max had gone off to Philadelphia to live with the Movement for a New Society community. Their presence and energy were noticeably missing. It was also March and the cold weather was dragging on.

It was great being back at Dandelion, and I got the feeling that the members were counting on me to help revive the Dandelion spirit. I was a little nervous about such an expectation but was eager to help the community get back on its behavior path.

Jane and Gordon were the first to welcome me, "We really missed your positive energy, Dicky. I'm eager to hear about what you learned at Los Horcones," Jane said.

Gordon added, "Yes, we are all dying to hear what actually goes on down there. Are they really as behaviorist as your letters said they were?"

I smiled and said, "Yes, there is so much to share. I'll review my notes and make a presentation tomorrow night."

The following day I set up a meeting to present all I had learned at Los Horcones. I got the sense that the members would support most, if not all, the ideas I was about to propose.

After my presentation, Gordon inquired, "Wow, a lot of good information, Richie; nice job. What would you say was the most important thing you learned down there?"

"I think there were two main things, Gordon. First, Los Horcones systematically gives members feedback on their behavior in a continuous and positive way. Second, their behavior code is much more specific in regard to what is considered appropriate and inappropriate behavior."

Jane perked up and asked, "Can you give us some specific examples of what you're talking about, Dicky?"

"Sure. First, they have behavior meetings twice a week, right after supper. It is usually a positive fifteen-minute meeting. Members get to report on how members are following, or in the rare instance not following, their behavior code. They particularly reinforce any advancement towards specific behaviors the community is working on as a whole. This is helped immensely by their detailed behavior code."

"Exactly how different is their behavior code from ours?" Julian asked.

"Well, they usually have both a positive expectation and a negative statement written for particular behaviors. For example, our behavior code states, 'Clean up after yourself.' At Los Horcones, for keeping the kitchen clean, theirs said, 'Wipe off table after using. Remove any items that were not there before.' That way the member or visitor has a very clear idea of the behavior expected. It can also cut down on arguments."

Gordon added, "I can see how that would work. When you have a broad statement such as 'Clean up after yourself,' that leaves it open to personal interpretation. Do I have that right?"

"Exactly," I replied.

Members started getting excited about this simple realization. Mory added, "That seems like a good way to make sure everyone knows exactly what the community expectations actually are. It would be especially good for visitors in helping them get oriented to our community norms." I smiled as I saw others smiling around me. This was going better than I expected.

"What are you proposing, Richie? That we break our code down into smaller steps?" Jane asked.

"Exactly. The other piece to this more-detailed behavior code would be to have regular behavior meetings. These would be like Los Horcones, short meetings after supper. No more than fifteen minutes. People would have a chance to say what they observed during the day. It wouldn't be anything like a 'Big Brother-is watching-you' type of thing. Our positive verbal commitment should make it a little easier."

This was the biggest change I was proposing and worried that adding another meeting to everyone's overworked schedule would be too much to ask. There was more talk around the room as people discussed this new addition.

Mory stated, "So, it sounds like people are open to having meetings every night, at least on a trial basis, is that correct?" There were nods around the room.

I said, "Okay, why don't we try it out and see how it goes. And speaking of positive feedback, there is one other thing I'd like to mention. You all know we have an agreement to keep a positive verbal environment. When someone does a behavior we don't like, our commitment is to present the feedback in the least punishing way. What I found in the rare instance, if I reminded someone about cleaning up after themselves more than once, their reply would be, 'That's the second time you've reminded me, Richie, and it's starting to become punishing, so please stop.' which I always did."

I continued, "But, what I realized at Los Horcones is that if the community, as a whole, has an agreement to keep a clean environment, that applies to everyone. If one person were not abiding by that agreement, it was up to that person to change their behavior, as opposed to other community members tolerating that behavior."

Bill said, "Whoa, that sounds pretty heavy, man." The comment broke the tension in the air, and the members laughed at the cliché left over from the Sixties.

I Like It sheet

I responded, "Well, yes, it does sound 'heavy,' brother, but this is actually the kind of feedback a person would have gotten personally if he or she lived by themselves."

"What do you mean, Richie?" Mory asked.

"For instance, if I lived by myself and left the tinnery a mess, the next day when I went to work there, I would have to clean it up before starting. If I find the tinnery a mess, and don't know who left it that way, at the behavior meeting I could report that behavior. That way the person gets the feedback they would have naturally gotten if they lived by themselves. Of course, I would say it in the least punishing way possible."

There were more side conversations. I noticed the general excitement in the group as to how this might be an effective tool to help shape more communitarian behavior.

"I have one concern, Richie," Jane added. "If we do decide to have a more detailed behavior code and have nightly meetings, how can we balance out the occasional negative feedback and still keep it positive?"

Gordon said, "We could say that when a person does have a negative to report, maybe they could report three positives as well. Would that be okay with people?" There were murmurs of agreement around the room.

Gordon added, "I'm excited about this whole adventure, Richie. Can we get consensus to at least begin with breaking down our current behavior code?"

All heads around the room nodded and I said, "Okay, great. I propose we meet next week to go over our current behavior code and see which items can be broken down into behaviors that are more specific. All in favor?"

Everyone responded, "Aye."

After the meeting, individual members thanked me for my presentation. We all seemed eager to approach this new chapter in the life of Dandelion.

Behavior Code Madness

The following week, the community had its first Behavior Code revision meeting. I was once again facilitating, and I felt it was going to be a positive meeting.

"Okay, I want to first welcome everyone to the meeting. I get a sense that there is excitement as well as a little apprehension in the room." People smiled around the room.

"You got that right, Dicky. We're going where no man has gone before. Oops, I mean where no person has gone before," Julian reported.

I pointed to the large, blank newsprint paper on the easel and said, "So how about we start off with the first item in our original code?" I then read the actual item. "We clean up after ourselves and return articles to their proper place so they can be enjoyed by others. What can we add to that to make it more specific?"

Mory responded, "How about something like, hang up clothes you have taken off, don't leave them on the furniture or floor."

Thus, began the breakdown of Dandelion's original Behavior Code. Over the next two weeks, we met and hashed out what Dandelion's new expectations would be. Because of the more detailed emphasis, our original one-page code became twenty pages. The next step would be having actual behavior meetings.

We agreed that the new code and new behavior meetings would go into effect on the coming Monday. There was a sense of anticipation/excitement/curiosity as how effective the new code and nightly meetings might be. I wondered if there would be a long-term commitment to the nightly meetings, or if members would reach a saturation point, burn out and stop attending meetings. I knew there was only one way to find out—experiment.

Monday arrived, and it turned out to be an ordinary day. After supper, as people drifted into the kitchen to clean off their dishes, I called out that the behavior meeting would start in five minutes. I had ordered a new notebook and wrote, "Behavior Meeting, Monday, March 18, 1979."

Members gathered in the living room, and I said, "Okay, who would like to start?"

There was silence for about ten seconds. Then Gordon piped up and said, "Well, I like how clean the living room has been throughout the day. Moreover, I liked supper tonight. That about sums it up." He smiled. I wrote down Gordon's name and recorded what he said.

With the ice broken, it seemed easier for the next member. Mory added, "I like how people seem to be keeping better track of their petty cash slips lately. It makes it a lot easier for me to add up totals at the end of the week. Thank you." Timothy followed and said, "I like how clean the tinnery has been lately. The floor has been swept after tinnery shifts and gloves have been put away in appropriate places. It makes it much more reinforcing to return to in the morning." I continued to write.

Jane added, "I like how clean the kitchen has been all day long. I like that Maura helped me unpack all the groceries dropped off earlier. I like how people have been handing in their labor sheets on time. I like the joke Dicky shared with me earlier." She smiled at me.

"Which joke was that, Richie?" Julian enquired. I simply stated, "What did the farmer say when he opened his mailbox and saw a bunch of ducks inside? Bills, bills, bills." There were groans around the room.

As the meeting continued, there was a general sense of relaxation coming over the members. People were worried that this might have been some sort of "Big Brother" campaign or something more negative, but as it turned out, it was a way to emphasize more of our positive verbal environment. I breathed a big sigh of relief. My instincts had been correct.

After the meeting, a couple of members came up to me and thanked me again for taking the lead in this new chapter of Dandelion. The next couple of weeks went by with no hard adjustments to the new ritual. Members began to report a few negative observations but were becoming more comfortable doing that ("I found an apple core left on the couch this afternoon and someone forgot to cover the oatmeal bin.") I then shared that I had been keeping data on the number of items left out the week before the code went into effect. Every day at two o'clock, I recorded the number of items left out in the living room. I kept data on the following week after the code had been in effect and there was a significant difference. (I figured it out statistically with a two tailed T-test performed.) Members smiled when I posted my paper regarding my scientific findings.

Spring 1979

Spring was approaching, and all the members were in good moods. As usual, the warmer weather brought an increase in visitors. One of them was Jeffrey Alexander, who arrived in early April. Jeffrey was from Columbus, Ohio, an Air Force veteran and a professional carpenter with a terrific sense of humor. I discovered this when I was giving Jeffrey a tour of the community and pointed out the still-frozen garden. Jeffrey wryly commented, "That, I assume is where the iceberg lettuce is growing."

It took me a moment to interpret Jeffrey's comment, then smiled widely and said, "Yes, you are correct, sir." We both smiled.

Jeffrey was the first new visitor since the new behavior code and meetings went into effect. To our amazement, he took it all in stride and accepted it openly. He said he got the impression it had always been that way.

As part of Dandelion's long-term strategy, twice a year we met to discuss and set goals for the next six months. These meetings were usually held in the spring and fall. For this spring's six-month plan, along with the usual industrial goals (such as planning for production of hammocks and tinnery as well as building projects), all kinds of other new projects were proposed. It was an exciting time to be at Dandelion.

One project I proposed was the addition of a large, cement swimming pool in the backyard. My reasoning was that on hot summer days, the community always paid for gas to drive communitarians to the local pond which was five miles away at the town of Bellrock. If you added up the wear and tear on the van and lost time going to and from Bellrock, it didn't make much economic sense. In addition, by the time we got back, we were usually all hot and sweaty again. The new pool would also raise our standard of living, which would hopefully make Dandelion a more attractive place.

To the amazement of everyone, we somehow were able to budget three thousand dollars for a pool. To reinforce this idea, I cut out pool pictures from magazines and put them up all around the shop. I also proposed on my birthday that the community hold a "hammathon" in my honor.

The hammathon would be like Jerry Lewis's annual telethon to raise money for kids with Muscular Dystrophy and would take place for ten straight hours, beginning at eight a.m. and going through to supper at six p.m. I said I would be happy to facilitate the event and round up live entertainment.

My birthday arrived and all was set. I was at the entrance to Aduki wearing a bowtie and greeted members as they entered the shop. "Welcome to Dandelion's first annual hammathon. Thanks for coming; nice seeing you."

Members began weaving hammocks, waiting to see what the entertainment would actually be. I stepped into the middle of the room and said, "Ladies and Gentlemen, for your weaving pleasure, won't you please welcome our first guest, Guido Manicotti (a recent visitor named Ron), who will be singing a popular song from a Broadway play."

Timothy then put *Henry Mancini Greatest Hits* album on the stereo and the instrumental *Some Enchanted Evening* began to play. Using an empty rope spool as a microphone, Guido broke into singing the words to the song and began waltzing among the jigs, serenading the weavers. It was quite amazing, as he knows all the words. Guido finished his song to loud applause and cheers.

The imitated sound of a phone ringing occurred. Jeffrey picked up another empty rope spool and announced that it was our first pledge, "A hippie from San Francisco wants to weave hammocks by astral projection." Everyone groaned, but there were smiles all around.

Next up was my impression of Kirk Douglas in various careers. One as a short-order cook: "Your *friiiiies* are ready." Everyone groaned. Next I did John Wayne as a baker, "Okay, pilgrim, we're gonna round up the loaves and were gonna put them in a circle in the oven." Everyone groaned again.

Between acts, Timothy was running a request line at the stereo, taking in all musical requests. The rest of the morning had dramatic readings ranging from Shakespeare to *American Graffiti* to *Zen and the Art of Motorcycle Maintenance*. Hammocks continued to be completed and hung up for inspection.

At lunchtime a cold buffet appeared. A little while later, a car appeared at the back entrance of the shop and Jane disappeared to deal with the local Jehovah's Witnesses. They gave her the latest issue of *Awake*, which reviled disco music as the work of the Devil, and Jane shared that with the crowd. Jeffrey left.

A few minutes later, he returned and he had been transformed by a walking stick, a turquoise sports jacket and white shoes (all gathered from Community Clothes) into that famous Southern evangelist, the Reverend Merrill Lynch.

He began his sermon. "Well, friends, I come

Jeffrey on his way to do some building maintenance

here today to talk to you about the evils of Disco music. Today every kind of place imaginable is being turned into an immoral discotheque, a den of inequity, and many have rushed to cash in on the profits. Now let me tell you what the prophets say about the profits. Well, they say give me the profits, brothers and sisters!"

This impromptu sermon by Jeffrey went on for ten minutes. Shouts of "Yeah, brother!" and "Hallelujah!" and "Tell it like it is!" echoed around the room.

Just then, the pool contractor showed up, and hearing the shouts inside, thought he was visiting an evangelical tent revival session. Jane went out to deal with him as well.

The rest of the afternoon had various other acts, which made the hours go by quickly, and by six p.m., we had woven fifty-five hammocks—the most ever woven in one day.

Front Porch Gatherings

With the warmer weather now in full swing, the place to hang out was the front porch. In the evenings, after supper, dishwashing and milking, it was always the place to be. Singing accompanied with guitars was often the main event. Visitors always added new instruments and voices.

With the advent of the new behavior code (and Dandelion's amazing ability to make fun of ourselves), there began to develop a humorous underground "revolt" to the behavior code.

One evening on the porch as the sun was setting, there was an impromptu song written and played on guitar by Jeffrey, who had now become a provisional member. Inspired by the influence of some punk rock band, he called it "Behavior Code Violator." Some of the verses were, "I'm gonna leave my shoes and dishes all over the place. Last night I kicked a plant right in the face. I don't plan on pleasant activities with nobody soon. Gonna just lock myself up alone in my room. Cause I'm a behavior code violator, not much of a circulator, just a no-good violator. Don't want no arbitrator, or even a facilitator, gotta be a violator!"

> *"When a free man dies, he loses the joy of living.*
> *When a slave dies, he loses the pain."*
> —Kirk Douglas in the movie *Spartacus*

The gardeners and woodcutters often "temporarily" borrowed the gloves used in the tinnery. For various reasons, however, the gloves often failed to make it back. As tinnery manager, I attempted to modify this behavior by attaching two-foot lengths of black chain to the gloves (using duct tape) and then nailing the other end of the chains to the tinnery table.

This arrangement had an unintended visual affect, however—whenever a worker sat down to do tinnery and slipped his or her hands into the gloves, it looked as if the worker was chained to the table. The chains were quite noticeable, as they looped over laps and sometimes hung down legs.

One day, Jane was giving a tour to a group of visitors from the local village. They entered the workshop and went first to the tinnery room.

As Jane began her story about "freedom of work choices" and "positively reinforcing workers," the visitors were staring at Julian and Timothy apparently chained to their workstations, cutting cans. At the same time, the song *I Robot* (by the Alan Parsons Project) was softly playing over the speakers, with the lyrics "Freedom, freedom, we will not obey. Freedom, freedom, take the chains away." (This song was the informal anthem of the tinnery, and many members often played the album while working there.)

The visitors must have thought to themselves, "What kind of place was this really, some kind of cult with brainwashing going on? Were the rumors going around town actually true?"

Jane made some rambling comment about "gloves walking off" and this was the tinnery manager's attempts to remedy the situation. She then diplomatically steered the group into the larger hammock workspace area.

Here the visitors saw large masses of tangled rope hanging out of large boxes, half-painted walls (the shop budget had run out of money to finish the walls), and a window with a large crack in it.

Gordon was weaving a hammock chair and Mory was weaving a hammock on a different jig. Both were wearing headphones and their backs were to the visitors. The eerie affect this had was that except for the sound of the hammock shuttles going back and forth to make the hammock or chair, there was silence in the workshop area.

As Gordon and Mory had their backs to the visitors, they were both unaware that they now had an audience. Gordon would occasionally sing out loud to the song he was listening to, and Mory did as well. The unintended effect was that the visitors would hear nothing as Jane continued her talk about equality and the labor system, and then, all of a sudden, Gordon would burst into singing the chorus to *Macho Man* with words like "Hey! Hey! Macho, Macho Man. I want to be a Macho Man." He started bouncing up and down at his jig with his long hair swinging wildly in the air. Then, over at the other side of the room, Mory started singing out loud the song she was listening to, which was Donna Summer's recent disco hit, *Bad Girls*, with the lyrics "Bad Girls, huh huh. Talking about Baddddddd Girls... huh huh. I got what you need. You got what I want." The crisscrossing of lyrics went echoing around the room like two people who had Tourette's Syndrome.

Against this bizarre-although-common occurrence in the workshop, Jane was now talking to the visitors about breaking down sex-role stereotyping, equality, and trying to create a positive culture in which to raise children.

As the tour slowly headed for the large swinging doors at the back, Mory and Gordon suddenly realized what was going on. They both instantly clammed up with sheepish looks on their faces, briefly smiled at all the visitors and tried to look as normal as possible.

Jane led the visitors out the back doors and there the visitors saw me crossing the bridge wearing my dress plaid pants, steel-toed boots, and a very old white,

Cath with visitor weaving hammock

faded, t-shirt with holes and red stains in it. I was carrying a chain saw in one hand and a hard hat in the other hand. Goggles were on the top of my head. My right index finger was bleeding and I caught the visitors looking to make sure all my fingers were there.

"Is everything okay, Dicky?" Jane asked hesitantly.

"Yeah, sure, I accidentally dropped a log on my hand."

As I walked off, the visitors tried to make sense of my outfit, and Jane talked about clothing options and how one was free to wear anything they wanted at Dandelion. She also added that I had a weird sense of humor.

Over on the other side of the building was Klaus (a current German visitor), banging a hammock stretcher hard against the ground while singing the German drinking song, *Ein Prosit*. Jane noticed that there was a huge pile of broken stretchers lying on the ground. She explained to the visitors that this was the way the wooden stretcher part of the hammock was tested to ensure that the wood was strong enough. She also correctly realized that Klaus was applying too much pressure for the testing.

"Um, Klaus, excuse me?" Since he was singing *loud* and so into his current mission of destroying as many stretchers as possible, he didn't hear her, so she tried again, *"Klaus!"* That caught his attention and he stopped to look around. With his German accent he said, "Ah, Jane, gude morning."

Jane then diplomatically suggested he see the hammock manager before he continued testing the rest of the stretchers. "Ah, yes, okay."

As Jane led the visitors to their cars, they saw a small, cracked rowing boat in the tiny creek beside the bridge, which was half-filled with water. A few of the visitors stared at it, but Jane decided to ignore it and make no comment about it.

As Jane was bidding them farewell, they could now hear Gordon's voice coming from the hammock shop as he sung the lyrics to *I Am Woman* ("I am woman hear me roar, with numbers too big to ignore.") In addition, Mory was now singing *Love to Love You, Baby*, with Mory singing along with the orgasmic sounds of Donna Summer.

The visitors all had smiles plastered to their faces as they said good-bye and Jane worried what they might be thinking. "Do you run an insane asylum here as well?" and "Do you allow members access to sharp objects, especially chain saws?"

Jane wished them well and went up to the farmhouse.

Tee Shirt Inequality

Every Summer one issue always came up—that men were able to work bare-chested in the garden (next to the public road) while women still had to either wear their shirts or drop down out of sight whenever a car passed by.

The men realized that since this was another privilege they were automatically given, they agreed that whenever they were working in the garden with a woman, before taking off their own shirt, they would first ask the woman if that was okay. Not once in six years did I find a woman who objected, although they did appreciate the solidarity.

There was a woman visitor, however, who must have somehow gotten the rules mixed up. One day she and I were working in the garden together and she asked me if I minded if she took off her shirt. "Mind? No, I don't mind," I said with a straight face. However, inside I was smiling. (No matter how hard I tried, there were certain things even living in an egalitarian society could not change.)

Visit of Gerry

Gerry, a kindergarten teacher from Connecticut, had been corresponding with the community for a couple of months. She was deeply interested in visiting Dandelion after the school year ended. She finally made it to Dandelion at the end of June for a two-week visit.

Gerry was multi-talented and besides being a teacher, she was also a skilled carpenter, a musician (she played guitar and dulcimer in a small Celtic band), and an extraordinary cook. She had a great sense of humor and fitted into the wacky world of Dandelion immediately. (She scored extra points with me, as she also liked basketball.)

Gerry's carpentry skills were quickly put to use. In preparation for our upcoming communities' conference (to be held in August that year), she and Jeffrey were assigned to build a new four-seater outhouse across the road in the wooded area. They accomplished this in three days and the community was quite impressed.

I quickly became infatuated with Gerry. She was the first woman I had ever met who actually looked like me, and I was very attracted to her. She had long brown hair, brown eyes, and was about five feet tall. (I often wondered if her similarity in looks was her main attraction.)

After a week of some serious flirting, we ended up in my room one night. Before that night, I had found a queen-sized piece of foam-rubber padding in the barn, and placed it over my bed and cot. This seemed to work out fine for sleeping, but that arrangement took up all the extra space in my room. I would have to come up with a better plan.

Gerry was an erotic lover and we spent every night together after that. I had not been with a woman since Maple the previous fall, and I began hoping that Gerry might decide to join Dandelion.

On one of our walks together, we had a serious discussion about it. "I would really like you to consider becoming a member, Gerry. You know you already fit in well with the other members. You share so many of the values we have and have the skills we really need. Plus, you know how I feel about you and it would be a big like for me personally."

Gerry said, "Oh, Richie, you are something else, so open to life. I am really enjoying spending time with you and getting to see what Dandelion is all about. However, I would need much more time to think about making such a serious commitment to Dandelion. I have my responsibilities back in Connecticut."

I nodded.

"I understand your situation, Gerry. I just hope you consider us as a serious alternative."

"I do take it seriously, Richie. In the meantime, let's enjoy our remaining time together as much as we can." She smiled enchantingly.

"Take as much time as you need, Gerry. You can go back to Connecticut and come back later in the summer for our conference. You can even help run the childcare program if you like. In the meantime, let's go play some basketball."

During the last few days of Gerry's visit, we spent as much time together as possible. We made love every night, took showers together, worked together and played together.

At night, she would sit on the porch, playing her guitar and singing. She built some sorely needed shelves for the basement and cooked some mouth-watering meals. By the end of her visit, everyone was asking her to join Dandelion.

At the same time my love affair with Gerry was unfolding, Jeffrey and Jane had started up their own relationship. This was something I first noticed one day when I stopped to talk with Jeffrey as he was fixing the rototiller by the barn.

He spontaneously said to me, "Man, is this what they call 'peace of mind,' Dicky? I don't think I have ever felt so centered or been so happy in my entire life. Everything I do here seems to have some kind of purpose."

I smiled and said, "You got it, Van Door (one of Jeffrey's new nicknames). Dandelion does tend to bring out the best in people, eh?"

Jeffrey smiled, winked and said, "It looks like Gerry is bringing out the best in you as well, eh, Dicky?"

I smiled and said, "She does indeed. I am so hoping she will decide to join us."

"Has she talked about doing that?" Jeffrey asked hopefully.

"Well, it has come up in our conversations. She has so much going for her in Connecticut, though. She says she definitely would like to come back for the conference in August. We'll see what happens, but I'm hopeful."

Meanwhile, the pool was gradually starting to take shape. First, the bulldozer showed up and dug out a large hole behind the farmhouse, about fifty feet to the right of Tamari. Then the cement truck showed up and poured the foundation. The pool workers showed up the next day and began building the pool, which took about two weeks to complete. When it was finished, a large water truck arrived and filled the pool. What started out as slimy/green water soon became clear, as the chlorine pump kicked in.

A chain-link fence was bartered with some local contractors (for five large hammocks), and a fence soon surrounded the entire pool. The pool was officially opened in early August.

The pool brought smiles all around the community and was one of those things that really added to the quality of life at Dandelion. It never ceased to amaze the constant visitors, usually with surprised delight. What kind of hippie commune was this?

There were a few visitors though, who did not quite appreciate the pool. Some visitors would show up and on their tour of the grounds, see Gordon out in front of the farmhouse pushing the community gas-powered lawnmower (making the usual obnoxious noise). Then, when they went to the back of the house and saw the large, cement pool (with diving board) they would exclaim sarcastically, "Looks like your typical suburban household, with all the trimmings."

When it was explained about the trip to Bellrock, how much gas that wasted, and how much the pool was enjoyed on the hot days, the visitor usually accepted the advantages, especially if it was a hot summer day.

The one drawback was that since most of us skinny-dipped in the pool there was the occasional Canadian Air Force helicopter that seemed to pass directly overhead to get a glimpse of the naked hippies. In addition, there was also a day when Jane was giving a tour to some local nuns, and she deftly maneuvered the tour around the pool when she realized there were communitarians swimming in it.

That summer Jonathon Stokes became a member. Jonathon brought an unbelievable amount of energy to the community, that even his daily five-mile jog was hard to dampen. He was also a trained artist and started up a cartoon strip in our newsletter starring "Dandi" the likeable communitarian.

I went off to Dearborn, Michigan to attend the Association of Behavior Analysis annual meeting with the hope of meeting some potential recruits. Jane, along with Donald, Deirdre, and four thousand others, attended a demonstration against the building of a new nuclear power plant in Darlington, Ontario. With her strong passion and commitment to this cause, Jane was arrested (for trespassing on government property), and spent two days in jail.

Dandelion's gardens had their best produce in years and our apple and plum trees produced abundantly.

New Moneymaking Schemes

Gordon and I often brainstormed on new ways to help the community make money. When I became tinnery manager, I often thought about new ways we could use the tin cans. We had our standard items like candleholders, lampshades, planters, and pencil holders, but I was looking for something bold, something daring.

Then one day it hit me. I was sitting on the toilet at the time and said, "Eureka! What about personalized toilet seats made out of recycled tin cans?" I finished up in the bathroom and then went out to find Gordon.

"Gordon, I've got it." I said and then described my idea in detail, "First we get a bunch of cans, flatten them and then weld them into the shape of toilet seat covers, to fit perfectly over the seat you sit on. Then we take them to craft-shows. Once at the show, we would tell people that we could customize the tinnery seats to have their own saying cut into them. Here are some I came up with already: Best seat in the house or Welcome to the Jones Throne, or simply, Have a nice Day." (This last one, obviously inspired by the 70s.)

I continued, "Once the saying is cut into the seat, we would then have a true piece of art and the fun would really start when you used it. After sitting on the seat for a few minutes, your weight would make the chosen expression imprint on your butt. Then, when you stood up, you could look in the mirror and see whatever saying was on the seat, transposed for the entire world to see. You could even collect a whole series of them, take turns and trade them with your friends, etc. What do you think?" I was very proud of myself and couldn't wait to tell my parents.

Obviously inspired by my wild imagination, Gordon said, "Wow! That sounds cool, Richie. We could call it 'Human Print Media'." And here's an idea I've been working on." He began explaining his newest idea.

"You know how people are always talking about great energy fields supposedly located under pyramids? Well how about we build a small pyramid over the pool? It could be a simple structure, built out of two-by-four studs. We then advertise in the National Enquirer newspaper and tell people we have this great pyramid in our backyard. For a $2 donation, they can ask us any question and we will go under the pyramid and come up with an answer for them."

Gordon continued with the details. "We could have a member lie on an air mattress located directly under the center of the pyramid. Another member would be sitting along the edge of the pool, open the letters and read them out loud to the member on the mattress. The member on the side of the pool would then write down the answers to the question and send it off. Both members would earn labor credits for their time."

"That sounds fantastic, Gordon. I think it could really work." I grabbed Gordon by his shoulders and began shaking him back and forth saying, "Let's bring both ideas up at the next community meeting."

We did bring both ideas up, to our astonishment, we did not get the response we were hoping for.

"Why would anyone in their right mind want to imprint a message on their butt?" Jane asked. Then Mory said, "For the pool idea, wouldn't we really be exploiting people, who actually believed we had some magical power?"

Feeling rejected and disappointed, Gordon and I headed toward the front porch to debrief after the meeting.

"What's wrong with those other members, Gordon?" I asked with obvious disappointment. "Can't they see what great moneymaking schemes those are?" We reached the front porch and sat on the couch, watching the sun go down. We were silent for a few minutes, mesmerized by the beautiful sunset we were witnessing. Then I began speculating out loud, "What about lava lamp pens?"

Rocky Horror Picture Show Trip

The *Rocky Horror Picture Show* had gained cult status by the time the movie was showing in downtown Kingston. Donald had first reported about it on his return from Aloe Community last Fall. "Unbelievable zaniness, the crowd in the theatre actually talks back to the screen and throws popcorn at it. People come dressed up in all kinds of silly costumes. They usually show it at midnight."

I began imagining all kinds of things that we might do at such a show. I organized a movie trip for a weekday matinée, so it would coincide with Dandelion's weekly trip to Kingston and we would not spend extra money on gas.

I encouraged everyone going to dress up in something special. I got out the old wooly bear coat and found a gorilla mask. I also brought along a baseball bat. Jonathon put on a sports coat and bowtie. Julian wore shorts and Mory wore a dress.

On the trip down to Kingston, we picked up an eighteen-year-old male hitchhiker. He came in the side door of the van and sat on the bump over the back wheel. I was sitting across from him wearing the coat and gorilla mask. Julian just sat in the back of the van staring out the window.

The hitchhiker expressed his appreciation for the lift and started some casual conversation. He was a little uneasy with me just sitting there with the baseball bat on my lap. Jonathon was closest to the hitchhiker and politely answered his questions.

I then began to moan in a high-pitched voice, "Mmmm." First, in a low voice that gradually got higher and more agitated, "MMMMMMMMMMMMM."

Jonathon continued his conversation with the hitchhiker and just ignored me. After my moans became so loud you could not hear the conversation anymore, Jonathon kicked out his leg in my direction and said, "Cut that out!" I stopped moaning for twenty seconds, and then began moaning again, this time tapping the bat in my hand yelling, "MMMMMMMMMMMMMMMM!" Jonathon perked up and said, "Shut Up!" Then he turned to the hitchhiker and said, "Don't mind him. He doesn't know his manners." Julian continued to stare out the window with a blank look on his face.

"So, where are you all going?" The hitchhiker asked with a slight quiver in his voice. "We're going to see the *Rocky Horror Picture Show*," Jonathon replied.

The hitchhiker smiled and with relief in his voice said, "Ohhhhhh, now I get it." Before he could say much more, we reached the place where he needed to get off. "Thanks for the lift and enjoy the show."

We reached Kingston and were all excited as we walked down the street in our full costumes with me carrying the baseball bat over my shoulder. I was sweating like a pig, but I knew the theatre would be air-conditioned.

We got to the theatre, took our seats, and then realized that there was only one other couple in the whole place. The movie began and we shouted out at the appropriate places of dialogue, but with only the other couple in the theatre, it just wasn't the kind of event I had imagined it would be. I was very disappointed, but at least we had tried to honor the tradition.

Open Door Policy

With so many people sharing the one bathroom in the house, the norm was always to leave the door open, including the personal time members needed for peeing or having a bowel movement. Visitors usually closed the door for privacy and we always respected that.

This norm came as quite a shock to me when I first visited. "Now wait a minute, I'm all for the equal sharing of resources, but isn't this taking the sharing bit a little too far?"

Part of the norm evolved out of trying to make members feel more comfortable about natural body functions, which sounded fine in theory, but in practice was another story. The other reason was that it was just plain practical, as members used the bathroom constantly.

Communitarians usually tried to respect the semi-privacy of using the toilet, but sometimes, this general norm was ignored due to busy schedules or unforeseen circumstances. This morning was one of them.

I entered the bathroom to take my morning constitutional, feeling lucky that it was unoccupied. I was sitting there a couple of minutes, just getting things started, when Jonathan showed up at the bathroom door. "Sorry to intrude on your personal space, Dicky, but I'm on a rush to meet with our sales rep for hammocks. Is it okay with you if I just take a quick shower?"

"Yeah, sure, do what you gotta do, man."

Jonathan stepped into the bathroom and immediately began stripping off all his clothing right in front of me (which was literally three feet from where I was sitting), thus giving me the unintentional privilege of a full view of Jonathan's naked backside. "I never realized how hairy your ass is, Jonathan, thanks for sharing that," I commented sarcastically.

To which Jonathan (who was going bald at an early age), replied, "Yeah, I wish what was growing so wild on my ass could have moved to my head." We both chuckled. Jonathan then hopped in the shower and began singing *Old Man River*. I returned to my original mission.

One minute later, Jeffrey came into the bathroom, went straight to the sink and began brushing his teeth. Recognizing Jonathan's singing he said, "Jonathan, Julian is going into Kingston to pick up supplies for the week. Do you think we should order more of that medicinal cow wash for Chrissie's udders?"

Richie and Jonathan

Jonathan (cow manager at the time) replied, "That probably wouldn't hurt, just to be safe."

Julian, who was cooking breakfast in the kitchen right outside the bathroom heard the conversation and came to the doorway to give his take on things, "I think there is an extra case of that stuff in the storage barn actually."

To which Jeffrey replied, "Oh, Julian, I think we used that up last week."

Then Jonathan, with his head under the shower, piped up and said, "Are you sure about that? I think Julian is right. I thought I saw a case there two days ago."

I stared straight ahead, noticing that my bowels had now frozen up and that I was in the middle of another God damn meeting. I was flabbergasted that all three of them continued to carry on about what or what not to order as if it were some kind of gigantic crisis. Hello? Didn't they notice there was a communitarian sitting on the bowl, trying to relieve himself?

Mory entered the kitchen and overhearing the conversation, now came to the bathroom doorway (standing next to Julian) and put in her two cents as well, "Just so you know—our cash flow is very tight this week. If we could postpone any purchases until next week it would be greatly appreciated."

I stared straight ahead in total bafflement, feeling like a piece of discarded furniture.

Jeffrey finished brushing his teeth and began brushing his hair. Jonathan popped out of the shower and began drying himself giving me an encore presentation of his hairy ass.

While drying off, he stopped a moment to look at himself in the mirror and said, "I think …"

Finally, having had enough of this meeting, I cut him off saying, "Excuse me? Could we take this outside or maybe up at a meeting? Maybe we could reach consensus by then?" All heads turned towards me as if noticing me for the first time.

"Oh, so sorry, Dicky," Mory said, smiling.

With my bowels now permanently paralyzed, I resigned myself to coming back later when there wasn't a meeting going on. I looked around for some toilet paper and to my dismay, found there was none. I sighed loudly and said, "Geez, Jeffrey, would you mind throwing me a roll of TP please?" He reached up on the shelf and tossed a roll, accidentally hitting Jonathan in the head. The roll bounced off Jonathan then rolled out the bathroom door under Julian's legs, unfolding ten feet as it rolled across the kitchen floor.

Gordon happened to walk in then, picked it up and walked over to the bathroom door, handing the roll to my outstretched hand, appearing between Julian's and Mory's legs. "Party in the bathroom!" Gordon yelled out excitedly. Jane, who was in the living room, strolled over to the bathroom to see what was going on.

After wiping myself and standing up, all the communitarians clapped and praised me. I stared down at the minor deposit I had left lying at the bottom of the bowl, shook my head in disappointment, and flushed the toilet.

"Don't get up on our account, Dicky," Jonathan said, smiling, as he took a friendly snap at my ass with his towel.

"Ha-Ha," I replied sarcastically and then elbowed my way out between Julian and Mory, who were now in a heated discussion about what else they could afford this week. What a way to start your day.

In August, we were the host for the Federation Assembly. Members came from all the other communities to share ideas and cooperate on various endeavors. It was our first time hosting it and went all out to make sure it was a very reinforcing event.

Kat Kincaid was one of the representatives from Twin Oaks Community, and she had never been to Dandelion before. Kat was one of the founding members of Twin Oaks and, like me, she was a dedicated behaviorist. She also had written the book, *A Walden Two Experiment*, which chronicled the first five years of Twin Oaks. That book had also inspired me to try out community. When she arrived, I very much enjoyed talking with her and took pride in showing her around.

I also met Laird and Annie from Sandhill Farm, and Malon from East Wind Community. Fernando from Los Horcones was also there. The highlight of the conference was the party at the end of the three-day assembly.

One of the things proposed by Fernando was that Los Horcones would be happy to host a five-day seminar on behavior principles applied to Walden Two Communities. The seminar would take place at Los Horcones in February. There was much excitement about this possibility, but it was hard to determine if it was the topic or the small fact that the seminar would be taking place in Mexico in February.

The Federation had also been in contact with the kibbutzim federation in Israel, and the kibbutzim was proposing to sponsor six members from Federation Communities to a six-month scholarship in any kibbutzim in Israel. This would include airfare as well.

The annual Dandelion Community Conference followed the Assembly. To my great disappointment and regret, Gerry did not make it back to Dandelion for the conference. It was a last-minute thing and she explained that she just did not have the funds to make the trip.

Transitions

The end of the summer turned out to be a time for more change in the community. Jeffrey left for Aloe Community after he returned to alcohol as a way to deal with his problems (which the community tried helping him with) but was not successful.

The inside of Tamari was almost completed and there were now five new bedrooms located in the basement. These were open to members and I claimed one for myself in the far back corner. That way, with the open space in the middle of the basement for the wood-burning stove, I at least had a little privacy, which I was valuing more and more.

It was the first time in almost two years that I would have a queen-size bed (in fact it would be the first time in my entire life I had one), and I was hoping to make up for some lost time.

I was still carrying my torch for Gerry (we had been corresponding over the summer), and still hoped she would join the community. When it became clear that she would not be able to visit us in the fall (due to job commitments and money), I made the bold decision to go visit her. I would spend all my saved up allowance to purchase bus fare to Connecticut. After visiting her, I would then take the train to visit my parents. I contacted Gerry and scheduled a visit for a couple of days in September.

I arrived at the bus station in Connecticut at six p.m. It had been a long journey (having left Kingston at seven A.M.), and even though I felt tired, I was excited to see her again.

When I stepped off the bus, Gerry was not there, and I ended up waiting for over an hour before she showed up. Her cheeks were very swollen, and she looked like a chipmunk.

She apologized profusely saying, "I am so sorry, Richie. I had two of my wisdom teeth pulled yesterday and the pain meds have had me sleeping on and off all day." Her words came out somewhat slurred, as she was still under the effects of the pain medication. "That's okay, Gerry. It's great seeing you again." We hugged each other affectionately.

"My car is this way."

As we walked toward the car, I debriefed about the trip down and brought Gerry up to speed with how Dandelion was doing. I emphasized how much people missed her and were still hoping she would return as a member. I noticed that she smiled at that remark but did not make a comment.

I switched the subject and turned to the more practical side of Dandelion. "The outhouse you and Jeffrey built was put to good use at the conference."

She smiled at that and said, "How is Jeffrey doing anyway?"

I told her how he had returned to drinking and had ended up going down to Aloe Community for the winter. "We're not sure if he will make it back to Dandelion. We're still processing that whole situation."

"That's too bad. I'm sorry to hear that. He seemed like he was doing so well there."

"He was, for a while. Dandelion does tend to be a very supportive place, although we really are not set up to be a therapeutic community."

We reached Gerry's house, which was a beautiful ginger-bread-like house, out in the woods, which she rented from a friend of hers. Made all out of wood, with flowerpots in front of all the windows, I felt like I was entering a house in a fairy tale.

Once inside, Gerry gave me a tour. There was a small living room, small kitchen and a small bathroom. Everything on the inside was made of wood as well, the walls, floors and ceiling. She explained that the previous owner was a carpenter and had designed the house and personally made all the extras.

Her bedroom in the back of the house looked out over a small garden surrounded by trees. There was a large five-foot-square skylight in the ceiling, directly over her bed. I looked up and could see some stars.

For me, Gerry cooked up some rice and beans and for herself, just sipped some soup through a straw. We continued to catch up over dinner.

To my surprise, she started talking about a new friend of hers named Peter and how he helped her around the house. I was a little confused by this turn of events and at first, thought she was talking about just being "friends" with this guy. As the conversation wore on though, I began to get the sense that Gerry was trying to tell me something, that maybe Peter was more than a friend. I felt even more confused.

By nine o'clock, we were both ready for bed. I was hoping to take up where we had left off and had assumed we would be sleeping in her bed together. I made a bold move, grabbed her by the waist and said, "Gerry, you know I have been thinking of you the whole summer. I'd like to pick up where we left off."

I leaned in to kiss her, but she turned her head and said, "Oh, Richie, that's so nice to hear. I just need some time to process what I have been going through lately. In addition, my teeth are hurting. Can we talk more about this in the morning?" She smiled and hugged me.

Being the gentleman, I said, "Sure, whatever makes you comfortable."

"I think it would be better for me if you stayed on the couch this evening, okay?"

I put on my best face and said, "Sure, that's fine, Gerry. I understand." (Inside I felt like my heart was breaking.)

Gerry then put out a sheet and some blankets on her couch, which was long enough to fit me. As I was nodding off to sleep, I began rehashing the trip so far. First, I thought, out of all the weekends to get her wisdom teeth removed, why had she picked this one? Also, if she was now involved or getting involved with this guy Peter, why didn't she tell me that before I spent my entire year's allowance to come visit her? I would have to wait until tomorrow to find out more.

We both slept in the next morning with me finally getting up around nine a.m. Gerry had gotten up earlier, taken a shower and then started some scrambled eggs for both of us.

"Breakfast is ready, Richie. I hope you like it." Her words still came out slightly mumbled, but at least the swelling had gone down.

"So, what is on the agenda for us today, Gerry?" I asked cautiously over breakfast, not knowing what to expect.

"Well, I thought we could take a short walk around here and just see how my energy is doing. We could pick up some food for lunch and supper. This evening I was hoping we could go see that movie "Godspell," if that's okay with you."

"That all sounds great, Gerry. I could use some walking and get the cramps out of my legs." I smiled at her and she smiled back.

"How did you sleep last night?"

"Fine, no problem. I was exhausted from the trip. But, today, I feel pretty good." We cleaned up the dishes and I took a shower. Then we set out for a walk.

Gerry answered more of my questions about how work was going for her, but she seemed somewhat preoccupied. I thought it had something to do with her teeth, as well as with Peter.

What really brought it all home, was on our walk, I put my arm around her shoulder and she immediately turned her shoulder, in effect pushing it off.

"Whoa, what was that all about, Gerry?"

"I don't know, Richie. I just need time to process what I am going through." She stopped walking and said, "Richie, I had a beautiful time at Dandelion and I was so grateful to meet you and spend time with you and get to know you. However, when I got back to my life here, I realized that I was living in some kind of dream world at Dandelion. I think my real life is down here. I'm so sorry."

I let out a long sigh and just nodded my head. I felt tremendous sorrow, but managed to keep a straight face and said, "It's okay, Gerry. I understand." Inside though, I was in turmoil. As I was already committed for the rest of the day, I would just have to make the best of it. "You know, Gerry, I was thinking of taking the train tomorrow to visit my folks. Do you think you could drop me off at the station tomorrow, by 9:30?"

She did not attempt to disagree with my plans and simply said, "Sure, that would be fine."

The rest of the day was a jumble of confused feelings for me. I participated as best I could, but inside, I couldn't wait to leave. I slept on the couch again and was not even interested in getting intimate with Gerry.

She drove me to the train station the next morning, dropped me off, and I never saw or heard from her again.

When I returned to Dandelion, all the members were excited to hear the latest news regarding Gerry. I responded only by saying, "It didn't work out." The members felt so sorry for me. They all assured me that my turn would come again. I nodded slightly and went to my room.

After my disastrous trip to see Gerry, I felt different when I returned to Dandelion. I was not only dealing with my heartbreak over Gerry but with other things as well. With Donald and Jeffrey gone, (along with Maple, Dondi and Max), there were now large gaps in life at Dandelion.

I just immersed myself in my day-to-day routine. Julian and I would end up having intense conversations while doing tinnery. (Although, no matter what subject we started on, we always seemed to end up talking about women.)

We would be talking about behaviorism, Marxism, feminism, space colonies, solar technology, nuclear disarmament, but always seemed to come back to the subject of being a single/celibate male in community. Sometimes we would even come up with elaborate fantasies where ten women would be giving us a massage.

To help deal with my mental pain, I ended up doing a lot of physical work. I cut a lot of wood that fall (keeping my clothes on), doing building maintenance, and worked on finishing Tamari. The days just seemed endless to me, but eventually, even though I got back some of my normal emotional balance, I noticed a change in my perceptions of Dandelion.

I started asking myself, "Why are such good people always leaving? Moreover, why are we having such a hard time attracting and keeping members, let alone behaviorist members? Where are all the so-called pioneer behaviorists I thought I would meet here? On top of that, why had Gerry decided not to join Dandelion and stay with me? Had she lost her attraction to me or to Dandelion?"

The fall was not all negative for me as the community had attracted a couple of interesting visitors. There were Craig and Casey, a fun couple originally from Buffalo, New York, doing the "grand tour," trying to find a community that would fit their dreams and lifestyle. Craig was committed to meditation and Eastern philosophy. Casey was a hardworking, assertive woman with long blond hair. I liked her sense of humor.

Another visitor, Maura (from Toronto) had decided to apply for membership. She was multi-talented and was a professional cello player. (She and Julian later developed a very nice relationship.)

The most exciting news though, was that Jane (with help from Gordon), had become pregnant and hearing that lifted my spirits immensely. It also brought along an optimistic sense that the community had matured and developed to a point where it now felt it was stable enough to have a child.

The other big news was that the seminar at Los Horcones was coming up, which also boosted my spirit as well.

The winter Solstice came and passed, with members visiting various relatives and friends, and then came New Year's Eve, 1979. Since it was the last day of the 70s, I found a disco version of *Auld Lang Syne* on a cassette. As midnight approached, a bunch of us were in the kitchen, and I played that version of *Auld Lang Syne*. My last thought, as the clock struck midnight was, "What better way to end the decade."

Maura and Julian thumb wrestling

January 1980

I began the new year determined to put what happened with Gerry behind me. It was a new decade and there was a lot going on at Dandelion. I had the joy and awe of watching Jane's body change to accommodate the baby growing inside her.

That month, we also had our second annual "Process." (I had missed the one last year when I was visiting Los Horcones.) The Process was a three-day event where we took a break from our usual work routines to focus on interpersonal issues. It was a time to step back, to look at how the members affected each other, and to learn some new coping and interpersonal skills. With that accomplished, we then focused on long-term goals and the steps needed to achieve them.

Our outside facilitator, Sydney, who had led the same process last year, returned to facilitate this three-day event as well. She used several methods to help people get "clear," with various meditations, sociograms and counseling.

Social relationships became clearer as the group stood in a circle and responded to questions like, "Who is the most responsible?" Members responded by placing their hands on who they perceived was the most responsible.

That question addressed the question of "power" in community. (Who had the most, who had the least, etc.) As usual, each person had different associations with the concept of power. Talking about this, the community was able to help differentiate personal power from power structures (i.e., how things got done.)

The community examined whether its egalitarian system had managerships, which gave some people more power than others did. That was decidedly not so. Even though the finance managership may have been more critical to the survival of the community (vs. the cow managership), both managerships contributed to the success of the community. It was determined to be more about having the experience and confidence in using personal power, or just being more assertive.

Overall, it was a very worthwhile experience and many misconceptions were put to rest. After those three days, there was a renewed sense of community throughout Dandelion.

The one thing that surprised me, while in the circle, was my response to the question about who we were most attracted to sexually in the community. I placed my hand on Casey. She had smiled at me when I did that, even though her hands were on Craig and another person. She was in her primary relationship with Craig, however, and I was not going to get involved in another three-way relationship.

January also brought some exciting visitors. Dakota Morningstar visited from Boston, and she made an instant hit with me because her sense of humor and craziness matched mine. She was also positive, a leader, a hard worker, and well-liked by all members. The issues she had a passion for were feminism, anti-nuclear power, cooking, and behavior psychology. I felt very comfortable with her, and we would often have long conversations while cutting cans.

The other benefit Dakota brought with her was that her long-time friend, Brian Otto, stopped by for a visit as well. Within one hour, he was helping with building maintenance projects and fixing wiring in Tamari. A recent college graduate, Brian had been involved with social change for years and was now interested in finding a community that fit his values. I welcomed his crazy sense of humor and together we would often do comedy routines. Thus began our life-long friendship.

The Los Horcones Seminar was coming up and the details for that trip were worked out. Not all members could obviously go, so at a meeting, we decided who would best benefit from attending that conference.

By consensus, the community agreed that Jane, Gordon and I would be the lucky ones to go, along with Dakota (who had officially become a long-term visitor) and had voluntarily agreed to donate her van for the trip if she were allowed to go. The community readily agreed.

The only hesitancy I had attending the seminar was that in the last phone call from my parents, my dad had matter-of-factly stated that he had colon cancer. "Well, Rich, I found some blood in my stool, and the doctors checked it out and they found some malignancy in my large intestine. Looks like I'll be going in for some surgery in February."

When I heard the date, I realized it was the same time I'd be in Mexico. My heart sank. "Geez, Dad, that is the same week I'm supposed to be in Mexico."

"That's okay, son. I don't want you to change your plans. You go down to Mexico. You can call your mother on the day of the operation to check in, okay?"

When I got off the phone, I was tormented with guilt. Shouldn't I be down in New York with my mom, in case anything went wrong with the operation?

At a men's meeting, I debriefed with Gordon, Craig, and Julian. They all reassured me that if caught early enough, colon cancer was a curable disease. That, along with the fact that my dad was only fifty-seven years old, gave him a good chance that he would survive the operation and beat the odds for long-term survival.

I heard what they were saying. Realizing that the Los Horcones seminar was a once-in-a-lifetime event, I decided to continue with my original plan. With all the preparations for the trip and worrying about dad, January went by very quickly.

In early February, we piled into Dakota's van and headed for East Wind Community. (Gordon would fly down later and meet us in Mexico.) To avoid having to pay for motels and having enough room in the van to lie down, we traveled straight through, stopping at gas stations to fill the gas tank and use the bathrooms. We took turns driving.

Two days later we reached East Wind Community in time for the Federation Assembly. Jane and I were the official Dandelion representatives. It was at this meeting that Sandhill Farm (located in Missouri), became part of the Federation, which brought the number of communities in the Federation up to six.

For me, it was nice being back at East Wind and catching up with acquaintances I had made the previous year. Here, we also picked up Malon, a long-term member of East Wind who would join us on our trip to Mexico. I also spoke with Durin, who was now officially a member of East Wind. When I asked him why he and Dondi had eventually broken up, he looked over the rim of his glasses and simply said, "We both realized we had absolutely nothing in common."

A day after the three-day assembly, we took off again, this time heading for the Mexican border. Another thirty-hour trip and we were at the gates of Los Horcones.

Behavior Seminar

The Behavior Seminar at Los Horcones was an experience I will never forget. I felt this was what my life journey had led me to—getting more knowledge about behavior analysis applied to communal living. I was so excited to be there and knew that Jane and Gordon were happy to be there as well.

As an expectant mother, Jane had a keen interest in learning more about their childcare program. I was glad that Jane and Gordon were there to share this experience, as I knew we would all present a united front when we returned to Dandelion.

Other communitarians attending the conference were Chip from Twin Oaks and Piper from Aloe Community, also Robert and Anita (who had visited Dandelion two years earlier) and had been there for two months. They liked the community so much that they were considering joining and would present one of the workshops.

Also visiting were Rob and Donna Jewett (two other behaviorists from Ohio), who had been invited to the seminar, since they were interested in joining a Walden Two community. Their three young children accompanied them. In addition, there was another behaviorist, Marian, visiting from Winnipeg, Canada, who was working on her dissertation about Walden Two communities.

The first seminar began at ten a.m. the following morning, and we gathered in a large classroom in the school building. To everyone's surprise, Juan started the first lecture in Spanish, with Fernando translating in English. (This was unexpected, as we understood Juan when he spoke English.) When questioned about this, Juan explained that he felt more comfortable expressing his thoughts in Spanish and then having them translated.

The first lecture was an overview of basic behavior principles and the philosophy of behaviorism. Juan emphasized that these principles had all been determined through experimentation. He went on to explain how science could give us "values," or more accurately, "behavior," which was actually what people meant when they talked about values.

Then he passionately talked about how at Los Horcones (and by implication, other Walden Two communities), science was the only place one could look to for values. He was speaking very fast and Fernando barely kept up translating into English.

Juan then went on to state that real Walden Two communities would be based on the science of human behavior—not on Skinner's fictional novel. (This statement came as quite a surprise to many people and later started some intense discussions outside the seminar.) He also stated that "lack of agreement" on this point was one of the main reasons the members of Los Horcones decided to build their own community rather than join one of the established ones in North America.

Juan's lecture immediately sparked several responses from the participants. "I agree with you that getting values from science is often a practical way to go." Gordon said, "On the other hand, I think it may unnecessarily alienate good potential members to require agreement that values must come directly from science. What is important is the values/behavior themselves, and there is solid broad-based agreement on both."

The discussion that followed made many of the guests begin to challenge their own assumptions as well as those of Los Horcones. Many of the participants began to wonder if there might be a real difference between the members of Los Horcones and the North American communities, based on their cultural upbringings. (One point that came up in a later seminar was that all couples at Los Horcones were monogamous, whereas couples in the other Federation communities often had open relationships.)

After the evening meal, many participants gathered at the community recreation building to discuss the seminars of the day. We first tried to make sense of why Juan had decided to communicate through Fernando, when he had an obvious mastery of English. Was there something more to that than just feeling more comfortable expressing his thoughts in Spanish? Might it be something else like some kind of informal power trip? I personally had no problem with it and thought the important thing was the knowledge expressed.

The rest of the week covered topics such as "Work Behavior," "Childcare," "Interpersonal Relationships," and many more. I found all the workshops valuable and thought provoking.

Later in the week on the day of my dad's operation, I called Mom to see how things went. "All went well, dear, no complications. The surgeon believes he got all of the cancer."

"That's great news, Mom," I said with a big sigh of relief. The Universe was in balance.

By the end of the seminar, I had gone through some emotional turmoil in thinking about leaving Dandelion and joining Los Horcones. Los Horcones just might be the place for all the pioneer behaviorists to make a stand together, I thought. It might possibly have a better chance than Dandelion.

It was hard even to think about leaving Dandelion, but that thought stayed with me. I decided I would use the last of my vacation time to spend an extra two weeks at Los Horcones before heading back to Dandelion. That would give me time to think things over and experience more of Los Horcones.

After all the seminarians had departed, I was the only communitarian left from the Federation.

Robert and Anita had decided to join and were talking about returning to New York, selling their land, and coming back down sometime in the summer. Rob and Donna were considering joining as well. I had long discussions with all of them. Marian, too, was now thinking of joining.

Los Horcones had purchased forty acres of land, located twenty miles away, to be the new site of their community. I became part of the work crew that was clearing the land there and putting up fences. That meant cutting down some hardwood trees, which, as the name indicated, were very hard and difficult to cut.

On those work crews, I got a chance to continue my talks with Robert and Anita, as well with Juan, Fernando, and Ramon and explore the possibility of joining Los Horcones.

By the end of my time there, I had concluded that Los Horcones was the place the pioneer behaviorists could build a real Walden Two community, although I still had some doubts. I felt like I was riding an emotional roller coaster. What would I be giving up to live there?

I knew I considered Dandelion my second home, which was only a day's bus ride from my parents. If I did move to Mexico, how often would I get a chance to visit them and my brother? How would I keep in touch with Dandelion?

By the end of my two weeks, I had decided that I had to give Los Horcones a chance. When I shared the news with the members of Los Horcones, there were cheers and smiles all around. They would be very happy to have me as a member.

Bus Ride to New York

At the end of my second week, Los Horcones scheduled a trip to Tucson, Arizona, with Robert and Anita driving. It was to pick up some material things that weren't available in Mexico, as well as to drop me off at the bus station. I said my goodbyes and told everyone I would see them later in the fall.

On the trip to Arizona, I brainstormed with Robert and Anita about how the summer might play out and they invited me to stay with them at Alpha Research. That way, I could work with them (cutting and selling firewood) and give me a chance to earn the $400 entry fee that Los Horcones required of all potential members. (This was another difference between Los Horcones and other communities in the Federation, none of which required any entry fee.)

By this time, Rob and Donna had decided to join Los Horcones as well. After selling their house, they would move to Alpha Research and planned to be there for the summer. Therefore, along with Rob & Donna (and their three children) there would be eight Americans moving to Los Horcones. The plan was to head out early in the fall.

Robert and Anita dropped me off at the bus station and I purchased a bus ticket to New York, planning to visit my parents. The bus ride took three days and was another unforgettable experience. The bus was packed. The ride started fine, driving along miles and miles of desert through Arizona, with temperature in the seventies. But as the trip wore on, babies began to cry and young children whined. The book I had brought was hard to read with all the noise and bumpy road. I tried napping, but with all the crying and whining, I was not successful.

Driving through the night, the bus kept stopping to pick up new passengers and new bus drivers. It stopped in St. Louis around two a.m. and the passengers were instructed to leave the bus so it could be cleaned. (At two in the morning? Who came up with that bright idea?) All the kids (who had finally gone to sleep) were suddenly awake and again began to wail.

I finally made it to the Port Authority of New York City Bus Station at five in the morning. My bus to New Rochelle would not leave for two hours, so all I could do was wait in the station. As I waited, I observed homeless people sleeping on benches, and small gangs walking the station. There were cops on patrol as well. The gangs and cops seemed to be performing some kind of intricate ballet where they would in perfect synchronization, manage to miss each other. The station was huge, had multi levels and was at least a quarter-mile long.

I finally made it to New Rochelle, where my mom picked me up mid-morning. I was so happy to see her again, excited to tell her about my new plans, and wanted to know how dad was doing. We hugged each other.

"How is Dad doing, mom?"

"He seems to be doing fine, dear, although he is still very tired. He sleeps most of the day but is gradually getting better."

"That's good news, Mom. I'm sure he is going to be fine."

When we got to my parents' apartment, I immediately went to see dad. I found him in bed, and leaned over to give him a hug. I was taken back by how gaunt and old he looked. It was the first time I had seen him as a "mortal" person.

"Ah, my traveling son has returned. Welcome back, son."

"Good to be back, Dad. Mom says you're doing better."

"Yeah, slow progress though. The body is not what it used to be."

After a small breakfast, I retired to my old room to take a nap and just recover from my long ordeal on the bus.

I awoke four hours later, refreshed and ready to share my new plans with my parents. When I outlined my plans to live in Mexico, my Mom tried hard to hide her sadness, but only said, "Mexico? That's such a long way from here. Are you sure that is what you really want to do?"

"Yeah, Mom, I'm sure. I gotta give it a try."

"Your friends at Dandelion will really miss you."

"Yeah, I know, Mom, but they'll be okay."

I tried reassuring them both that this was what I really wanted to do, would always make time to come visit them, and that my love for Dandelion would never change.

I realized that the current path I was on was so different from my friends and relatives. Some of them were now married, having children and buying their own homes. My brother had just entered law school and my friends were coming up in their professional careers. However, in my heart, I knew this was what I wanted to do. I took the bus to Dandelion the following day and thought about how I would let the members of Dandelion know about my change of plans.

When I got to Dandelion, everyone was happy to see me. I was told how much I was missed and how everyone was ready to apply behavior principles to Dandelion even more systematically. Inside, I was again feeling tortured about my plan to join Los Horcones and decided to hold off on announcing my decision. What made it even tougher was that Brian had joined Dandelion and Dakota was thinking about joining as well. There was a sense that Dandelion was really starting to grow again.

Spring 1980

The spring was another extraordinary time for Dandelion. With the warm weather approaching, there was a very positive feel in the air. Along with Brian, the community had two other new members, Gaye and Matt, a recently married couple who had worked in theatre in Toronto. They had become interested in communal living during the past year and wanted to try it out.

Matt was twenty-seven years old and Faye was thirty-seven, an interesting role reversal of older men hooking up with younger women. They fit in well with Dandelion's culture and were the main force behind another cultural renaissance.

With our interest in theatre, Matt, Brian, and I developed a strong bond. On the front porch, we would brainstorm about new theatre games, often with hilarious results. We came up with a game show called "What's My Oppression?" The premise was that people had to identify what kind of oppression someone was experiencing. One of the game show questions was, "An eighty-year-old black woman was denied service in a restaurant. Is this a form of ageism, racism, or sexism?" (As Brian pointed out, the show had limited possibilities.)

Although Dandelion had all these new members, Craig had left the community and gone off to New Zealand, exploring communities there. That meant Casey was now a single and available woman, a rare occurrence indeed.

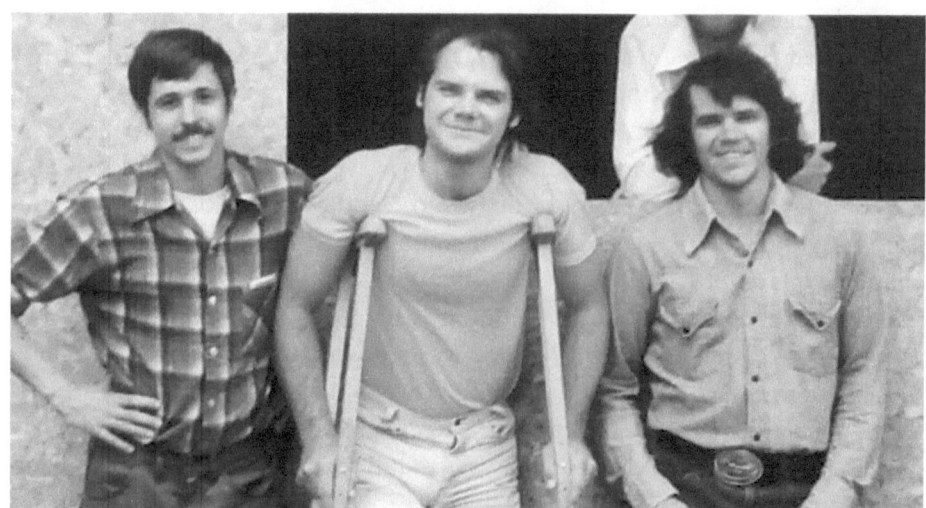

Richie, Matt and Brian

Casey stopped by my room the evening I returned and the next thing I knew we were in bed together making love. I could hardly believe it. (I hadn't been with a woman since Gerry.)

Along with my decision to leave Dandelion, I now had this new variable to consider. Suddenly, there was so much going on and so many good people joining Dandelion.

Alas, nothing was to come of my one-night stand with Casey. Three weeks later, she announced that she was off to New Zealand to join Craig and explore community there.

Cabaret Night

Having two professional theatre people at Dandelion certainly added to the cultural scene, and Matt and Gaye decided they wanted to host a Cabaret Night.

Cabaret Night was a night where members could display their various talents, from one-act plays, to live music, to comedy routines. It turned out to be a special night with many quirky acts.

The shop had been magically transformed, where the set designer had given much thought to the cunningly draped backdrop, ingeniously fashioned to resemble community bed sheets, which created a dramatically simple effect.

Matt, the host of the evening (dressed up in tie and jacket), introduced the first act. The community was back in the Wild West, following the escapades of Butch Cassidy and the Sundance Kid, with Brian (Butch) and Richie (Sundance) playing the title roles. Matt helped narrate the scenes with a running commentary.

At the end, Sundance says, "Australia? That's your great idea? What's so great about Australia?" After Butch explains the advantages, Sundance says, "But that's a long way from here, isn't it?"

To which Butch replies, "Everything's always gotta be perfect with you!"

With the audience now warmed up, a classical interlude followed, with Maura playing cello and her sister (visiting from Montreal), playing flute. It was an exquisite rendition of *Berceuse Slave* and Beethoven's *Minuet in G*.

Then Gordon treated the crowd to some original ballads he had written about social change and life at Dandelion in particular. (*I Got the Outhouse Blues* was one of them.)

After Gordon's amazing performance, I had the chance to play out one of my life-long dreams. Matt and I performed the opening scene from *Walden Two*. I played the soldier returning from World War II to ask his ex-professor some questions regarding social problems. Some of the poignant lines were, "What we don't see, sir, is why we have to take up where we left off. Why isn't this a good time to get a fresh start, from the very beginning? Why not get some people together and set up a social system somewhere that would really work? Why can't we *do* something about it?" Also, "It's a job for research, but not the kind you can do in a university, or in a laboratory anywhere. I mean you've got to experiment, and experiment with your own life. Not just sit back in an ivory tower somewhere as if your own life weren't all mixed up in it."

That line about "experimenting with your own life" had always inspired me and here I was, experimenting with my own life, living my philosophy, values, and principles.

Gabriel (another new member) graced the audience with his tin can harmonies (banging on different size tin cans with drumsticks), followed by Matt, Brian and I doing some improvisational comedy routines with suggestions from the audience.

The climax of the night was when unsuspecting Julian was "volunteered" to do a take-off of the TV show, *This Is Your Life*. Julian, sitting on a stool facing the audience was submitted to offstage voices talking about his childhood and college days. Donald (who was visiting) showed up wearing an old lady's dress (playing Julian's mom) and talked about the idiosyncrasies of her son, all the while pinching his cheek.

Then his childhood love interest, Phyllis Potts (played by Gordon wearing a dress), was delighted to see him again. In addition, the inevitable army buddy reminded Julian of the times they shared. (Julian had never been in the army, or any military branch.)

The night ended with a standing ovation for all the performers.

First Baby Born at Dandelion!

By far, the most amazing and dramatic event of that year was the birth of Parrish Dandelion on April 19. The anticipation of Parrish's arrival had been adding to the excitement around Dandelion for weeks. M'lissa and Larry had come up from Twin Oaks to assist Jane in the delivery.

In the fall, Jane had searched for months trying to find a doctor who would at least consider a home birth. Everywhere she went, doctors refused to take the chance. She finally found a doctor who agreed to be there, so long as there were no negative signs during her regular pre-natal appointments.

The night before Parrish's birth, most of us had gone out to Kingston to a local disco and in the morning, we were recovering from various degrees of a hangover.

It was eight a.m. and I was lying in my bed with my hair all fluffed up like a bird's nest when I heard the door in the hallway open. Then M'lissa's voice shouted out, "We're having a baby!" I immediately woke up, got dressed and went out to the farm house to see what was happening. I was so excited to be a part of this event.

I climbed the stairs to the second floor and went to the far room, which had been transformed into a nursery and had a mattress on the floor and a crib by the window.

Gordon and M'lissa were right next to Jane, with Larry and the doctor farther away. Brian and Dakota were in the doorway and I joined them. Other communitarians came up and we all took turns looking in.

The life energy in the room was just amazing. Brian commented that he felt it was going to be a girl.

Jane was still in the beginning stages of labor, so I went downstairs for a quick bowl of granola. I then went outside and moved the van to the front of the house, adding a mattress from the visitor room, in case Jane needed an emergency ride to Kingston.

The rest of the morning seemed to go as well as could be expected with no complications. I was downstairs and heard Jane scream. I became a little worried, but then realized it was just part of the process of dealing with the pain.

A little before noon (after only six hours of labor), Parrish was born—a boy. Everyone rejoiced in welcoming Parrish to Dandelion. The community had placed bets on the day and hour Parrish would be born, and I had won the contest.

I walked outside a little while later and was surprised to see Chrissie, with her head sticking inside the doorway of the front porch. "What the…" I stood there transfixed. I had heard of farm animals somehow being 'in tune' with women giving birth on farms, but thought that was just an urban legend. Now here I was staring at the community cow, with her head poking through the porch door. I gently led Chrissie back to the barn.

Jane and Parrish meeting Naomi and Jonathan

That night, the community had a welcoming ceremony for Parrish. We gathered in the living room where there was a large stainless steel bowl of water placed in the middle of the floor. One by one, we said wishes out loud for Parrish, and after making the wish, took a small handful of water and threw it up into the air. This was said to be an ancient Pagan ritual.

Some of the wishes were, "To have compassion, a sense of humor, appreciation of nature," "War is less a part of your world," "To be healthy and happy," "Tolerance," "Good listener, likes music, and has a happy childhood."

Afterwards, the community went out to the garden in front of the house. There, we dug a small hole in the middle of the garden, placed the afterbirth inside, and planted a small rose bush over it.

By the end of the day, there was a general sense of well-being in the community, and the members were well aware that this was the beginning of a new chapter in our journey.

The birth of Parrish had a profound effect on me in two ways. First, I was now even more conflicted in my decision to leave Dandelion. Second, I wondered if I would ever meet a woman with whom I felt I could have a child.

Over the next two weeks, I debriefed with Dakota about my values, personal goals, and behavior. I did not share my turmoil with other members, as I did not want to burden anyone else, especially with the responsibility of a new baby in community.

I Post My Leaving Paper

With the warmer weather coming, I felt I could no longer put off my decision to leave Dandelion. With emotions churning, I tried listening to what my gut was telling me.

My primary identity over the last couple of years had been as a radical behaviorist who was committed to building a real Walden Two community and I wanted to surround myself with other behaviorists who shared that same goal.

I tried putting into words what I was feeling, and it took me days to get the right words.

I finally wrote it all down, explaining how I felt, that I would leave in June, live at Alpha Research for the summer, and then head to Los Horcones in the fall.

The next morning, I posted it on the bulletin board in the kitchen. Dakota was washing dishes at the sink, and after posting it, I walked over and hugged her. She could tell by my eyes what I had just posted.

"Don't worry, Richie. Things will work out for you, and Dandelion will do fine." We hugged each other for over a minute, and then I went back to my room and cried.

As word spread around the community that I was leaving, there was a general feeling of sadness. My fellow communitarians wanted me to be happy, but they could not imagine life at Dandelion without me. Members came up to me shared their feelings, and I was again torn with waves of uncertainty.

In Dandelion tradition, I would have to have a "leaving" meeting. This meeting (more formally referred to as another "clearness" meeting) was a time to reflect on what a member had contributed to the community, offer wishes for the future, and discuss any unresolved issues that members might have. It was a poignant way to bring closure with a member who had lived at Dandelion. It also left a door open in case the member ever wanted to return.

At my clearness meeting, everyone agreed that Dandelion would miss me. Still, they understood my commitment to behaviorism and that I wanted to try out Los Horcones. It was a very dramatic meeting, as people shared memories of fun times working together and sharing how much I would be missed. With that meeting, I was officially ending my membership and felt quite emotional.

The next night, Julian and Timothy prepared a tinnery going-away ritual for me. I was to report to the tinnery at eight p.m. I entered the tinnery and found Julian and Timothy dressed up in judo outfits. (They were attempting to re-create a scene from the TV series *Kung Fu*.) Candles were burning in eight tin cans spread around the tinnery, giving a very warm glow. No lights were on.

They both bowed to me and led me to the cutting station. Julian said, "When you can rib and bend the can with no mistakes, it will be time for you to leave Dandelion."

I turned on the torch, ribbed the twelve-ounce can and then bent it. Julian and Timothy inspected the can, nodded to each other and smiled.

"It is time for you to leave. May you have a safe and interesting journey, my friend," Timothy said softly. They then turned and mooned me. I turned and mooned them back.

Two days later, it was time for me to leave. Dakota had generously made her van available to me. My plan was to take my stuff (there wasn't much, mostly clothes), visit my parents, and then drive to Boston and drop off the van to Dakota. She had decided to do some social change work in Boston for the summer. From there I would take the bus to Alpha Research.

I packed Dakota's van, said my final good-byes, and headed down the driveway. As I passed Aduki, I noticed six of the members (with some other visitors) stood by the driveway. As I approached the bridge, all of them mooned me goodbye, giving me a great send-off to my next adventure.

The Summer of Alpha Research

I had tears in my eyes as I left Dandelion and drove through the town of Enterprise one last time. I thought of all the great times I had there, the passionate people I had met, and particularly the women who had become my lovers.

I reviewed my life journey so far. If someone had told me when I was twenty years old that I would live in Canada (on a commune), present my thesis at a national conference of psychologists, have a film of mine shown in American Embassies around the world, been a grape picker in France, lived in Mexico for a while (on another commune), and become lovers with some beautiful women, I would have thought that person was crazy.

However, that was my life journey so far. If that were my twenties, what might my thirties bring? I again thought about how many of my friends and relatives were now married with children.

Then I started to think more about where my life was now headed. What would life at Los Horcones really be like? What new skills would I learn there? What new friends would I make? How would the summer at Alpha Research unfold?

I made it to Mamaroneck by suppertime, and my parents were happy to see me. Over supper, I filled them in on my upcoming plans. My parents (who always loved and supported me), were most curious about Los Horcones. My mom seemed more worried than my dad about my living in Mexico. I assured them that Los Horcones had a high standard of living, was located out in the country, and was a wonderful place to live. I again emphasized that I wanted to live with other pioneer behaviorists and build a Walden Two community.

After a couple of days with my parents (and with tears in my mom's eyes) we said our good-byes, and I was off to my next adventure.

I drove to Boston and dropped off the van with Dakota. We had a nice reunion and the next day I took the bus to Alpha Research.

I arrived at the Canton (New York), bus station at seven p.m. and was warmly greeted by Robert and Anita. They took me back to Alpha Research and broke out a large bottle of Colt 45 beer.

"So, how did things go at Dandelion, Richie? Was it difficult to leave?" Robert asked.

"More difficult than I imagined it would be, but I still feel like I made the right decision."

They both smiled, and Anita said, "Well, the Jewetts should be arriving in two weeks. We figured you could stay in the pump house. It is small, but at least you will have your privacy. We plan on putting the Jewetts up in the log cabin."

Robert added, "We realize the living quarters will be tight, but it is only for the summer."

In the morning, I got a tour of the land. The main property surrounded a small pond and the landscape was picturesque with tall oak and maple trees everywhere. The sounds of birds could easily be heard, as there were no traffic noises.

Alpha Research was somewhat primitive. It did not have indoor plumbing—only an outhouse away from the main building. Their outdoor solar shower was fine for limited use, but I wondered what they did in the winter. (I later found out they took sponge baths.)

The financial plan was to cut wood off the land and sell it. That way the community would have enough money for each of the members to pay their Los Horcones entrance fee. Anita and Robert would put Alpha Research up for sale in the fall after we had all left for Los Horcones and keep that money for themselves.

There was no formal labor system such as Dandelion had. Instead, a list of projects was posted, and members chose what they wanted to work on. We spent most of our time felling dead trees and then cutting them into logs. We also took turns with cooking and dishwashing. (On average, we worked about eight hours a day.)

By the end of the first week of cutting wood, I now referred to myself as a "logger" and took pride in knowing I was getting into the best shape of my life.

A week later Donna and Rob arrived (with their three kids), and there was general excitement. It felt like all the pieces of the puzzle were coming together. After the kinks of labor and living situations settled, the community got into its own sense of rhythm. In the evenings, we would often brainstorm on what we had to offer Los Horcones and pinpoint what strengths we each brought to the endeavor. We took turns reading to the kids.

To lighten the load of cutting wood each day, members took on nicknames. I became "Hanging Moon," Rob became "Spoke Too Soon," and Anita became "Babbling Brook."

The wood piled up over the summer and Robert began making contacts to sell it. He also contacted a real estate agent to begin the process of selling their land.

As the departure date came closer (second week in September), there was a general sense of anticipation. I wondered if this was what pioneers heading out to settle the West might have felt.

We began counting the days to our departure date. We inspected the two vans and two cars. In addition, any last-minute details (checking out maps for the most efficient route to travel, getting food, supplies, etc.) were all completed.

It was late afternoon in early September, and Anita had just returned from picking up the mail. In the mail was a large manila envelope from Marian, the Canadian living at Los Horcones. Anita opened it and out spilled a twenty-nine page hand-written letter. It began, "Hope this letter reaches you all." Thus, began the most dramatic letter I had ever read in my life. Marian explained that she was no longer living at Los Horcones and detailed what had happened to her over the summer. She painted a very bleak picture of the reality of Los Horcones, at least from her perspective.

I was sitting at the picnic table (along with the others) and the pages were passed around, one by one. I could not believe what I was reading. Marian reported that the criticism about the American Walden Two communities was intense. Los Horcones members believed theirs was the only "true" Walden Two community and that the other communities in the Federation were not worth spending time with. She went on and on about the derogatory comments said about the American communities.

She then reported about members (Rene and Roberto) and other visitors who were kicked out, and that even she was forced to leave under adverse circumstances (she was told to leave as soon as possible and to not come back). On and on she went about aversive control, critical comments, and that life at Los Horcones was not what it had been like when she first got there.

As I read the letter, I felt my heart breaking. I could hardly believe that what I was reading could be true. However, I also sensed that Marian was telling the truth.

I read the last page, walked off to find some space on my own, and ended up on a large boulder overlooking the pond. I felt the tears brimming in my eyes, which turned into a flood, and then I was sobbing uncontrollably. What had I done? I had left Dandelion with the hopes of joining a more behaviorist community and now it seemed all I believed in was crashing down on me. I didn't know what to do, but I was sure I wanted nothing to do with community ever again.

The next day I shared with everyone that I would not be going to Los Horcones. All the others understood and said that they would not be going either. We began brainstorming about starting a community there at Alpha Research. I told them that I was not ready to make that kind of commitment and just wanted to go visit my parents for a while.

Alpha Research was kind enough to give me one thousand dollars (for all the time and energy I had spent cutting wood that summer), and I left the next day with my duffel bag of clothes and took the bus to New Rochelle, New York. For the first time in my life I felt I was going into a deep depression.

Living in Rochester

After visiting my parents for a while, I ended up staying in Rochester (New York) visiting friends there, living off my small savings, and just trying to decide what I was going to do next. Folks at Dandelion contacted me hoping I would return to Dandelion, but I was just not ready to make any kind of commitment.

In Rochester, on December 8, I heard the news that John Lennon was dead and felt devastated by that news. I kept thinking, out of all the people to kill, why a musician in his prime? I had such a hard time dealing with that, which just added to my own emotional turmoil.

Christmas came around, the weather was getting too cold for me, and I had had enough of living in Rochester. I went back down to visit my parents (who were worried about me), but I again tried my best to reassure them that I just needed time to get my life back together.

I had been in contact with ex-Dandelion member Jeffrey, who was now living in North Carolina working as a painter. He invited me to come down to stay and work with him. We would catch up and have a good time. He was currently living at Aloe, which had folded as a community and was now renting out the property. I felt I had nothing to lose and would appreciate the warmer weather. Therefore, I decided to go visit him for a while.

After the holidays, I took a bus to Chapel Hill (North Carolina) where Jeffrey was waiting for me. As I got off the bus, Jeffrey said, "Dicky, the right reverend Merrill Lynch welcomes you to North Carolina!" It was great seeing him again, and his sense of humor boosted my spirits immediately.

Jeffrey's idea of working together as painters didn't materialize. "Things seem to have slowed down, Dicky. Sorry about that." A couple of weeks later, Jeffrey fell in love with a woman and moved in with her. That left me all by myself, with no car, no job and my money running out.

It was now February and I had no idea what to do next. At least the weather was turning warmer. I knew I would soon have to get a job somewhere, but I had no idea where.

By pure luck, I found out that a small farm down the road needed help with the spring planting. This would be off the books and I talked to the farmer about my farming experience at Dandelion. The farmer and his wife took a liking to me and offered me the job. The farming job turned out to be just what

I needed. The physical work of planting seeds, weeding, and other farm chores, was exhausting, but helped kick me out of the depression I had been wrestling with since September. I felt like I was getting balance back in my life.

In April, Brian, along with his new girlfriend Alison (old friend of his and recent visitor to Dandelion) came down to visit me. Brian and I immediately connected over old times and he talked about how much everyone missed me. They gave me an update on how Dandelion was doing, talking mostly about how Parrish was walking and talking and the overall positive effect that had on the community.

Plans for a new children's building were underway. Ira (the long-time member of Twin Oaks Community) had joined Dandelion, along with her daughter Raphy. Some other recent visitors talked about returning as members as well. In addition, Peggy, who had arrived at Dandelion on her motorcycle, had just joined.

The community had made a commitment to become much larger and it was a time of high energy and optimism.

I could sense the excitement in Brian's voice and realized how much I missed living at Dandelion. Brian said the community would gladly welcome me back if I decided to return. "It will be like old times, Richie. We could really use your positive energy and it would mean a lot to me personally if you came back."

Brian and Alison returned to Dandelion, and a couple of days later, I decided to leave North Carolina and visit Dandelion in June. I would take some baby steps and see how I felt being back there.

Summer of 1981

I returned to Dandelion the end of June (after stopping off to visit my parents and brother) and Brian picked me up at the Kingston bus station. It was a joyous reunion.

"Great seeing you again, Richie," Brain exclaimed.

"Yeah, great seeing you too, bro." We hugged each other affectionately.

On the ride back to Dandelion, Brian gave me an update on Dandelion. On the minus side, Matt and Gaye had returned to Toronto to pursue their theatre careers. Maura had gone there as well. Timothy had left for work back in New York and Julian had gone off to Seattle to be with friends for a while. Jonathon and Mory (along with their newborn child), had moved to Ottawa, where they hoped to start a publishing company.

On the plus side, there were several new members. There were Tony and Joni, two eighteen year olds, who brought a lot of idealism. Also Michael, a young man from Quebec who was good with his hands and liked to work in the tinnery at night, and Peggy (the one who had arrived via the motorcycle), a mother with young daughters searching for an alternative lifestyle. Her two daughters (Sandy and Chelsea) were living at Dandelion for the summer. In addition, Alison had become a provisional member.

Larry had become a dual member, spending half his time at Twin Oaks and half at Dandelion. There were also some long-term visitors for the summer, such as Billy and his thirteen-year-old daughter Shadow from Chrysalis Community in Indiana, which was thinking of applying for membership in the Federation. Also, in hopes of attracting more members, Dandelion had decided to include meat as part of their diet.

The van came to a stop in front of the farmhouse and I stepped out. It was a warm, June day and all the flowers in front of the farmhouse were in full bloom. Sprouts of vegetables were beginning in the garden and I breathed in the fresh clean air.

Gordon came up, gave me a big hug, and said, "Richie, so nice to see you again."

"Same here, Gordon, it's been too long."

Gordon helped me unpack my bags and as we walked into the farmhouse he said, "There's enough space that you can stay in your old room. We thought you would like that."

"Thanks, Gordon. Truly appreciated."

"It has bunk beds in it now, and you may have to share it with someone, as we are filled to capacity with so many visitors these days."

"No problem."

On the way through the farmhouse, everyone happily greeted me. Jane said, "Welcome home, Dicky."

"Good seeing you too, Jane. Can't wait to see Parrish!"

"You'll be surprised how much he's grown. Did Brian tell you he's talking and walking now?"

"Oh, yeah, I can't wait to see what words he has picked up around here." We both smiled.

After being at Dandelion for a couple of days, I felt like I was coming alive again. My spirit was soaring just being back at my second home. The weather had been perfect throughout June and continued into July. The pool was always in use on the hot days.

I was pleased to see that nightly behavior meetings were continuing. It took me a couple of days to adjust to all the changes, but by the end of the week, I was beginning to feel like I had never left.

The most thrilling change for me was to see how much Parrish was thriving at Dandelion. I was so grateful for that. Just watching him smile and interact with all the members was a joy. When I first saw him, I was surprised at how much he had grown.

After days of numerous interactions with members and hearing their stories, it sounded like Dandelion had become an entirely different place. In my contemplative moments, I wondered if I could really fit back into Dandelion, but the other side of me was saying, "Let's see what the summer brings."

A week later, the phone rang, and I picked it up. "Good morning, Dandelion Community. This is Richie."

"Hi, this is Pat. I'm scheduled for a visit tomorrow and just wanted to confirm my pick-up at the train station."

"Let me check the calendar, Pat, hold on. Yes, you're on the schedule for a pick-up at 4:30. Where are you coming from anyway?"

"Queens, New York."

"Ah, great, I'm originally from Brooklyn, myself. It will be nice having another New Yorker here."

"Oh, really, what part of Brooklyn?"

"I grew up in the projects off of Knapp Street, in Sheepshead Bay."

"Oh, I know where that is. Nice area."

"Yes, I remember it well. Okay, we will see you at the train station tomorrow afternoon. A guy named Brian will be holding a sign saying Dandelion Community."

"Thanks. I'm looking forward to meeting everybody."

"Have a safe trip up."

The following day, I was sitting on the front porch in the late afternoon when I saw the van pulling up the driveway. Brian parked the van near the workshop and got out.

The door on the other side of the van opened and out stepped the most beautiful woman I had ever seen. She was about five feet tall, had brown eyes and waist-length black hair that glistened in the sunlight. She had high cheekbones and the body of a Greek goddess. She was wearing cut-off green shorts, black shoes and a paisley brown and white shirt. I was captivated. She put her backpack on, Brian picked up her suitcase, and she followed him up the driveway.

When they approached the porch, I knew it had to be Pat. I wanted to make the best impression that I could. This would be hard, as before I returned to Dandelion, I had shaved off my beard, mustache, and gotten a crew cut. My hair was in that "in between" stage of looking like a wild man. Nevertheless I spoke up.

"Hi, you must be Pat. I'm Richie. I spoke with you yesterday on the phone and feel like I almost know you already. Welcome to Dandelion."

Pat smiled and said "Hi. It's nice meeting you as well." Then she followed Brian into the house.

Pat was another Antioch student coming up for a three-month internship; she would get three school credits for spending the summer at Dandelion. In her letter to the community, she said she was a psychology major, particularly interested in the positive verbal environment and learning more about behavior principles in practice. She also had a passion for health and was an artist who loved painting and drawing.

Pat fit in so well that after three days she was treated like a member. In addition, she and Michael hit it off immediately. Within a week, they were Dandelion's newest couple.

A couple of days later, another visitor from New York named Tango arrived as well. I was weaving a hammock in the shop when Jane walked in with some new visitors. "This is the main shop where we weave all our hammocks and hammock chairs. This is Richie."

Tango stepped over to me, reached out his hand and said, "Hi, I'm Tango."

I had read Tango's visitor letter and said, "Oh, you're the guy from Rye, right?"

"That's me."

Turning to Jane, I said, "Rye is right next to Mamaroneck, where I grew up after we left Brooklyn." Tango and I exchanged a few more words and then Jane continued the tour.

After supper, I met Tango on the front porch and we immediately hit it off with our warped sense of humor being the main attraction. "So, Tango, I was a beach boy at Westchester Country Club for a few summers. Ever been there?"

Tango smiled and said, "Oh, yeah, my parents were members, and we used to hang there every summer."

It had been over ten years since I was a beach boy, so I knew all the other beach boys I had known were long gone. "They still have the 'Long Island Whitefish' wash up on the shore every day?" I asked and smiled wryly.

Tango laughed and said, "Oh, yeah, nothing like seeing a used condom floating in the water to make you want to just dive in and go for a swim." He then broke into a line from the movie *Apocalypse Now*. "Just love the smell of napalm in the morning, the smell of victory."

From that night on, we would often do lines from movie or comedy routines we both enjoyed, especially from the movie *Dr. Strangelove*. (With lines like, "Mandrake, do you know what fluoridation is?" or "Where the hell is Major Kong?")

A couple of days later, Theo (a German visitor) arrived, as did Janet, from Toronto, another artist. They were both upbeat people and along with Pat and Tango, added much to the positive atmosphere of Dandelion.

In addition, Mert (another friend from college) came up for a visit. She was an artist, had spent time on a kibbutz in Israel, and was interested to see what communes in the Federation were like. She had a great sense of humor and many co-operative living skills.

Tango, Sandy and Peggy

My 30th Birthday Celebration

Donald was coming up for a week-long visit the first week in July. Along with Donald's visit, and since I had not celebrated my 30th birthday in any serious way, Brian proposed that Dandelion throw a party in honor of that important event. Everyone agreed. To add some extra fun, I proposed that people come up with any "acts" they might like to perform at the party.

Donald arrived, and he had tears in his eyes.

"So nice seeing you again, Richie."

"Same here, Donald. It's been too long, eh?" We hugged each other and after catching up, we started talking about what we could do for the party. Since we were both amateur jugglers, Donald proposed that a juggling routine would be perfect. Our two alter-ego French jugglers, Jacques and Pierre, would perform. We practiced daily for a week and by the time of my party, we had almost perfected our act.

The night of the party arrived, and it was another magical evening. With all the visitors, about thirty people were gathered in the shop, ready to have a good time. The party began and people were instantly on the dance floor. After about a half hour, Brian announced, "We are now in for a special treat, folks. Would you please give a warm welcome to the amazing French jugglers, all the way from Montreal, Jacques and Pierre!" The crowd applauded loudly as Donald and I entered the main room. We bowed deeply.

We had both stuffed our juggling balls down inside our underpants and Donald, speaking with a French accent said, "Ah, *oui, merci*. We are ze French jugglers Jacques and Pierre and, as you can see, we have no balls." (Groans were heard around the room.) "Can we please have someone come up from ze audience to verify that we have no balls?"

Several hands enthusiastically shot up in the air. Donald pointed to Janet and she walked up with a big smile on her face. She patted us both down (discreetly avoiding our crotch areas) and then turned to the audience and said, "Yup. They have no balls." The audience burst out laughing and applauded loudly.

Donald and I then turned our backs to the audience, pulled out our juggling balls, turned back around and with surprised looks on our faces as Donald announced, '*Mais, oui!* We *do* have ze balls!" This was followed by more applauding and shouting.

We then performed our routine almost flawlessly, dropping our balls only three times. The audience was quite impressed, especially when we began to pass (and catch) the balls to each other. We did this while simultaneously saying out loud to each other, "Self, self, self, pass, self, self, self, pass."

At one point, Donald went into the dipping room (just off the main room) and I began to throw the balls to him. As I passed the balls to him (which only I could see), I described the balls Donald was juggling. "*Mais oui, mon frère* is now juggling four balls." I then began throwing in more balls one at a time. "Now he is juggling five balls, and now he is juggling *six* balls! *Mon Dieux, c'est incredible!*" All the time, the audience could not see Donald juggling anything.

After I finished describing Donald's phenomenal act, he then began throwing them back at me. When he finished, he came out and we both took a long bow. The crowd enthusiastically gave us a standing ovation, which was not too hard, since everyone was already standing and ready to get back to dancing.

And dance we did. The energy there that night was legendary, as everyone was dancing, drinking, and having a fabulous time.

Later on, in the night, the other event took place that no one would forget. Theo, Larry, Tango, Joshua, and I did a dance version to *Age of Aquarius* from the Broadway show *Hair*. Although for our dance routine, we changed the words to *Age of a Hairy Ass*.

As the song began, we started out with all of us kneeling on our knees, gradually rose in tempo with the song, and then spread our arms up in the air. Then when the chorus started, we turned our backs to the crowd, dropped our shorts and underpants, then began singing *Age of a Hairy Ass,* all the while moving our hairy butts back and forth. The crowd once again went wild with cheers, whistling and applauding.

However, the ultimate performance of the night happened around midnight, when I turned the music down and shouted to the dancing crowd, 'Okay, everybody listen up. I've always wanted to dance naked at a party and the time has come. In addition, people on the outside think we dance naked all the time anyway, so let's do it! For the next song, all the lights will be turned down low and anyone who wants to dance naked with me, come on down!" The lights were turned down as low as possible and Robbie put on the record *Hari Krishna* from the play *Hair*.

Since it was late at night, and people were mostly in their shorts and tee shirts (it was a hot July night), I prayed that I would not be the only one taking off the rest of my clothing and dancing. Just as I finished removing my underpants and was stepping out into the middle of the room, I saw with great relief that Tango, Brian, Joshua, Seth, and Theo were joining me, all naked. Jane and

Mert were also brave enough to join me and we all met in the middle of the floor and began dancing.

At first, each person was just dancing individually. Then we gradually formed a circle and put our hands on the shoulders of the person in front of us. We were all smiling and laughing. I was thinking to myself, "So this is what it's like to dance naked? What a feeling!" (I felt the same way I did when I was naked, cutting down trees with the chainsaw; totally free, breaking down societal norms.)

Certain body parts, on both men and women were flopping freely around, but nobody cared. Other people who had kept their clothes on were dancing just as wildly all around us, and everyone was laughing and having a good time. It was probably the closest I had come to participating in an orgy.

The night ended with a bunch of people going to the pool for a midnight swim. I would never forget that party. I remember it as another fun way to welcome me home.

The New Children's Building

There was so much going on that summer. By this time Gordon was divorced from Jane and he was soon to marry Peggy who had just announced that she was pregnant and expecting next April. The need to have Dandelion's first children's building became apparent and plans for such a building began.

The first blueprints of the building (done by Gordon and Larry) showed that it would be smaller than Tamari and have only one floor. This would include one large living room, two small bedrooms, a kitchen, bathroom, and a laundry room, would hold the washer and dryer. There would be windows all along the southern wall and built in the field behind Tamari.

We were excited about this new project. Whenever a new building went up, it was a visible sign of the community's growth.

To get the building built, the community had to find someone who would be brave enough to take on the role of building manager. The manager would be responsible for everything—ordering supplies, dealing with lumber and cement companies, organizing and supervising work crews, and so on. It was a huge responsibility. The only person mad enough to take on the project was multi-talented Larry.

The word went out to other communities that Dandelion was looking for help with the building and would welcome any experienced carpenters for labor exchange.

Tomo showed up (back again from Twin Oaks) along with Hook from East Wind, who also had experience as a construction worker. (He also happened to be an ex-marine sergeant, but you wouldn't know it by his serene, gentle manner.)

Those two were to share a room together in Tamari, until Tomo found out (the hard way) that Hook was a snorer. In fact, he snored so loud, that Tomo was forced to yell at him between snores to wake him up. "Hook." Snore. "Hook!" Snore. "*Hook!*" "Huh, what?" Tomo ended up staying on the living room couch until another room became available.

As usual, before the actual work on the building began, we would have to come up with a name for the building. We held a naming party and many names were proposed. Tomo thought "Frog Hollow" would be nice, as there were many frogs in the area. Jane proposed "Sprout," since it was an obvious choice for a community named Dandelion. After much debate and other names proposed, the community finally voted and Sprout won.

The building of Sprout began, but unfortunately, one disaster after another occurred. First, the cement truck hired to pour the foundation became stuck in a muddy bog, which led to a huge tow truck coming to pull that truck out.

Then there was the small cement mixer Dandelion owned (for smaller projects) and was used on Sprout after the main foundation was poured. The motor on the mixer burned out on the second day and Dandelion did not have the funds to replace it.

Since money was tight (and there was an abundance of labor in the form of many visitors that summer), Larry came up with a novel idea.

Instead of replacing the motor, the work crew first moved a twelve-foot folding ladder next to the mixer. Then, to keep the mixer rotating (keeping the cement wet), visitors took turns climbing up the ladder and then stepping onto the top of the cement mixer. Then using the ladder to hold onto for balance, they carefully began walking slowly to rotate the mixer. This turned out to be quite efficient.

To make it look like we were not exploiting workers, I tied a carrot to the top of the ladder, so it looked like they were walking towards a reward.

On one of my construction shifts, I got into a discussion with Hook about what we had learned from our fathers. Hook's father was a boilermaker and lived in Missouri.

Larry and Janet work on Sprout

My dad was an insurance agent most of his professional life and had grown up in Brooklyn. Hook said that the motto his dad taught him was, "Give no shit and take no shit." This contrasted sharply with the advice my dad had given me, which was, "Never stand when you can sit, and never sit when you can lie down."

The building of Sprout occupied the main energy of Dandelion that summer. We all took turns working on the building, from which many great stories and friendships resulted. In addition, the speed with which Sprout went up was amazing. By the end of September, the basic building had taken shape and the plumbing and electrical wiring had begun.

Moon Madness

The summer of 1981 at Dandelion was the place to be on the planet. There was so much positive energy there, which contributed to so many accomplishments. On the work side, was the building of Sprout, weaving hammocks outside, taking care of the garden, cutting wood and doing craft shows. On the fun side, there was swimming in the pool, volleyball games, hanging out on the front porch, spontaneous singing groups forming, and runs to the local convenience store for ice cream in the late evening.

Several long-term friendships were developing as well. Tango, Theo and I would often hang out together and do comedy routines. We would work together and sing together at parties. Pat and Janet developed a friendship based on their mutual interest in art.

It was as if a wave were cresting at Dandelion that summer and many people were riding that wave and seriously thinking about joining (Alison, Pat, Janet, Tango, Mert and me).

Maybe it was something in the water or the alignment of the planets or just the right chemistry had appeared, but that summer we had an outbreak of what the community later called "Moon Madness."

It started innocently enough when over dinner one night I began telling stories of my wild high school days and how mooning was a "rite of passage." I told them how my friends and I would sneak onto the grounds of the Westchester Hills Golf Club and have wild drinking parties. The local police were often called and when they showed up, they would shine their spotlights onto the course. There they would see ten human moons, close to the pond, with the mist surrounding them. My friends and I would then disperse and stay hidden until the cops disappeared. I was proud to report that there now stands a ten-foot high chain-link fence around that golf course.

After that story, people seemed to be hanging moons everywhere. The women started getting into it as well, but they had their own slant on it. Along with mooning, they would sometimes lift their shirts up and flash someone.

One day, while I was painting the trim on an inside window at Tamari, Mert grabbed a ladder and climbed up the outside wall of where I was working. When she reached the top of the ladder, she lifted her tee shirt and pressed her ample bosom against the window. I was caught by surprise and smiled appreciatively. She winked at me. With my mind now elsewhere I accidentally painted a wide brush stroke across the window instead of the window frame. Her mission accomplished, Mert nonchalantly retreated down the ladder and left me wiping the paint off the window.

There was some extra cement left over from the foundation of the children's building, so we poured it off by the side of the driveway right next to the workshop, to fill in a deep rut.

Tango and I took it upon ourselves to leave a "lasting impression" and spontaneously dropped our shorts (and underpants), and gently placed our buns into the wet cement. When it hardened, you could easily see our four butt cheek indentations.

When Theo got in the van and left Dandelion in September, fifteen members and visitors lined up along the driveway for his send-off. As the van began driving down the driveway, we all turned around and exposed our rear ends. We referred to it as a "twenty-one bun salute."

Moreover, just as appropriately, Theo stuck his butt out the window as he was driven off into the sunset.

Before Theo left, Tango and Theo and I made a solemn oath, based on an ancient Ukrainian ritual. The ritual (which I had learned from Halia, a visitor from the Ukraine), was that each person was to pick out a star or planet in the sky and claim it as their own. Then, when you parted company with your family or friends, whenever you looked up and saw "their" star, you would think of them.

Theo, Tango, and I decided that whenever we saw a full moon, that would remind us of the fabulous summer of '81 and we'd think of each other. In addition, we would turn around and moon the moon.

There also happened to be a young man from France visiting during that time and being "exposed" to the mooning craze, he came to believe that mooning was a common normal cultural practice of North Americans. When it came time for Pierre to leave, I drove him to the airport and walked him to the waiting area inside the airport. We said our good-byes and then Pierre turned around, lowered his pants and underpants, and mooned me, within easy view of several passengers in the waiting area.

I was quite taken back by this public display of good will and wasn't quite sure how to respond. Mooning at Dandelion was fine, but here out in public? I didn't want to offend the foreign visitor, but then again, here I was in the middle of an international airport, with hundreds of people walking around. I quickly weighed my options. Could I be arrested for indecent exposure? (What really was indecent about a rear end anyway? We all have them, right?) Would I get arrested and Dandelion get its name in the paper? Would that ruin our reputation? I was perplexed for a moment, but then sighing, did the only proper thing I could do, and not wanting to insult the friendly international visitor, turned around and mooned him. "Right back at ya, Pierre, and Bon Voyage."

The few passengers in the waiting area who witnessed this unusual event were thinking what? Someone recently let out of an insane asylum? The parting of two lovers? Who knows? Who cared? It was the summer of 1981 and the place to be on the planet was Dandelion Community, with all its crazy and eccentric people and rituals.

Pierre, now thinking that appropriate protocol had been met, smiled widely, waved and walked down the walkway toward his plane. I quickly left, hoping no security personnel had witnessed the event.

Dandelion Builds a Dome

As part of the preparation for conference that summer, the community planned to build a geodesic dome. Domes had become quite popular in California and were inspired by the physicist Buckminster Fuller. Gordon would oversee the project.

It would be located across the road in the main hay field and would be thirty feet in diameter and twenty feet high. The roof would temporarily be covered with large tarps, as that's all the community could afford.

The main structure would be made of eight-foot studs with the joints held together by metal clasps. (That was the theory at least.)

We gathered to assemble the dome and several members and visitors were there to help. We laid the studs out in the field in the shape of a large circle, attached the metal clasps to the ends of the studs, and then connected the studs together.

After three hours, the dome gradually began to take form. To connect the studs higher up, we stood on ladders.

Then, lo and behold, when Felix (another long-term summer visitor) leaned on some studs to finish connecting the last pieces together at the top, the whole dome slowly began to collapse, with Felix riding the wave down.

Many of the studs splintered and the metal clasps popped off or twisted into bizarre shapes. We watched in awe as what we had been putting together the last couple of hours slowly began falling apart.

Felix, holding on for dear life and imagining he was Major Kong in the movie *Dr. Strangelove,* went riding down, hollaring, "Yeeee-Hahhhhhh! Yeee-Hah-hhhhh!"

The dome slowly crashed onto the ground, spilling Felix onto his side grinning. "What the?" was all he managed to say.

After it was determined that no one was hurt, some members began laughing. Others just shook their heads. Most of us were just grateful that no one was seriously injured.

Gordon just stared at the mishmash of the now-piled-up struts and broken clamps, shook his head and simply said, "Well, back to the drawing board, I guess."

Brian piped up, "Ahhh, don't worry, Gordon. We'll just do it again till we get it right. Just like Thomas Edison did with the electric light bulb."

Others tried to boost Gordon's spirits as well.

"It was a good first try, Gordon. We'll make it better next time, don't worry," I said.

It was later determined that the clasps we had chosen were not strong enough and were replaced accordingly.

A week later, we made our second attempt on the dome, and this time everything worked according to plan. From that point on, we referred to it as "the dome that stayed up." We now had our own dome and felt we could make plans for even better improvements later, like enclosing the walls and roof.

Richie and the dome that stayed up

Night of New Games

Later in August, Billy and Alison organized an evening of New Games in Aduki. The New Games were a series of non-competitive games coming out of the New Age spirit, like Theatre Games, but more co-operatively based. Billy and Alison had swept the shop and made some chocolate chip cookies.

We gathered in the shop, played several games, and then Alison said, "Okay, for this next game we need everyone to lie on the floor and place his or her head on another person's stomach." To my surprise, Pat somehow ended up on my stomach.

Alison then said, "Okay, on the count of three, I want everyone to start laughing. Ready? Here we go, one, two, three!"

The laughing commenced and was at first all fake laughter, but soon, everyone was getting into it and then real laughter was happening all around the room. Members' heads began to shake up and down as the person's stomach muscles they were lying on began to contract and expand. We all looked and felt silly. The laughter bounced off the walls and since all the windows were open, it was heard way down the road.

Alison inspectiing a hammock

The games ended at 11 p.m. and the Billy said, "To close out this evening we have a special event planned out behind the farmhouse, so please follow me there." There were murmurs of curiosity.

I followed Billy up the driveway, and I was delighted to see that Pat was walking right next to me and we began debriefing about the games we had just played. "Those were awesome, eh, Pat?"

"Yeah, I really enjoyed that laughing exercise."

When we reached the location, Billy came to a standstill and requested silence from the crowd as we gathered around him.

"We are now going to go back to where it all began, way, way back to the time of our ancient hominid ancestors," Billy said.

He then pushed a button and a bright light lit up the area between the farmhouse and Tamari. And there, in the middle of the space, made from cardboard, stood a ten-foot replica of the monolith from the movie *2001: A Space Odyssey*.

The dramatic music from that movie began to play, with the drums pounding away and the French Horns blasting out loudly. Then Tango, slightly bent over and acting like a proto-human, began to re-enact the opening scene from that movie where the proto-human hesitantly approaches the monolith and touches it.

After he touched it, he began to screech and roll around on the ground like a monkey. It was a magnificent performance and the group applauded as the music faded. Then the light went out.

"Bravo!" I cried out. I turned and found Pat smiling at me.

"That was amazing," she said.

I smiled back and said, "Yes, and this whole evening has been amazing, Pat." That night marked the beginning of our love story.

Behavior Psychology

The following evening, while I was finishing up the supper dishes, Pat walked up to me and said, "Richie, I would really like to know more about behavior psychology and why you are so dedicated to it. Everyone here says you are the person to talk to."

I became very animated and replied, "I would love to share with you what I've learned, Pat. Just so you know, since there are so many new members, I've actually been thinking of teaching a short class on it in the fall." I put the last dish away, dried my hands and continued, "But since you asked, why don't we take a walk down to Sprout and I can share some of the basics with you."

Pat smiled and said, "That would be great. Let's go."

We walked down to Sprout (which recently had its walls and roof put in place) and walked into the large living room space. The openings for the windows were all in place, but no windows were in yet.

Pat walked over to one opening, sat inside it, with one leg up, the other draped over the edge, and leaned her back along the frame. Through the opening could be seen the green grass of an open field. The sky was beginning to turn pink as I paced back and forth in front of her.

"Well, let me start off with the basic rules or laws of behavior. There are only a few, but if you master them, you will see reality in a different way—at least I did." I smiled and thought I was being so clever, but I believed what I was saying.

"The main assumption of behaviorism," I continued, "is that behavior is shaped and maintained by its consequences—what happens after someone does or says something. We call the first law 'positive reinforcement.' What this law says is that when you do something and you get something you like as a result, you will tend to repeat it. For example, if you put a dime in a vending machine and you receive a candy bar, that would raise the probability of doing the same thing next time you wanted a candy bar. Or if an artist paints a painting and gets a lot of praise for it or even gets paid for it, that would be positive reinforcement."

Pat nodded and said, "Okay, I get it. That seems so simple. What else is there?"

"Next, we have 'punishment,' and that is what it sounds like. You do a behavior and as a result, you get something you dislike: you touch a hot stove and you burn your finger. You break a dish, and someone yells at you, or you drive over the speed limit and you get a speeding ticket. In those examples the result is that it tends to dampen that behavior, at least temporarily."

"Okay, that sounds straightforward as well. What else?"

"Well, here is the big thing—and if you get this, you will be on your way to becoming a behaviorist." I paused and smiled for effect. "The next law is called 'negative reinforcement,' and just about everyone confuses it with punishment. In negative reinforcement, you do something, and your behavior, removes something you don't like. My favorite example is taking an aspirin for a headache. You take the aspirin and it removes a dislike—the headache. That heightens the probability that you will take an aspirin for a headache in the future, so you are reinforced for taking the aspirin." I checked to see if Pat was following what I was saying, and she seemed fine with it.

"Other examples of negative reinforcement are: putting on a coat when you are cold, turning down the volume on a record player when the music is too loud, raising an umbrella when it start s to rain, becoming drunk as a way to turn off all the dislikes in your world, or lighting up a cigarette to soothe your cravings for tobacco—all examples of negative reinforcement."

Pat listened quietly to what I was saying and then said, "So, that would be a good thing, right?"

I smiled widely and said, "Yes, exactly; it has a reinforcing effect. People tend to confuse it with punishment because it has the word negative in it. They also confuse it because you start out with an aversive stimulus—the dislike—and you are trying to turn it off or remove it. Some psychologists even call it the 'terminating response.' I spoke with Skinner about this two years ago and suggested he should have named it 'relief reinforcement.' He said that to name it negative reinforcement just seemed to make sense to him as he was formulating his ideas."

Pat said, "Okay, I think I get negative reinforcement. So how does all this relate to *Walden Two* and Dandelion?"

"Well, now you get into some fundamental ideas about society and how it works. Do people go to work because they get a paycheck at the end of the week, positive reinforcement? Or do they go because if they don't go, they will lose their job (punishment)? Or do they do it to turn off all the negative things not having a job would mean? Let me ask you this, Pat. During your time here, have you felt like you were at some kind of job?"

"No, not really. It almost feels like I've been away at a kind of summer camp or something."

I smiled. "Exactly. I feel the same way. In my entire time here, I have never felt like I was 'working.' I've always felt like I was building something. I think that is because we have set up such an egalitarian atmosphere here. No bosses. It gives one such a sense of freedom."

I continued, "Some other examples of what makes Dandelion different: Do people drive the speed limit because they like to, or do they drive the speed limit to avoid getting a speeding ticket? Do kids study hard at school to get a good grade or to avoid a low grade? If you examine our current school systems closely, you will see that a lot of it is based on punishment or threats of punishment. In fact, I believe corporeal punishment is still used in some schools today. What we are trying to do here at Dandelion is to base a society on positive reinforcement as much as we can."

"That's where the positive verbal environment comes in, right?" Pat asked.

"Exactly," I replied, with a big smile. "We find that emphasizing what we like, out loud, gives people a much more balanced idea of how they are doing. I remember when I worked at some jobs during college, how many times I did things right, but rarely was I reinforced for it. However, as soon as I needed negative feedback on my work, my supervisor was right there."

I continued, "At Dandelion, even though it sounds idealistic, people get positive feedback out loud much more often. Therefore, when a time comes for some negative feedback, which is inevitable in any society, here it is much easier to take in because our ratio of likes versus dislikes is much more in balance."

"One of my favorite examples of how this actually works at Dandelion happened before your time here. We had a new member who often swore a lot. This bothered me, and I was trying to figure out the least punishing way to give that member feedback. There were two ways I could have approached it. One was to say directly, 'You know, it bothers me when I hear you swearing around me, and I would like it if you didn't do it so much.' That way, I pinpointed the behavior and stated what I would like instead. The other way was to wait until that member was not swearing and say, 'You know, I really like that you haven't sworn around me in the last half hour.' In both cases, you are giving the person feedback, but the second way, which I chose, was a little less punishing and kept the interaction positive. In addition, our kids here are growing up hearing about likes and dislikes rather than generalized goods or bads."

Pat said, "Okay, thank you, Richie. I think I am beginning to understand a little bit better what Dandelion is about."

"One last thing, Pat, and it again has to do with language and how it shapes our reality."

"Go on."

"Well, I know when you've read to Parrish, you've seen how we whited out all the generic-masculine pronouns in our children's books and replaced them with more neutral terms. We wanted to make sure our kids actively heard a non-sexist language growing up."

"Yes, that certainly wasn't true in my childhood."

"Mine either. It just sets up children, particularly young girls, to become confused when you talk about 'mankind' and you think that will automatically include women in their perceptions as well. The evidence indicates that the generic-masculine does not function neutrally."

Pat slowly nodded her head, and I could tell it was a lot to absorb in one night.

"There is a lot more to say about language, Pat, but I think that's enough for now. How about we go get some tea or something to snack on?"

"Sure, that would be nice. Wait—are you trying to reinforce my behavior?" She said with a smile.

"I'm reinforcing both of our behaviors. This has been a very reinforcing conversation for me, Pat."

We walked up to the farmhouse under the darkening sky. I felt like holding her hand, but knew she was involved with Michael, so I refrained.

Two days later, we were assigned to clean out the barn, which turned out to be a very enjoyable experience for both of us. As we worked together, we laughed a lot and shared stories from our childhoods.

Walking back to the farmhouse for lunch, I said, "It was great working with you, Pat."

"Same here, Richie." She smiled, and I got bold and placed my arm around her shoulder as we walked.

She immediately put her arm around my waist and said, "It's been great getting to know you Richie." I was gratified by that intimate gesture and compliment, and inside my heart was leaping.

Over the next couple of days, I seemed to find more and more time to spend with Pat. We would share an orange on the front porch in the late afternoon, or I would sometimes check in with her when she was on a meta shift with Parrish. (Childcare workers were referred to as "metas," after the Hebrew word for "childcare worker.") We wove hammocks together and did several shifts working on Sprout and the still-unfinished top floor of Tamari.

I was gradually feeling more and more drawn towards this remarkable woman but was determined not to get involved in another three-way relationship. If something was meant to happen with Pat, I would let it unfold in its own time.

Later that week, we spent the afternoon nailing shingles onto the roof of Sprout, she doing one side and I the other. We were close enough to the top where we could talk back and forth. Tango and Tomo were installing gutters and they joined in with the banter as well.

By the end of the day, we had covered the top of the roof. I was pleased at how much we had accomplished. Pat had become quite competent as a roofer in the few short hours she had been up there. "Nice job, Pat. You're on your way to becoming a professional roofer."

"Thanks, Richie. It's pretty easy once you get used to it."

We gathered our tools and then sat down next to each other on top of the roof, where we could see the back fields of Dandelion. Chrissie was in the distance munching on some grass and we could hear people splashing and laughing in the pool.

Tomo and Tango had finished up earlier, so that just left the two of us. Reluctantly, I knew it would soon be time to leave the roof and my connection with Pat would be broken for the time being.

However, before we left, Pat brought up an unusual subject, "So, Richie, if you had your choice of how to die, what way would you like to go?"

I smiled and said, "Me? Well, I guess it would have to be doing something physical like hiking or swimming. Something where I was using my body, doing something I really enjoyed. How about you?"

"I always thought that skydiving was the way I'd like to go. But something tells me I'd probably be hit by a car."

"Like in Queens?"

"Perhaps," was all she said, smiling.

"It's been great working with another ex-New Yorker and getting to know you these past couple of weeks, Pat."

"Likewise, Richie, and I really admire your passion for behaviorism and Dandelion."

We then heard Janet calling the five-minute warning for supper, retrieved our tools, stepped off the ladder and headed for the farmhouse.

Late August 1981

A week later, a new visitor named Marie-France from Quebec arrived. Michael and she hit it off right away, would often converse in French, and started hanging out more and more together.

A week after that, on a clear night, I caught up with Pat after she milked the cows and said, "So Pat, I was thinking of going over to the dome to watch the stars. Would you like to join me?"

"Yes, that sounds like fun. Let me just wash up and I'll meet you in front of the house."

One of the great benefits of living at Dandelion was the absence of streetlights. We could clearly see the Milky Way and so many other stars at night.

On the walk over she said, "Just so you know, Richie, Michael and I are no longer involved the way we used to be." My heart skipped a beat. I (and others) had noticed their drifting apart the last week and the developing relationship between Michael and Marie-France.

"Well, I'm sorry to hear that, but on the other hand it's been great getting to know you at such an easy pace."

"There's nothing to be sorry about, really. We had been drifting apart for a while."

We arrived at the dome and stared at the stars through the top of the dome. I pointed out some constellations. Then Pat said, "Just so you know, I've been thinking of extending my internship here through the fall. What do you think about that?"

I smiled and with my heart skipping another beat, said, "That would be phenomenal, Pat. You have made such a positive impact on the community. I think the community would love to have you stay on."

"I sent out a letter to Antioch two days ago, so I should have an answer by next week."

Then I said, "And just so you know, Pat, I have been thinking about re-applying for membership as well."

"Oh, that is great news, too, Richie. I know the community would love to have you back here." She smiled and we both looked into each other's eyes.

After a half hour of talking about the stars and constellations, we headed back to the farmhouse. This time I did hold her hand and she reciprocated. I felt so comfortable with her, that it seemed like the most natural thing to do.

In addition, with Michael no longer in the picture, I felt things just might work out for us.

When we got to the house, I said, "Why don't we hang out in the hammock a little while and do some more stargazing?"

She stared into my eyes, smiled shyly and said, "Good idea—it is so beautiful out tonight."

We did hang out in the hammock for a while and shared our first kiss there. It was slow and sensuous and with my arm around her shoulder, we watched the stars. "This has been the best summer of my life, Pat."

Gordon with son, Parrish

"Yes, mine, too. Let's see what the fall brings."

We began making out and Pat said, "Why don't we go back to my room?"

"That sounds like a great idea, Pat." We made it back to Pat's room and she invited me in. She lit some candles and then we immediately began taking each other's clothes off. I had seen her naked in the pool, and loved the way she looked, but when I saw her naked body in the flickering candlelight, my breath was taken away and I became rock hard.

She had all the right curves and her breasts were the perfect size for her body.

"Pat, you are the most beautiful woman I have ever met."

She looked deeply into my eyes and said, "Come into my bed, Richie Dandelion."

Fall 1981

September turned out to be a blur for me, spending all my spare time with Pat. At night, before making love, we would often read out loud sections from the O.U.R. behavior books. I loved the sound of her voice and hearing her read the words that had become my own personal philosophy.

In bed, we also read aloud *Tales of the City*, by Armistead Maupin. That book was a cult classic and had become a favorite at Dandelion. All the members ended up reading it. The story took place in San Francisco in the 1970s, with a cast of unforgettable characters and accurately described the craziness of that era.

I took on extra cow-milking shifts with Pat, just so I could spend more time with her. I also helped her when she was on a meta shift and often we would spend time with Parrish in the evening just because he was so much fun to be around. (Parrish had turned into an outgoing, curious toddler who wanted to know about and be involved with everything.)

When I was not spending time with Pat, Tango and I would often work together and continue doing our comedy routines. Our sense of humor became our bond. We would just bounce off each other making comments and burst out laughing. Going to the local dump together became a joy as we pretended we were real garbage collectors. We also shared an interest to see who could find the most interesting thing of value at the dump.

Along with Tango, another funny guy joined Dandelion that Fall. His name was Sean Hayes, a young man from Ontario who looked like the Irishman he was. He had a reddish beard, light hair, and a twinkle always present in his blue eyes. When he, Tango and I got together, something magical in creativity happened.

There was a real cultural revolution going on at Dandelion that fall as well, with plays, live music being heard at all times of the day, poetry readings, improvisation classes, cocktail parties, etc. It seemed like the high energy of the summer was spilling over into the fall.

In addition, Alison, Janet, Sean, I and a few others decided to become provisional members. Pat's request for a renewal of her internship was granted and the community was happy to have her continue as a long-term visitor. Sean and Janet had developed a nice romance.

To everyone's amazement, Sprout was finished by October. There was still cosmetic work to be completed, but the electricity was on and the bathroom was fully functional. We had a big open house party to celebrate.

In November, the play *Dreams & Schemes*, originally written by me but added to by other members of the Dandelion Theatre Troupe, made its world premiere. The play had three acts, each portraying a different version of Dandelion as perceived by a visitor dreaming of what Dandelion might be like the night before her actual visit. It took place in the Sprout living room.

The first act was a nightmare parody of Dandelion's positive verbal environment. At this community, called "Poison Ivy Community," members were all dressed in black, with frowns on their faces. An "I Hate It!" sheet was posted, with comments such as "Life is horrible," "People are useless," and "Get depressed" scrawled on it. The Behavior Manager was a dictator, and everything had to be done his way.

The visitor's second dream sequence took place on the stereotypical commune called "Buttercup." Here, members talked with the carrots, consulted mood rings, and hugged each other every minute. "Groovy!" "Oh, wow!" and "Far out!" were sprinkled throughout the dialogue. In this scene, Tango was a "breathatarian" who didn't eat any food because he got all his nourishment from just breathing.

The third act took place in the future on the first Federation space colony. Here all kinds of problems occurred, with deflector shields down and Pat (from the women's space construction crew) in peril as her safety line broke and she was left floating in space with a dwindling oxygen supply. This bit incorporated a superb dance routine, performed by Pat, Janet and Alison, with the *Blue Danube Waltz* playing in the background.

Parrish, as a grown man now (played by me) was the star of this scene. In addition, Tango played a funky computer that kept the audience laughing using familiar lines from the current Dandelion vocabulary.

A lot of old *Star Trek* lines were used in this act as well, such as my favorite: "I can't change the laws of physics. I've got to have thirty minutes."

The play ended with a happy conclusion, as Parrish and the space construction women saved Pat. The play received a standing ovation.

Other things happening that fall: I taught my first behavior psychology class. This class went one hour a week for six weeks. Both new and long-term members attended it. Pat always showed up and took notes.

There was a French class being taught by Janet and new member Isabelle (by this time, Michael and Marie-France had left the community), which was also well attended. Overall, it was a fall of creativity with a real sense that the community was moving forward.

Wind Spirit

On our days off, Pat and I began taking long walks to view the magnificent fall foliage. We walked for hours along dirt roads, way past the town of Enterprise.

One day we started out with no real destination in mind. The wind was blowing strongly and there was the hint of cold weather in the air. The sun was breaking through the clouds and I felt as if I were entering a movie or dream.

We walked along the dirt road, avoiding crushed snakes and flat frogs, talking about various things. We came to the railroad tracks and walked along it hand in hand. In the short time we had spent together, I wondered how close we could get.

I soon imagined that we were the last two people on Earth after a nuclear war or plague, looking for signs of civilization. We stopped and listened. The wind was the only sound we heard.

We looked up, saw "Think Ledge" (a rock ledge overlooking the railroad tracks) and climbed up to it. When we reached it, the wind was now strongly blowing all around us. We held each other and became one with the wind spirits.

We stood facing the sun, and I felt an indescribable attraction to Pat and my environment. I yelled out, "I love you, Pat." It was picked up by the wind and scattered to the far corners of the world. "I love you, Pat, I love you, I love you," echoed in my mind. I stared into her eyes, feeling so grateful that I had met this amazing woman.

"I love you, too, Richie." We hugged each other and just stood there a few minutes, entranced by the moment.

We headed back to Dandelion a little while later, and when we got to the bridge, I knew another magical moment with Pat was ending. I was glad it happened and that we just might have shared the last warm day of fall together. I was sure there would be other days to share.

Staying or Going

Later in November, Pat posted a paper requesting a two-week labor exchange at Twin Oaks Community. She said she needed time away from Dandelion to sort through her feelings about staying here or going back to school. She felt that she could not ask Antioch for another extension, and that if she decided to stay at Dandelion, it would be as a permanent member. The time away could give her a clearer picture of what she was really feeling.

The community agreed it would be good for Pat (as well as for the community), since Dandelion owed so many labor exchange hours to Twin Oaks. Everyone also wanted Pat to take the time she needed to make sure she was making the right decision.

The day before she left, Pat and I took another long walk to talk about things. She said if she decided to stay, she would wink at me when she returned. If she decided to go back to school, she would close both her eyes.

December 1981

The two weeks she was gone just dragged by for me. I lost sleep trying to guess what her decision would be. We talked on the phone a couple of times, but she was still undecided. Better to wait with no expectations, I told myself. However, wouldn't she have said she was staying if that had been her decision? On the other hand, maybe she wanted it to be a surprise for me and see my reaction.

The two weeks ended, and I was waiting for Pat when the train pulled into the station at Kingston. People were getting off and my eyes scanned the crowd carefully. I thought I heard someone call my name from behind, and there, with a big smile on her face, was Pat.

She was wearing a grey granny dress and I thought she looked like a waif from a 1920s Charlie Chaplin movie. We had an awkward hug as Pat was wearing her backpack, with me trying to put my arm around it. "It's so good to see you, Pat. I really missed you."

"Missed you too, Richie." I took her suitcase and we walked back to the car. "How was the trip?"

"Fine, no problems. I really enjoyed my time at Twin Oaks, as it is so much bigger than Dandelion and so much more to do. They have thirty cows now."

I gave her an update on Dandelion, but the whole time, I was hoping Pat would wink at me.

When we reached the car, she took off her pack and we embraced each other hungrily. "Wink, Pat, please wink," I was saying to myself.

We got in the car and I began kissing her repeatedly. As we kissed, I could tell that Pat was in the same mood. That must be a signal, I thought excitedly. Wasn't she just then talking about some fantasy she had on the train and wanted to show me rather than just talk about it? We finally managed to stop kissing each other and drove off.

We decided to go out for dinner, and we went to a Chinese restaurant in Kingston. Once we were eating our wanton soup, I could no longer put it off. I had to know, or I would go crazy.

"So, please tell me, Pat. Are you staying or going?" I could hear the desperation in my voice, wanting and not wanting to know at the same time.

"Okay, are you ready, Richie?" She looked at me and then slowly closed both eyes.

I felt my heart drop out of my chest. She was talking, and I was trying to concentrate on what she was saying (something about how she felt it important giving school a second chance), but all I really heard myself thinking was, "She's going, she's going. Dandelion has failed again to hold onto another special person."

Pat was saying not to let it change things between us or spoil the moment. I had heard things like this before and set in motion my programmed internal dialogue, "Okay, if she's really going, I'll make it easy for her. I'll just bury my feelings deep inside." I carried on the rest of the conversation and even managed to smile a little, putting her leaving out of my mind.

Back at Dandelion, Pat jumped out of the car, eager to get back to her home. I began to unpack the car as Pat entered the house ahead of me. When she walked in, all the members were there, and a huge roar of joy bellowed out the door. It was such a spontaneous and loud response that Parrish broke out crying. Everyone was so happy to have her back.

The next couple of days were torture. I put Pat's leaving out of my mind as best I could and just tried to concentrate on my daily activities. I knew how I would feel once Pat left and I was dreading that. I had been in similar situations, but never to this extent.

Alison's activist friend, Christopher, came to visit the following week and really boosted the spirits of the community. He ended up having informal discussions with different members and counseled Pat as well.

After her talk with Christopher, something changed with Pat. I wasn't sure what it was, but Pat again started talking about Dandelion being her home and feeling that it wasn't time to leave yet.

My heart skipped a beat again, feeling frustrated at the same time. *Don't get me started again, Pat, please,* I was thinking. Then she told me that she wanted to have another talk with Christopher to clarify what she was really feeling.

I was in my bed reading when she returned to my room an hour later. She came in and lay down beside me, putting her arm over my waist. She then sat up, stared at me, and then smiled and winked at me. I stared at her for a long time, feeling the blood rapidly pulse through my veins. "Wait a minute, does that mean what I think it means, Pat?" But she was out of my room running down the hall, laughing.

The other big change that month was that Tango had decided to return to school and pursue his dream of becoming a lawyer. He would leave at the end of December. Even though that affected me deeply (another member we could not hold onto), I wanted Tango to leave with a ceremony honoring the time he had spent at Dandelion.

I rounded up Brian and Sean and together we brainstormed a while and came up with the idea that in honor of Tango, we would build a non-sexist toilet against the outside back wall of the farmhouse.

In the barn, we found an old cracked toilet seat, took it to the farmhouse and nailed it to the wall. We set it up so that it could fold down in case a woman wanted to use it. That was it. Men would just stand and aim against the ground below the upright toilet seat.

The day before Tango left, we had the unveiling ceremony. The toilet seat "memorial" was covered with an old sheet. It was late in the afternoon and the temperature had dropped into the single-digit numbers. I had asked Gordon to be the informal "mayor" who would give a speech about Tango's impact on the community and the significance of the memorial that would be left behind in his honor.

I chose Gordon because he had a great reputation as a critical thinker and philosopher. But he could sometimes belabor an intellectual point until he beat it into the ground. That was exactly what I was hoping he would do in his speech regarding Tango. Gordon delivered the goods.

As the fifteen members plus visitors gathered around the back of the farmhouse, Gordon droned on and on about the accomplishments Tango had given to Dandelion. "We will always remember and appreciate the "bio-wipes" (large green leaves) he had so generously collected in the summer and left in the bathroom. In addition, who could forget the "impression" he and Richie had left in the cement down in the driveway, and all the comedy routines that he, Richie, Sean and Brian had done over and over and over and over?"

After ten minutes, Gordon was still droning on about Tango and members were shivering by now and really starting to feel the effects of standing still in the freezing weather. The crowd grew restless and started yelling out, "Come *on*, Gordon, speed this *up*! We're freezing out here!"

Nevertheless, Gordon, playing his role as mayor to perfection, ignored them as if nothing was happening. Sean (a big fan of the Canadian Air Farce radio show), yelled out, "Eat it raw!" To which Gordon responded enthusiastically, "That's right, just what we need around here, more spirit, rah, rah, rah!"

Then Brian yelled out, "What is reality?" I piped in with, "I'm Spartacus!" The whole crowd began to yell out all kinds of irrelevant statements. Gordon took it all in stride and finally finished saying, "Whenever we use this memorial, we will be thinking of you, Tango. Thanks for all you've done and have a safe journey."

Then, with a great flourish, Gordon walked over to the memorial and pulled off the sheet. Members shouted and applauded, even though all they were staring at was an old, beat up toilet seat nailed to the wall. Then Gordon magnanimously stated, "I now declare the Tango Dandelion Memorial Toilet open for business." As most members scattered inside to get warm, Sean, Brian, Tango, Gordon, and I lined up to use the toilet. To my disappointment, however, not one woman seemed interested in testing out the seat.

January 1982

Pat had decided to become a member and the community joyously accepted her. Along with her, the other new members were Alison, Janet, Sean, John and I. John was a tall quiet man from Tennessee and his Southern accent had a very calming effect on the community.

It was wintertime, and the days were short, but the community continued to have an abundant amount of positive energy.

In mid-January, a rat invaded Dandelion. A few traps were set up to deal with the situation, but the rat seemed too smart for us.

One morning, while I was cooking my breakfast of two eggs, I went to the breadbox to get some bread to toast. The breadbox was old, and we used a string to hold the lid up. If it were not tied tight enough, a gap of about three inches was left open.

I began to pull down the large front lid that covered the breadbox and saw two eyes staring back at me from around the loaf of bread in the center of the box. "Whoa, a rat!" I immediately closed the lid and tied it shut.

Looking over at my eggs, I realized they were starting to burn. I quickly flipped the eggs onto my plate and then wrote on a sticky note, "Rat inside, do not open," and pasted it on the breadbox. I went to the living room to eat my breakfast.

A few minutes later, Brian entered the kitchen to cook his breakfast and saw the note on the breadbox. He came into the living room, "So, is there actually a rat inside the breadbox, Richie, or is this one of your wild jokes?"

I calmly replied, "Oh no, it's no joke. It's for real." I went back to eating my eggs and reading the newspaper.

As more communitarians came in for breakfast, and repeatedly asked if there really was a rat in the box, the whole thing morphed into a big, community issue. As a community, we now had to reach consensus on how to deal with the rat.

Questions flew. The meat-eaters speculated whether it would be safe to eat, which totally grossed out the vegetarians. Could we let it loose in the wild somewhere? If we did, would it come back? Should we destroy it? And if so, what would be the most humane way to do it?

Could we somehow rationalize killing it by saying rats were part of the food chain (for the cats) and let them have it? What if we opened the box from the third floor of Tamari, let the rat fall to the ground, and let the cats have it after that? What if we put the breadbox inside the freezer and left it there for a couple of hours? Suppose we brought the box to the shop and gassed the critter? All kinds of strategies were proposed and evaluated.

I finally declared that since I was the one who had discovered the animal, I would take responsibility for it. No one disagreed with that statement and I decided to drown it in the stream.

Pat accompanied me as I carried the box to the bridge and saw a two-inch layer of ice covering the stream. I put the box down, and Pat said, "I'll go get a broken stretcher, Richie." She returned and gave me the stretcher.

I pointed the sharp edge of the stretcher at the ice and smashed a large hole into it, then positioned the box so that the opening faced down towards the water.

I untied the string, and the bread and rat fell into the hole in the ice. The rat immediately came back up to the surface, and I beat it off with the stretcher. The rat turned away, swimming back under the ice, and it never returned.

We never saw Aqua Rat again, although some say, on a moonlit night, deep in winter, if you look closely enough at the stream, you just may catch a glimpse of the ghost of Aqua Rat.

Janet, Sean, Alison, (visitor in back), John, Isabelle, visitor, Mark, and Richie holding hands before dinner

Quest for Firewood

A film came out that year called *Quest for Fire* and made a big impact on the communitarians, but mostly on me. It depicted how our cave-dwelling ancestors might have lived and how sacred fire was in their lives.

After watching the film, I started referring to the firewood crew's goal as "Quest for Firewood." Moreover, we came up with new names for the piles of wood we gathered; a low amount was a "petite load," a medium amount was called a "shit load," and a full amount was a "beaver load."

In our zeal for firewood, a few communitarians accidentally ended up cutting down some trees on our neighbor's property. We were embarrassed about this and agreed to reimburse the Gainsekes for the wood we mistakenly took. It was the least we could do, as the Gainsekes had always been kind to us. Earlier that winter, they had graciously let us get fresh water from their faucets when our pipes froze.

Randy and Louis cut firewood

Spring 1982

March turned out to be a completely zany month for Dandelion. To combat cabin fever, the creative Dandelions came up with many memorable events.

The first one was celebrating St. Patty's Day. Sean wanted to honor his Irish roots and on March 17, large, green, paper shamrocks appeared everywhere—including the walls, hammock jigs, and milk buckets. He encouraged all members to wear and eat something green that day. To accomplish that, he put green food coloring in the milk and potatoes that night. Jane, who had just returned from Twin Oaks, topped off the day by importing a Twin Oaks tradition, presenting Sean with a green whipped cream pie in the face.

He also told Irish jokes all day long. His favorite was the one about the Texan who walks into a pub in Dublin and says, "I hear you Irish are pretty good drinkers. I'll bet five hundred American dollars to anyone who can drink ten pints of Guinness in a row." There is silence across the bar and no one takes him up on his bet. One man gets up and leaves.

A half-hour later the man returns and approaches the Texan and says, "Is the bet still on for the five hundred dollars for drinking ten Guinness in a row, sir?"

"It sure is, buddy. Do you think you can do it?"

"Let's see. Bartender line 'em up." The bartender pours the ten pints and the Irishman drinks every single one of them.

The Texan is quite impressed. "Well, I'll be, nice job," he says. Here is your five hundred."

"Thank you, sir."

Then the Texan says, "If you don't mind my asking, where did you go that half-hour you were gone from here?"

To which the Irishman says, "Well, I had to first go down to Murphy's pub to make sure I could do it."

The big event that day was that Sean had told everyone that he would be starring in a dramatic world-premiere three-act play that would take place that evening in the living room.

After a fabulous dinner of green potatoes, green milk and green cake, the dining tables were removed, and the living room was set up with the fifteen kitchen chairs facing the large window. Sean had emphasized that the play would start at precisely at eight p.m. He encouraged people to be on time so as not to miss any of the play.

Members began showing up at 7:45 and Janet, using a flashlight, escorted them to their seats. The whole community was present and excited to see what Sean had in store for them this time.

At precisely eight p.m. the houselights dimmed and Sean walked into the middle of the floor. He had a black cape over his shoulders and a black plastic mustache taped under his nose.

He turned to an imaginary figure and shouted, "Pay the rent, *pay the rent!*" He then ripped off the mustache, took the cape, wrapped it around his head (making a hood), and then turned the opposite way he was originally facing. Using a high-pitched female voice, he quivered and humbly said, "I can't pay the rent, I can't pay the rent."

Sean then turned, threw the cape on the floor, stood up boldly and said in a heroic, manly voice, "I'll pay the rent!"

He then turned to the audience and bowed profusely. The whole play had lasted less than twenty seconds. There was at first shock and confusion, which quickly turned into laughter and shouts of approval as we realized we had witnessed the entire play. Sean had pulled off another captivating event.

Three days later came the celebration of the spring equinox. This was the same year that Earth Day was celebrated around the world.

Dandelion was heated by wood in the farmhouse, Tamari and Sprout, with the goal of becoming less reliant on non-renewable resources such as oil and gas. Aduki had an oil heater to warm the workspace quickly when needed.

To ensure the best use of resources, every fall, the windows on the farmhouse and Aduki were covered with plastic sheeting. Some windows had see-through plastic, but most had a thicker, heavier plastic covering, that prevented a clear view through the window. (Tamari and Sprout had double-insulated windows, so no plastic was required.)

For fuel efficiency, this all seemed to work quite well. By the end of winter, though, not being able to see clearly out the windows just contributed to the oppressiveness, and March madness became a true phenomenon.

The morning of the Equinox I was in my bedroom listening to the song, *Age of Aquarius* on my radio. Reflecting back to my birthday celebration, I began singing *Age of a Hairy Ass* and got inspired.

Continuing to sing the words, I went out, found the other men in the community, and told them to meet me at my bedroom in ten minutes.

I then went off to Comedy Clothes, pulled out several ski masks, and returned to my room.

Five minutes later, six men showed up. "What's up, Richie?" asked Brian.

"I have a great idea."

The men groaned in unison. By this time, they had all learned to be cautious of my great ideas.

"What is it this time, Richie? Toilet seat covers made from tin cans?" Brian asked.

"No, no. Much better than that," I said, smiling, and continued, "You have all heard of streaking, right?" There were some uneasy nods around the room. "Well, we're on a commune and I believe it's time we tried it." Two of the men left, but Brian, Sean, John, and a visitor remained.

"Here's the plan. We are all sick of winter and all that plastic covering the windows, right? Well, I say it's the first day of spring and we should go and rip all that plastic off. We're close enough to warmer weather, right?" John, looking out the window saw the three inches of snow against it. He shook his head but said nothing.

I continued, "We go out wearing only boots and ski masks so no one can identify us, singing *Age of a Hairy Ass*. What do you say? Are you with me?"

The four remaining men shouted, "Hell, yeah!" Excited, we took off all our clothes, put on the ski masks, boots, and headed out the door. When we stepped outside there were three inches of snow on the ground and the temperature was just above freezing. The frigid air immediately caused certain body parts to shrivel, but, hell, we didn't care as we were having too much fun. We began singing *Age of a Hairy Ass*.

Brian said, "Hold on a second." He ran over to the farmhouse, picked up a banana, tied it to the side of his belt (which was the only thing he was wearing), and rejoined us.

We ran down to the hammock shop and burst through the door, joyfully singing our new mantra. Many of the women members were there busily weaving hammocks, having interesting conversations about women's liberation and racism. They took one look at us and almost in unison began shaking their heads in disbelief. Alison jokingly commented, loud enough for us to hear, "These are the men we are counting on to help us gain equality?" The women smiled and continued to weave their hammocks, intentionally ignoring the wild, rampaging men ripping off the plastic around the room.

Sean yelled out, "Come on, ladies, sing it with us!" However, the women just kept on weaving, so it was only we men who were singing, *Let the Sunshine In*.

After finishing our mission in the shop, we left and headed for the main farmhouse. Inside the farmhouse, after ripping off the plastic in the living room, we went running into the kitchen. The kitchen floor had just been washed, and John slipped and fell flat on his ass. This caused an immediate pile-up of our five naked bodies and we all laughed at the absurdity of the situation.

Brian's banana was crushed in the melee, and Sean slid into the table, causing the large bowl with the fruit in it to fall and spread its contents all over the floor. John picked up an apple, washed it off and began munching on it.

With our bodies now damp from the kitchen floor, but mission accomplished, we returned to my room to retrieve our clothes. We debriefed about what we had just done, and all agreed that since we had such a great time, it should be an annual occurrence.

After that, the real spring equinox celebrations began. Donald, his new girlfriend, Helena, and Robbie had all come for the weekend to celebrate.

At eleven a.m., the first event was the hoisting of the Earth Flag that my mom had so generously donated. Members gathered in front of the farmhouse and watched as Pat and I stood on the roof and hoisted the flag atop a small flagpole (that Robbie had helped build) on top of the farmhouse, where it could be seen for miles around.

In front of the farmhouse, Peggy had set a large steel bowl with water. Members then began making wishes for the planet and after each wish, would take a handful of water and throw it up into the air.

Then the fun began. First up was the Dandelion outdoor egg-relay event. (Dandelions had chosen the egg as the Pagan symbol of spring and returning fertility of Mother Earth.)

In honor of that, a "sacred" hard-boiled egg would be passed from member to member as it journeyed around Dandelion. Mark and Isabelle had planned several activities while the egg was making its journey. The first challenge was that the egg had to be held on a spoon in one's mouth the whole time. The second challenge was to do it in fewer than thirty minutes.

Mark making cheese

The relay began in the front of the farmhouse. Mark held the egg on a spoon in his mouth as the oven timer was set for thirty minutes. The whole community followed him as he walked to the solar shower where two plastic pails of water were waiting.

He carefully tilted his spoon and dropped the egg into the spoon John held in his mouth. The community held its breath and watched as John received the egg. He bent and lifted the pails and carried them to the cows in the barn.

Inside the barn, Gabriel received the egg onto his spoon and then shoveled a heaping of Chrissie's dung over the fence. Alison, on the other side of the fence, received the egg and then proceeded to haul a hefty bale of hay up to the woodpile outside the farmhouse. There, Robbie accepted the egg and then biked down to Aduki—all the while balancing the egg on the spoon in his mouth—and gave it to Bronwyn, who took the egg in her spoon and then went inside Aduki and wound two shuttles of rope.

The crowd was loudly cheering all the participants now, as time was running out to beat the clock. Bronwyn gave the egg to Janet, who snowshoed up the driveway and passed it onto Brian. Brian pulled Parrish on a toboggan to Tamari. There he gave it to Isabelle, who then shoveled off the walk. She passed it onto Donald, who then went down to the composting toilet and put a ceremonial portion of peat moss into it. He ran up to the third floor of Tamari where Helene waited spoon in mouth and hammer in hand. She climbed a ladder, hammered in a nail, and then rushed downstairs where I was eagerly waiting. I took the egg, picked up a hula-hoop, and hopelessly tried twirling it around my waist as I walked down to Sprout, balancing the egg in the spoon as I went.

When I got there, I then spooned-off the egg to Gordon who rolled the hula-hoop and carried a potty full of pee (donated to the cause by Isabelle) back up to the outside of Tamari, where Pat waited. She had the last leg of the race, and with two minutes remaining to beat the clock, the tension was really mounting.

She took the egg from Gordon and with difficulty walked slowly through the rungs of a ladder laid out on the ground. When she got to the last rung, she shoveled three rocks into a waiting wheelbarrow, pushed it to the front of the farmhouse and placed the egg gently into a waiting carton. The task was finished in just under thirty minutes, and the crowd cheered joyously.

The last event of the day (before the scrumptious, communal dinner feast), was the egg-rolling contest, which took place late afternoon in the living room. It was a race to see who could push a hard-boiled egg across the living room floor using just his or her nose, and it was open to any member who wished to compete. Sean witnessed the event and reported the following story in *Pappus*:

> What started out as a fun event quickly deteriorated into an almost barroom brawl. Said Richie, "I've seen rats behave better, with less conditioning." Richie was referring to the unbelievable events that shocked the egg-rolling world during the finals that startled spectators and athletes alike.
>
> As all followers of non-competitive egg rolling know, funky colored eggs must be pushed across a dirty carpet from one makeshift basket to another, using only one's nose. As in most non-competitive sports, pushing, shoving and general bloodletting are far from the call of the day,

except for what happened on this otherwise happy equinox.

The confusion began early, when the athletic participants refused to participate. Said one athlete: 'This is silly—I'm almost thirty.' Suddenly, out of nowhere, and for no apparent reason, two roller derby lacrosse-minded head-butting individuals dove to the carpet in a frenzy. Patski Pelikin, renowned for her keen peripheral vision and cute nose took the lead pushing her beautiful grade-C egg in a winding pattern along the carpet. Janet 'The Planet' took out her multi-colored souped-up 'chicken stopper' and hurriedly followed suit.

There are varying stories as to what happened next. Some state that Pat accidentally stomped on Janet's egg in her excitement of having found a dime on the carpet. Others claim that Janet intentionally caused a scene in order to substitute a soft-boiled egg under Pat's nose. Due to the cloud of dust that arose from the unswept carpet, nobody will ever be certain of what occurred on that sad day in the non-competitive kingdom.

After several screams and jostles of excitement, the crowd rushed to the floor to preserve the spirit of the event. Everybody (but the two rebel-rousers) converged on the basket of unbroken eggs and communally and delicately in sweet co-operation, transported the eggs across the carpet in harmony as the sounds of eggshells cracking rang out beside them. The day ended with a fabulous meal, vegetables or something."

The Dandy Awards

Both Sean and I were enthusiastic fans of the cinema. We continued to bounce off favorite movie lines with each other, and came up with the idea of having an annual recognition dinner (like the Academy Awards), to honor the accomplishments of individuals at Dandelion. In addition, instead of winning "Oscars," members would win "Dandys."

We got all excited about this and it was all we talked about for weeks. We even planned the Dandelion Awards Dinner to occur on the same night as the Academy Awards.

In my spare time, I made some trophies made up of recycled tuna cans turned upside down, which I used as a base. On top of that, I welded stick figures made from leftover scrap tin cans.

Sean and I brainstormed over what categories we would have to win trophies. The main categories we came up with were: most overplayed record, machine that gave us most trouble, grossest dinner conversation, best response to an emergency, best director of a project, most overworked saying, most aversive job, most embarrassing moment for the community, best burper, and most unusual occurrence. We then made copies of all the categories and had people anonymously vote for the winner in each category.

The night of the awards came and the whole community gathered in the living room to see who had won what. Using a small cardboard tube as a microphone, Sean began, "Welcome to the first annual Dandelion Awards. We know all of you are as excited about this event as Dicky and I are."

Members applauded and smiled, and someone yelled out, "Eat it raw!" To which Sean replied, "Yup, that's right, rah, rah, rah. Without further ado, let's go to the first nomination. Alison, if you please."

Alison stepped up to the front of the table and said, "I'm *sooooo* excited to be here. Feels like I'm in Hollywood or something. Okay, the first category is: Most overplayed record or tape." She then proceeded to name the nominations. After stating the last nomination, she picked up the sealed

Sean Purcell weaving a hammock

envelope, slowly opened it and said, "The most overplayed record or tape at Dandelion Community this past year goes to…Barde."

The audience clapped and cheered. Since Alison was the biggest fan of Barde, Sean stepped up and said, "Alison will accept the award herself since she played it most often."

Alison accepted the award with a big smile on her face. 'I'm so excited! Thank you! Thank you! I'm gonna go play Barde right now."

I announced the next category, which was "Best Director of a Project." This award easily went to Larry for his tremendous work done on Sprout and he stepped up to receive his Dandy and humbly said, 'I accept this award in honor of the current children at Dandelion and to the future children of Dandelion. Thank you."

The audience loved that line and responded appropriately with loud clapping, whistles and shouted, 'You rock, Larry!"

"Way to go, Larry!"

"Thanks again, Larry!"

The next category was "Weirdest color room." Sean won this category for the color "green-sort of," and I called him up to accept his award.

But wait, what was this? Coming to the podium was Sean dressed up in the shaggy black coat. He waddled into the middle of the room, took the fake microphone and said in a serious voice, "Hello. My name is 'Running Hog' and I represent all the oppressed groundhogs around this community." He then upped the tempo and began a rant about how the groundhogs of this community were not treated as equals. "You call yourselves egalitarian? Well, what about US? Your centuries of oppression have kept us groundhogs underground for too long." (A loud, collective groan was heard from the audience.) Sean continued. "Things need to change, and they need to change now!" And with that final statement, he grabbed the trophy and stormed out of the room.

The categories and winners flew by. One of the trickier categories was "Most embarrassing moment for the community." Tango won this award for that hot day in August, when he was washing tin cans on the side of the farmhouse (in the nude) and thought no one would see him.

However, some older women from Enterprise stopped by to buy some tinnery and he was the first person they found.

Tango just slipped on his shorts and escorted them to the shop. Tango also won "Most unusual occurrence of the year."

Pat and I won "Best response to an emergency" for the way we dealt with Aqua Rat.

The night ended with another dance down at Aduki and afterwards everyone proudly carried their awards to their rooms.

Cruise Missile Blockade

Not all was fun and games for the community that spring. On the serious side, in late March, Sean and Janet joined an affinity group in Kingston who joined other activists in blocking the road to Litton Systems Industry, which was responsible for building cruise missiles. (The cruise missile was intended as a first strike attack weapon, not a defensive weapon.)

Sean wrote about his experience in *Pappus*:

"When we arrived, it was agreed that there would be five waves of protesters. (This was among 200 people who had shown up for the protest.) The first protesters lay down in front of the entrance to the plant. The police arrived and arrested a bunch of us on trespassing charges. I was arrested, and Janet tried to be arrested as well, but the ever-so-polite police officers just kept picking her up and moving her to the side. I was released later that day on my own recognizance. We all find our own battles against the machinery of war."

Tapping the Maple Trees

We processed maple syrup from the trees grown on our property and there was talk of that becoming a possible new industry. But as we would need forty quarts of maple sap to produce one quart of syrup, the economics of scale made that adventure cost prohibitive. Nonetheless, we were committed to make enough for our own consumption.

In early April, Pat and I were assigned to switch the buckets on the maple trees that were now abundantly producing sap. The sun was shining brightly with a hint of spring in the air. There was still snow on the ground, but small patches of green grass were beginning to appear in various places.

It was early in the afternoon when we started out and the temperature had shot up to the mid-sixties. It was so warm we did not need jackets.

The maple trees were located out beyond the far fields behind the farmhouse, where there were no public roads, and we had complete privacy.

We were carrying empty buckets as we headed out across the snow-covered fields, talking about the gorgeous weather and our upcoming plans for the summer. We were hoping to do some camping in one of the local providence parks.

Pat had her luxurious hair tied up in two braids, with the tails falling onto the front of her chest. Half way across the field, she stopped and put her buckets down. I stopped as well and was mesmerized as I watched her slowly unbutton her blue and white plaid shirt and then tie it around her waist. She was wearing no undershirt or bra and now her braids were hanging down over her perfectly formed breasts. The way her hair and skin contrasted with the white snow and blue sky was breathtaking. "Ah, that feels better," she said. She then picked up the buckets and we resumed walking across the fields.

The effect this simple action had on me was forever burned into my memory, as I was now madly in love with this renaissance woman. My heart soared like the eagle.

In my wild imagination, I was now joyously walking with a Native American woman and humbled to be in her presence. I temporarily forgot what we were doing or where we were headed, and kept saying to myself, "I am so lucky, so lucky, so lucky to have met this gem of a woman."

After we had switched the buckets on the trees, we headed back to the farmhouse with buckets full of sap. I causally said to Pat, "Seeing you take your shirt off in the middle of that field is the coolest thing I have ever seen a woman do."

She smiled back and said, "Wish I could do that more often. What an awesome feeling having the wind blow on my skin."

Devon's Birth

The biggest news that spring was the birth of Devon. She was delivered at Kingston Hospital with no complications. The community had many of the same celebrations for Devon as we did for Parrish. Members took turns making wishes for her and her life journey. In addition, it again added that special energy to the community that only a newborn can bring.

Devon

My 31st Birthday

The following month was my birthday, and this was to be a less-intense party than the year before with *Age of a Hairy Ass* and the French jugglers (who had no balls), and dancing naked. Could anything ever top that party? No, nothing could top that. This party was to be a quiet gathering for Dandelion and celebrated in a more appropriate way for a mature man turning thirty-one.

This year, I took no part in planning the celebration. If there were to be anything, I would leave that up to the other members. I heard that a cake had been baked in my honor, and we were all to gather in the living room at 8 p.m. That was all I knew.

That evening I was on the living room couch reading the newspaper waiting for the others to show up and Pat sat next to me reading *Ms. Magazine*. A few minutes later all the members and a couple of visitors showed up.

Janet went to the kitchen and returned carrying a large double-layered chocolate cake and placed it on the table. I noticed that oddly, no one brought in either plates or forks. Pat said, "We hope this is a birthday celebration you will never forget, Richie." She kissed me on the cheek.

Brian said, "Yeah, Sundance, get ready for a special treat!"

Larry made a short speech about how much everyone appreciated my commitment to Dandelion and what a wild and crazy person I was and how much people appreciated my sick sense of humor. He then lit the candles on the cake. Everyone sang *Happy Birthday* and I blew out the candles.

Larry then made an unusual request, "Richie, you are here among some of your closest friends and we have a special celebration for you tonight." He then placed one of the kitchen chairs in the middle of the room and continued, "So, will you first please sit in this chair and take off your shirt and shoes." I got all excited and complied, thinking, "Is this the beginning of the orgy I have so long fantasized about?"

Next Larry said, "Now, please take off your pants and socks." I got more excited and did what Larry requested. I looked around the room at all the smiling faces to see if my suspicion of an orgy might be confirmed, but if there was to be an orgy, no one else seemed to be showing it on his or her face.

Larry continued, "Now, for the last part, would you please remove your undershirt and underpants and lie on the floor?"

Summer 1982

June turned out to be another spectacular month. There were so many new visitors along with all the new projects started. With the increase of long-term visitors and potential new members, we decided that having an extra outhouse would help with preventing the septic systems in both the farmhouse and Sprout from overflowing.

Pat and I were assigned eighty labor hours to build a two-seater outhouse to be located halfway between Tamari and Sprout. Along with help from Billy (the communitarian from Chrysalis Community who had returned for a two-week visit), we brainstormed several designs.

"I always thought an outhouse should be designed with a window overlooking some peaceful scenery. That way, one could be in a relaxed mood and not need to strain while pooping. So, I suggest we include a large window in our design," I said.

Pat said, "That sounds like a good idea, Richie. I would also like to see us design it with a partition in the middle, so visitors and members don't end up sitting next to some total stranger."

An experienced carpenter who had helped build several buildings in his own community, Billy said, "Those sound like great ideas. I also think that we should shingle the top of the outhouse and have a plastic pipe connected to the bottom to allow for ventilation and composting." We all agreed on the final design blueprint.

Part of the plan was to dig a hole that was six feet long, four feet wide and eight feet deep. After that was accomplished, we found some discarded railroad crossties (confiscated from the local train track) and laid them along the outline of the hole. This would be the foundation for the rest of the outhouse.

With the left-over lumber from Sprout, we put together four walls and a roof. On the east side of the building, we built the frame for a large three-by-five window. That way there would be some nice morning light coming into the window with a view of open fields. Our neighbors the Fenwicks heard about the project and they donated two old toilet seats they had in their barn.

When the outhouse was completed, we were very proud of our work. Before we officially opened it for business, we had a small cocktail party there to celebrate the newest addition to Dandelion. In honor of the Fenwicks, we named the outhouse after them.

Fall 1982

In October, new member Cath joined the community. She was a big fan of John Lennon and in honor of his legacy, wanted to do something special for John's birthday on October 9. She proposed that we have a campfire, that people come dressed up as a Beatles' song, and then sing each of those songs.

Members loved the idea and on the evening of John's birthday, we gathered around a small campfire next to the farmhouse. We did come dressed up as various Beatles songs and some of the costumes were quite creative.

Sean, with two straws sticking out of his nose, came as *The Walrus*. I kept tripping over the ground portraying *Day Tripper*. Gordon showed up with his arm in a sling and people finally guessed he was *If I Fell*.

Another new member named Sean showed up with a bunch of maps protruding from his pockets and he was *Nowhere Man*. Cath arrived wearing a creative mélange of dress, shawl and scarves expressing *Lady Madonna*.

The positive energy present that night was palpable, and the spirit of Lennon was there as the communitarians sang his songs, drank beer and danced around the fire.

The sad news that Fall was that Jane and Larry had decided to move to Toronto, taking Parrish with them. They were both interested in becoming full-time midwives and would be working with a midwife in Toronto, attending births and learning a lot.

This news was greeted with much sorrow and disappointment. (I got a sense of what members must have felt when I left.)

As in many other communities, when a long-term member reached his or her seventh year (which both Jane and Larry were in), it was a time for much reflection and change.

After having Jane and Larry's separate clearness meetings, we realized their choice would be best for both of them and wished them well.

However, this news had a deep impact on me. It now left only Gordon who was among the founding members. I also knew with Jane and Larry gone, we would suffer an immense loss of skills, knowledge and history.

Everyone was smiling and cheering, but I was thinking, *Now hold on here. If this is supposed to be an actual orgy, why am I the only one taking clothes off?* I began to feel a little uncomfortable with that last request as my idea of an orgy began fading. What was going on here?

What made me feel uncomfortable was that there were two new visitors present (one of them a woman) who I had only met the day before. Then Brian said, "Aw, come on Sundance, we've all gone skinny-dipping together. We know what you look like, man." I took a big breath, removed my undershirt and underpants and lay down on the floor, to cheers and applause.

Larry then took the cake off the table, squished it onto my face, down onto my chest, and said, "Okay, whoever is a true friend of Richie, step right up here and lick this cake off him!" Eight members strode towards me with big smiles on their faces. I could not believe what was happening and just watched as people licked the cake off me.

Only in community, I thought to myself. *Only in community.*

Craft Show Madness

This time of year also found the community gearing up for all the holiday craft shows coming up. There was a giant push in progress for the making of as many hammocks, hammock chairs and tin cans as possible.

As hammock manager, Gordon oversaw finding members who would be good at selling at the wholesale and retail level. He realized that most of the members were not really business types, but he had a good sense of whom he could count on.

He approached me one day while I was sweeping the floor in the tinnery. "So, Richie, it's that time of year again and we are looking for some folks to take on our big craft shows. I was wondering if you and maybe Pat might be interested in doing some together?"

I paused a second, realizing the major commitment Gordon was asking of Pat and me. I had done holiday craft shows before and knew the craft shows at malls usually went from ten in the morning to ten at night, seven days a week. There was also the hassle of finding cheap places to stay along with limited money budgeted for food. Some of the shows lasted weeks.

"Yeah, sure, Gordon, I would be happy to help out the community."

"That's great, Richie. Thank you. I knew I could count on you. Do you think Pat would go for it as well? I think you two would make a dynamite team."

"Well, I would have to talk to her about it, but I think she would be up for it, Gordon. Give her a chance to see more of Canada, meet some new people. What fairs are you thinking of?"

"There's the big one in Toronto and one out in Windsor. Toronto goes for one week and the other for two weeks. I was also thinking that maybe on the slow days Pat could stay with the booth and you could do some wholesale marketing at local stores in the area. What do you think?"

"Sure, Gordon, I'll check with Pat and get back to you."

I talked with Pat later that day and was relieved when she said, "That sounds great, Richie. I'd be happy to do them with you. I know I've only done a couple of weekend shows in Kingston, but this sounds like it could be an adventure."

"Well, just so you know, Pat, these aren't your usual two-day shows. The shows in malls can be brutal, sitting under fluorescent lights for hours, seven days a week. Then we have to find places to stay, usually with friends of community or other craftspeople we meet at the shows. There won't be that much money for eating out, either. On the plus side, we can build up a lot of overtime quota and earn some extra vacation time."

"I understand Richie, and I think it would be great to do it together. Count me in."

We did end up doing those two shows and for the most part, managed to enjoy ourselves, but there were issues that came up. For starters, at the one-week craft show in Toronto, in mid-November, it was eight p.m. and we still had not figured out where we would stay that night. None of the other craft-show vendors had offered us a place to crash, and we were considering sleeping in the van that night. We had brought sleeping bags, but it would be cold that night and we needed to make sure we got a good night's sleep.

Luckily, at that time a customer stopped by and was very interested in buying two of our large hammocks. I perked up and said, "Well, just so you know, we are open to bartering and are actually looking for a place to stay for the week. We would be happy to trade two hammocks for that. We have our own food, so just need a room to sleep in."

The woman thought a moment and said, "Well, this just might be your lucky day. My husband and I have a small room in our basement, which just has a bed in it. It even has its own bathroom. For two hammocks, you would be welcome to stay there for the week if you want and we live just two miles from here."

Relieved, I smiled and said, "That sounds terrific. You will hardly notice we are there."

For the rest of the week, the routine we worked out was we would both work the booth together in the mornings and evenings. In the afternoons (with hammocks in hand), I would visit various businesses around town that might be interested in purchasing hammocks wholesale, mostly furniture and swimming pool stores. Late in the afternoon, I would return and give Pat a break.

I had never done wholesale marketing before, so Gordon had coached me on what to say. On my first contact (at a pool store where we had done business before), I went into the store practicing my speech and upon meeting the manager said, "Hi, I'm Richie from Dandelion Community."

Before I could continue, the owner said, "Dandelion Community? You got any hammocks with you? I'll take ten if you got 'em."

I could hardly believe my ears and said, "Sure, yes sir, I'll be right back." I practically skipped out the door. "Man, this is going to be so easy," I thought to myself. But as I found out later, going cold turkey to other stores did not produce the same results.

When I returned to the mall later that afternoon, I was so happy to see Pat and share how my first wholesale experience went. She was happy to see me and shared that she had sold two hundred dollars' worth of cans and hammocks. We hugged each other tightly and kissed each other passionately. We were off to a great start.

The following day, while I was out making cold calls, the mall manager (an older gentleman in his late fifties), approached Pat and said, "Pardon me, Pat, but I need to speak with you regarding mall agreements around craft shows."

"Sure, what is it?"

"Well, it seems like you and Richie are just doing too much (he fumbled for the right words) well, public displays of affection. We got a complaint from one of the store managers and I need to ask you to tone it down a bit. I personally have nothing against it, but we need to respect the wishes of our regular customers."

Pat couldn't believe it. Out of all the things to notice (drinking, swearing, inappropriate dress, etc.) someone was raising such an innocent issue. "Okay, I will talk with Richie about it and we can keep an eye on that."

"Thanks so much, Pat. Truly appreciated and best of luck with the show," he said with relief in his voice.

Later, when I returned (with no success that day selling hammocks) Pat gave me a shortened kiss and explained the situation. "Well, you are not going to believe what we got feedback on today. Seems like we are doing too much of PDA. Can you believe it?"

I was stunned, but then started smiling. "Well, how about that. First time in my life that has ever happened."

"Me, too."

We did "tone it down" a bit after that, but we made up for it at night when we were alone. When I was at the mall, I sometimes blindfolded myself and then wove hammocks on the small jig we had in front of our booth to attract customers. This tended to attract children, who brought their parents along.

After a week of fluorescent lights, strange beds, and the occasional snacks from the mall food court, we were very happy to return to Dandelion.

Spring 1983

As usual, spring brought a lot of changes for Dandelion. On the plus side, Dandelion picked up some interesting new members—Bede and Chantal from Quebec, Lewis from New York, Rene (a professional violinist) from Mexico, Alice (who changed her name to "Louis"), and Randy Friesen, the construction worker who had visited before.

On the minus side, Jane's leaving (along with Parrish and Larry), had a profound impact on Gordon and Peggy. With Devon now walking and talking, they had been thinking more seriously about the advantages of a larger community.

Lewis

After weeks of weighing the pros and cons of big versus small, they finally came to a decision. They posted a paper saying they would leave Dandelion and move to Twin Oaks at the end of May.

This was another blow to the community. With Jane gone, and now Gordon and Peggy leaving, there would be immense holes to fill. Gordon had been hammocks manager for seven years and Peggy had been Dandelion's accountant for three years, not to mention their strong commitment to the communal movement, from which Dandelion had so benefited.

At their clearness meetings, they both stated that they were looking for a larger community and felt it could offer more for Devon. Many great memories and best wishes were expressed.

They had one request and that was for the donation of the Volkswagen bug, so they could travel to Twin Oaks. (Dandelion had picked up an old Volkswagen for $400 last year.) It would certainly cut down the expenses and make for an easier trip for Devon.

There was a big discussion regarding the Volkswagen, and Gordon and Peggy were asked to step outside for fifteen minutes.

I said, "Well, considering all the time and energy Gordon has put into the community for seven years, including helping fund the original $10,000 down payment on the land, I think it is a reasonable request. Moreover, Peggy with her great accounting skills has also saved the community thousands of dollars."

One member responded, "Yeah, but what about our commitment to equality? What if everyone requested something like this?"

Brian spoke up and said, "That's a good point. The way I talk about it, though, is that the car would almost be the total cost of three bus tickets to Virginia. Besides, we hardly ever use the bug. We bought it as a spare in case we ever really needed it. Maybe we could regard it as a going-away present?" The community reached consensus and agreed to let Gordon and Peggy have the car.

For the next two weeks, we helped Peggy and Gordon prepare for their departure. It was an emotional time for everyone.

When the day came for them to leave, Gordon was stoic and unemotional. Pat and I walked him, Peggy, and Devon to the car. We hugged Peggy and Devon and when we turned to hug Gordon, he was already in the car.

I went over, pulled him out, and gave him one more hug. "Thanks for all you have done for Dandelion, Gordon. We'll really miss you." Gordon just nodded and returned to the car.

I had my arm around Pat and tears in my eyes as I watched them drive down the driveway. I was now the last behaviorist at Dandelion and the only one left who had known all the original members.

I began thinking again, about where all the pioneer behaviorists were and where the dream had gone. I thought about that the rest of the summer.

Playing in the barn: Brian, Parrish, Chelsea, Raphy and Jeremy

Summer 1983

We gradually adjusted to the loss of Peggy, Gordon, and Devon. Although it was just not the same, the community had all the positive energy of the new members to help Dandelion continue to flourish.

Live music seemed to be the dominant force that summer. You could often hear Rene and Alison playing their violins, sometimes in beautiful duets. Randy often played his mandolin on the front porch in the evenings, with me playing along on guitar.

There were always new visitors who joined the music scene. In addition, all the musicians gladly offered to teach other members how to play their various instruments, which members often took them up on.

Randy playing mandolin

Louis

Rene

Lost in Translation

As usual, Dandelion had many international visitors that summer, but there was one the community (and especially I), would never forget. He was from Japan and his name was "Masa," but in accordance with Japanese custom (to show respect), everyone referred to him as "Masa San."

Masa San had come from a small Japanese farming co-operative located in Northern Japan. He was a very friendly gentleman and immediately made a lasting impression on the community. He also spoke fluent English, which was a big plus.

In my quest to expand my knowledge of Japanese words (that I had mostly learned watching the TV series *Shogun*), I sat down next to Masa San during lunch one day and told him I was interested in learning some particular Japanese words. Being a typical, immature male, I wanted to learn the names of certain body parts.

Members who were sitting at the same table immediately became a little curious because they never knew what I had in mind.

Masa San was eating his tofu soup and salad as I casually asked, "So, Masa San, can you please tell me, in medical terms, what the Japanese word is for penis?"

Masa San seemed to take the question in stride as if it were part of a normal, everyday conversation. That was because Masa San thought I had asked about the word "peanuts," but was not quite sure, so he asked for clarification.

"You mean the kind you put in your mouth?"

I was quite surprised by that remark, misunderstanding that Masa San was thinking of food items you put in your mouth, while I was thinking of something entirely different. I was also thinking, *Geez, is that kind of event so common in Japan that was the first thing Masa San could think of for a clarifying example? Maybe I should move to Japan.*

An awkward silence enveloped the table as members held their breath, waiting for my reply. After contemplating the best way to answer Masa San, I replied, (with a grin on my face), "Well, yeah, sometimes—if you're lucky."

The whole table burst out laughing. People began shaking their heads in disbelief. Masa San was still confused, so I pointed to my crotch. Masa San then caught on and laughed out loud, too.

Brian said, "He's done it again—somehow managed to bridge two completely different cultures with humor."

After clearing up the miscommunication, Masa San then gave me the correct word I was looking for, *Dankon*.

After that conversation, I felt I could talk about anything with Masa San. A short time later, while weaving hammocks, I commandeered him for another Japanese translation. This time it was to translate the erotic moans of Yoko Ono on the last album John Lennon ever recorded (*Double Fantasy*).

When my turn came for music, I put on the song *Kiss, Kiss, Kiss* with Yoko Ono erotically moaning, and I casually said, "Masa San, I was always curious as to what Yoko was actually saying. Can you please translate for me?" I then turned up the volume really loud, to help.

Since it was summertime, all the shop windows were wide open and now the whole community had the privilege of listening to the moans of Yoko Ono. People stopped picking tomatoes in the garden and looked at each other. The cow popped out of the barn and shook her head.

Nevertheless, inside the shop, Masa San was taking his mission very seriously. His ear was next to the speaker and was earnestly listening to every moan breathlessly being emitted by Yoko.

"Hold me," Masa San said. "Touch me." Masa San kept his composure throughout the whole translation, appropriate for a gentleman from the Far East. After Yoko Ono was finished with her performance, I found myself breathing a little faster. I thanked Masa San and told him I was going to the pool to cool off.

Brian checking out the pool

That summer Pat had been in contact with Sandhill Community (the Federation community located in Missouri), regarding their request for labor exchange in September to help with their sugar cane harvesting.

Sandhill was a small community of five adults and one child who made their living through organic farming. They grew sugar cane to make molasses and had dozens of bee hives from which they sold honey.

Pat had been feeling the need to get away from Dandelion and had talked with me about it. "I don't know, Richie. I feel like things are piling up on me around here and just need a real break from Dandelion. In addition, I'm starting to realize there is so much I want to do with my life and don't think the community can provide for it. It's frustrating."

"Yeah, I know what you mean, Pat. For me it has been so different since Jane and Gordon left. I also miss the energy of Peggy and Larry and the kids. But the biggest thing is that I feel we have permanently lost our behavior emphasis."

"Well, we're still having behavior meetings though. That counts for something, right?"

"Yeah, I know, but still, there is something missing. Who lives here now that understands the difference between negative reinforcement and punishment? Or is even passionate about behaviorism?"

"Oh, Richie, I understand, there has been so much change for both of us here lately. So many people have come and gone."

"Yeah, I try to keep optimistic, but I just don't know. Other things are starting to bother me that I wasn't aware of before."

"Like what?"

"I just need more personal space. I'm tired of sharing the bathroom all the time, and I wish I had a larger bedroom."

"I understand that as well." Pat was silent for a few moments and then said, "Richie, I want you to know that I've been thinking more seriously about going back to school. I want to do more with my life than weave hammocks and milk cows, and I don't think it would be possible to live here and attend school at the same time." Pat sighed.

We talked more and agreed it would be a wise move for both of us to get away for a while and get the chance to see what Sandhill was like. We also thought it would be another great adventure. Therefore, we requested a month's labor exchange with Sandhill in September and the community agreed.

First, we had to decide how we were going to get there. With little personal spending money, we decided to try hitchhiking. Luckily, Tango had come back for a short visit before he returned to school in Ohio. He was able to take us to his college, where we stayed overnight. The following day, he dropped us off at the interstate exit. It took us two days of hitchhiking, but we finally reached Sandhill.

At that point, Sandhill only had the original small farmhouse, which was their main residence building, and currently all members had their own bedrooms. So, Pat and I were asked to set up our pup tent in the backyard.

The members of Sandhill included four of the original founding members, Laird, Ann, Stan, and Grady. They had a new member, Clarissa, and Ceilee, the six-year-old community child. Another visitor, Jake, on labor exchange from Twin Oaks, was staying in a small shed out behind the main farmhouse.

Sandhill had forty acres of land, used mostly for growing sugar cane. They also had four small gardens where they grew their own vegetables and soybeans. Construction on a new twelve-bedroom residence building was nearing completion.

Their diet included as many organic whole foods as possible. Most meals consisted of whole-wheat products, brown rice, vegetables and fiber. My digestive system was not accustomed to this diet and I sometimes ended up visiting the outhouse two or three times a day. These visits cleared out my system entirely.

A small pond located across from the farmhouse was a true blessing on those hot summer days. As at Dandelion, people using the pond usually went skinny-dipping. However, the only drawback Sandhill folk forgot to mention was that if you were out in the water with an inner tube, the fish would come up and nip at the hair on your butt. "What was that?" I asked myself when that first happened. Worried it might be a snapping turtle, I immediately headed for shore.

When I later asked Laird about it, he smiled and said, "Oh, so sorry, Richie. We should have warned you about the biting fish, nothing to worry about."

"Easy for you to say, Laird, but I'm not used to having fish bite my ass."

While we waited for the sugar cane to ripen, Pat and I worked in the garden and on the new building. Then the day came when the sugar cane was finally ready for harvesting. All the community members and visitors got on the old flatbed truck and headed out into the fields.

When we reached the field, Ann instructed the visitors on how to use a machete on the sugar cane, "You grab the cane stalk at the very bottom and just swiftly cut it. It usually takes just one swipe, but some of the larger ones might take two or three. Please remember to be aware of others around you when you swing the blade. We don't want to lose any more members." She paused and then grinned and we heard a twitter of laughter.

We began walking down our assigned rows, bending each stalk over, and then cutting it at the base. We would retrieve the stalks after we had finished the rows and load them into the wagon.

Stan began singing *The Midnight Special* and everyone joined in. "Well, you get up in the morning and it's the same old thing. Say anything about it, you get in trouble with the man. Let the Midnight Special, shine its light on me. Let the Midnight Special, shine its ever-loving light on me." That really boosted the mood and the band of workers began singing other songs, such as *Old Man River* and *Tis a Gift to be Simple*.

We worked quickly, finished the field by noon, and filled the flatbed truck with hundreds of sugar cane stalks. Grady drove the truck back as the rest of us walked back to the farmhouse to feast on a very filling lentil soup that Laird had made. We returned to another field after lunch and finished that one by late afternoon. We cleared the rest of the fields over the next five days.

At night, the fun really started. The cane stalks were inserted into the cane press to squeeze out the juice, which was collected in large white plastic pails at the bottom of the press. To insure the highest quality juice, the canes were pressed as soon as they returned from the fields. This process often lasted into the middle of the night. I got up to pee one night and saw Stan over by the press still inserting the canes. There was a lantern hanging from a tree, and he looked like an elfin creature.

Once the pails were full, we brought them to the Sugar Shack, a small building with a long metal trough inside it. A small fire continuously heated the trough and the juice was emptied into it.

Once the juice began to boil, it turned into molasses and was poured into individual jars. By the time we had finished, the community had processed more than five hundred jars of molasses.

During this time Pat and I seriously began talking about our future. One night, as she sat outside our tent looking up at the stars, Pat said, "You know Richie, being away from Dandelion these past couple of weeks has really had an impact on me."

"Yeah. Me, too."

"There are so many things I love about Dandelion, but it is just not the same place anymore."

"I know, Pat. Have you gained any more clarity?"

"I think so. I want to do something in women's health. You know I have a passion for that, and I just don't see that happening at Dandelion, at least not in the foreseeable future. In addition, being here at Sandhill made me realize how much bureaucracy there is at Dandelion. Filling out petty cash slips, filling out labor sheets, tracking down who made long-distance phone calls to take that money out of his or her allowance, etc. Here at Sandhill they just do what needs to be done and don't keep track of it. When you need money for something you just take it out of the cash box and the same thing for phone calls. It all seems to work fine."

"Yeah, well, maybe having so few members makes it easier."

"I understand that, and it just seems that it works better here."

Pat paused for a moment, and then continued. "At Dandelion the way labor is assigned always seems so unrealistic. We always underestimate how long certain projects will take, so I often feel like I'm rushing through my work. It does not fit reality."

I nodded. I had experienced the same thing ever since my first week at Dandelion.

"What else?"

"Currently I don't feel like I have any real close friends. You are the only one I share with how I'm really doing. I get along fine with most members, but it is just not the same community it was two years ago. Also, every time I want to do something extra, like take an art course outside the community, the decision must be made by the community. I'm tired of having the things I want to do be under the control of the group."

I sighed. I had heard all these arguments before and realized it was all about the tradeoffs—standard of living versus expansion.

"What about you, Richie? Have you reached any more clarity?"

"Yeah. I agree with all you've said, Pat, and I'm starting to feel the same way. Dandelion seems so different to me ever since Jane and Gordon left. I'm the only member now who identifies as a behaviorist. Along with that, I'd like to see long-term payoffs for people who make a lifetime commitment to Dandelion. We don't have any real plan in place to keep people here over time. If someone stays for a few years, then leaves and comes back later, he or she is treated the same way. There is no real incentive or pension plan in place for members to stay longer. I realize Dandelion is a new social system and is still struggling, but we need to find a way to keep long-term members."

Pat nodded.

I continued, "I've always wondered why we have such a hard time attracting new members, let alone behaviorist ones. I think it's because we have come to define ourselves so narrowly."

"What do you mean?"

"As I see it, we describe ourselves as a non-smoking vegetarian behaviorist community located in a rural setting. Because of that, we tend to weed out smokers, meat-eaters, non-behaviorists, etc. And we are poor, at least financially."

Pat nodded and said, "What else?"

"Well, I don't know if it's a function of getting older, but as I mentioned before, I just feel the need to have more personal space. I've been getting tired of having to share the living room, kitchen, and bathroom all the time. In addition, even when I go to my room to get away, that seems not enough for me lately.

"Then there's the issue of food preferences. I've enjoyed the food at Dandelion for the most part, but sometimes I just don't feel like eating what's for supper that night. On top of that is our low allowances. If I want to go into Kingston for dinner, that would wipe out two months of allowance saved up. Then I couldn't afford a bus ticket to visit my parents. Moreover, I agree with you about our limited work options. I always saw myself eventually teaching a course on behavior psychology somewhere or working with people with disabilities—maybe even getting an advanced degree."

"I understand what you mean, Richie."

I nodded, "There's one more thing, Pat. I always thought there would come a point where the Federation would have a much stronger impact on local as well as national politics. That we'd be large enough to affect the direction society was going in, even if we only bent that direction slightly. That just seems to be a pipe dream now—or something that might happen, but at a much later time."

Pat nodded, "Well, maybe that will eventually happen, Richie. Who knows? At least you have gotten the chance to experiment with your own life, yes?" She smiled.

I said, "Yes, I've also gotten the chance to meet you, Pat." I leaned over and kissed her. We continued talking inside our tent way into the night, trying to clarify what our next step would be.

October 1983

By the time we returned to Dandelion, our minds were made up. We would post our leaving papers and leave at the end of October. Where we were going next was not clear.

Billy had invited us to visit Chrysalis Community in Indiana, right outside of Bloomington. Chrysalis was a land co-op, where people shared the land but each person or couple had their own house. That might be more of what we were looking for.

Indiana University was also located in Bloomington, and Pat knew they offered a degree in nursing. Perhaps that could work out for Pat, and maybe I could get an advanced degree in psychology.

There was much sadness in the community when members heard about our plans. Everyone knew they would miss us. We had made Dandelion such a fun place to live, and an era was truly ending.

In my last couple of days there, I reflected on what had initially drawn me to join Dandelion. I'd felt I was making a lifelong commitment to build a Walden Two community, and I was sure that other behaviorists would soon join me. Together we would all make a stand against war, social injustice, poverty, and all the other things that had so troubled me in my younger years.

Richie leaving Dandelion for the last time

That now seemed to be a dream for future generations. Moreover, with Jane, Gordon and me gone, Dandelion's commitment to behaviorism would likely disappear.

Yet there had been a few years when Dandelion was a visionary community. We had designed social systems that did not discriminate against women or minorities. We had changed our verbal system with considerable success, and we had been a role model on what cooperative living offered.

I also reflected on the dramatic impact Dandelion had had on my personal life and how much I had learned there. I had lived an egalitarian lifestyle committed to social justice and equality, becoming less racist and less sexist. I'd learned better decision-making skills, become more aware of women's issues, did childcare shifts, learned auto mechanics, new cooking skills, gardening skills, managed a business, developed construction skills, welding skills and lived a lifestyle based on behavioral principles. In many ways, I had lived my original dream and had truly experimented with my own life.

In terms of relationships, some of the friendships I made there would last a lifetime. I had also met so many amazing women, some of whom I was lucky enough to become lovers.

Now, when I think about my time at Dandelion, I realize that there was no other time in my life when I had matured so much in so many ways while so immensely enjoying the process. I am indebted to that community and will forever treasure my experience there.

Where Are They Now...

Gordon: Moved to Twin Oaks where he still lives today. His daughter, Devon, lives in Charlottesville, Virginia and works as a musician.

Jane: She and Larry became midwives and practiced midwifery in Ontario for fifteen years. Jane became a leader in the midwifery movement in Canada working to bring midwifery into the regulated and publicly funded health care system in Ontario and British Columbia. They have lived on Vancouver Island since 1997. Jane now pours her passion into ecological education and restoration in the Cowichan Estuary, climate change action, and leading workshops on communication and relationships on Gabriola Island. Larry shares in this work as well and also works for Canada's Agency for Cooperative Housing. He hikes the West Coast Trail twice a year.

Parrish and his wife Joanna live, work and develop games in Toronto.

Jane and Larry's daughter Ariel and her partner Arnie are wildlife biologists, generally found studying birds in the wild.

Donald: Returned to school as he had planned, since he was only 18 when he joined Dandelion. The intellectual sub-current at Dandelion was a great preparation for university, and he found himself in medical school, eventually becoming a doctor in a teaching environment. Raising children in a nuclear family often left him longing for the co-operative and shared experience of community living. The simple, non-consumeristic way of life still beckons!

Maple: Worked here and there and became a lawyer working for the Canadian Human Rights Commission. Married, had three kids and moved to the suburbs.

Dondi: Lived at Twin Oaks for seven years. While there, got married and had two daughters. Left Twin Oaks and tried life as a nuclear family. Got a master's degree in Education, adopted two boys, and lived in Germany for twelve years. The past four years living in Seoul, South Korea, teaching Middle School for the Department of Defense.

Mory and Jonathan: Married and opened their own publishing company in Ottawa. Mory also worked for non-profit organizations and charities and is now working for the federal government. They have two sons and two daughters. Their daughter Naomi (who was born at Dandelion), is a senior economist with the Ontario provincial government.

Ira: Moved to Twin Oaks and continues to live there. She still carries her passion for gardening, became a writer and authored *The Timber Press Guide to Vegetable Gardening in the South East*.

Greg: Has been married to the love of his life for thirty years. ("Got so lucky!") Lives in Maine and had a career in publishing. Two daughters. One headed off to college, the other just graduated from the Maine Maritime Academy.

Brian: Married Alison and still together after thirty-seven years. Both very active in the local arts communities. Acting in a lot in community theater and indie films. Doing photography for theatre groups and mostly on travel destinations around the world. Still working for social justice.

Alison: Is a happy multi-instrument musician based in the Kitchen–Waterloo arts community, with strong ties to Tanzania and other parts of Africa. Still standing against injustice and working to change the world.

Julian: Changed his name back to "Bill" and now lives in the Pacific Northwest with his dog, Wishka. He volunteers as a master gardener, writes book reviews for the Alternative Library, and performs as the "noise band," Xenosterra.

Cath: Worked as the Executive Director at the Yolo Community Foundation. Also worked with a variety of other non-profits and on numerous community projects. She likes to think that while she no longer lives in an intentional community, in some way the ethic of community involvement has moved on with her into her larger community of 60,000 in Woodlawn, California.

Tango: Law became Tango's passion, and his career went on to litigate against drug and device companies on behalf of thousands of clients. For fun, he's passionate about gardening and foraging, things he learned at Dandelion (i.e. "organic gardening" = squishing cabbage worms.) He has vacation property where he's revitalizing an abandoned apple orchard. He also loves skinny dipping in his pond, another thing learned and repeatedly practiced at Dandelion.

Peggy: Lived at Twin Oaks for sixteen years after leaving Dandelion, doing economic planning, hammock weaving, forestry, cooking and childcare. She moved to Charlottesville, Virginia in 1999. Her primary occupation was doing accounting for non-profit organizations. She currently lives with her partner, Ann. They do urban permaculture, nurture neighbor connections, barter for much of what they need and accrue social equity. Retired for three years, they host various people from around the world in their AirBnB and WorkAway. She still does a small amount of accounting "for barter," volunteers for Hospice, gardens, food processing, cooking, practices Tibetan Buddhism and spends quality time with friends and family. Still building community after all these years.

Janet: Ran off and married Sean Hays. Three kids and thirty-seven years later, still in love and laughing. Working as an elementary teacher and artist in Toronto. Loves to get away canoe tripping and winter camping.

Sean: Pursued his love of the theatre, education and Janet. After several years on stage and many more in university, he now plays the role of a man who thinks he is as smart as the woman he loves. Sean and Janet have three children (all delivered by Jane and Larry from Dandelion) and live happily in Toronto.

Pat: Followed her passion and became a nurse practitioner and works in the field of women's health. She still has a passion for painting.

Acknowledgments

This book could not have been done without the generous support, technical assistance and encouragement of the following people…

Mike Reilly & David Robinson (My editors)

Kitty Werner (My formatting editor)

Robbie Sproule (Photographer for 99% of the photos.)

Tom Barber (All his computer help.)

Rachel Fisher (Publishing Manager at Onion River Press.)

Juliette Horton (Photographer for photo of me on back cover.)

John Darby (For all the feedback he gave me on my first draft.)

I thank you!

About the Author

After leaving Dandelion, Richie Graham attended Indiana University where he received a Master's Degree in education. He worked in the training department at Methodist Hospital in Indianapolis, then moved to Burlington in 1991, where he has been living ever since.

He has worked mostly for non-profit organizations dealing with disability rights issues, and also served for twenty years on the board of directors with Kids on the Block-VT, a puppet troop with each puppet having some disability/difference.

More recently he has become involved with the ecological movement and has been working to get Vermont branded as an Earth-friendly community. In his spare time, he writes, hikes, and sings at a karaoke bar.

www.ingramcontent.com/pod-product-compliance
Lightning Source LLC
Chambersburg PA
CBHW020122130526
44591CB00032B/333